# JAPANESE
# COLOUR PRINTS

## BY LAURENCE BINYON
### AND
## J. J. O'BRIEN SEXTON

FREDERICK PUBLICATIONS

# PREFACE

The plan of this book follows the plan adopted by Fenollosa in his *Outline of Ukiyo-ye* and in his *Masters of Ukiyo-ye ;* that is, we have not dealt with the subject school by school, or master by master, but period by period. Only by such a treatment can the true relation of one master to another be understood, or the whole movement of Ukiyo-ye through its many shifting phases, which affect all the artists at once, be appreciated.

In each chapter we give an account, with such biographical details as are available, from Japanese sources, of the artists beginning work within the period covered by the chapter. These data are followed by an account of the movement of Ukiyo-ye during the period, and an appreciation of the chief works produced.

The body of the work is prefaced by tables to facilitate the reading of dated books and prints ; an account of the Censorship of Prints ; a table of the *Mon* of the Yedo actors during the 18th century ; and a table of publishers' trade-marks and seals. These will, it is believed, be of service to collectors, since the information hitherto published on these matters has been meagre and often inaccurate. At the end of the book will be found brief essays on some outstanding problems, and a select list of important books printed in colour. Otherwise we have not concerned ourselves with the books, or with the paintings, by Ukiyoye masters, except when this was necessary to elucidate the text.

For permission to reproduce prints in their possession we cordially thank Prof. William Bateson, Mr. Ricketts and Mr. Shannon, Mr. Oscar Raphael, and the Trustees of the British Museum. Our thanks are also due to Mr. F. W. Gookin for permission to quote extracts from letters received from him ; to Mr. Carl Schraubstadter for permission to refer to a print, signed by the Second Kiyonobu, in his collection ; and to Mr. Howard Mansfield, Mr. Arthur Waley, and Mr. K. Tomita, for courteously supplying information on special points.

# CONTENTS

# LIST OF ILLUSTRATIONS

# LIST OF ILLUSTRATIONS

# LIST OF ILLUSTRATIONS

# LIST OF ILLUSTRATIONS

# LIST OF ILLUSTRATIONS

# LIST OF ILLUSTRATIONS

# LIST OF ILLUSTRATIONS

PLATE I

PLATE II

そめ　さくら　こ　は　な　ら　ひ　も　の　た　な　び　き

山ぶきの　花そ　しら　な　ちる

弓山吹

春信画

PLATE III

PLATE IV

湖
龍齋画

PLATE V

PLATE VI

PLATE VII

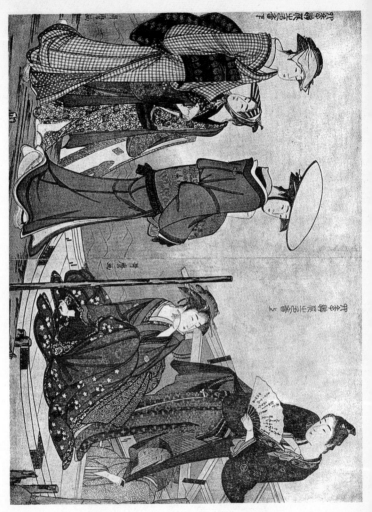

PLATE VIII

PLATE IX

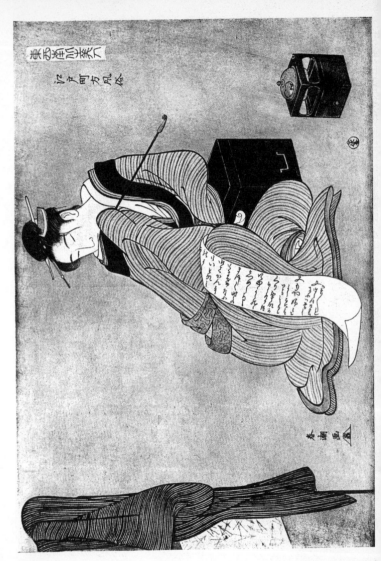

PLATE X

PLATE XI

PLATE XII

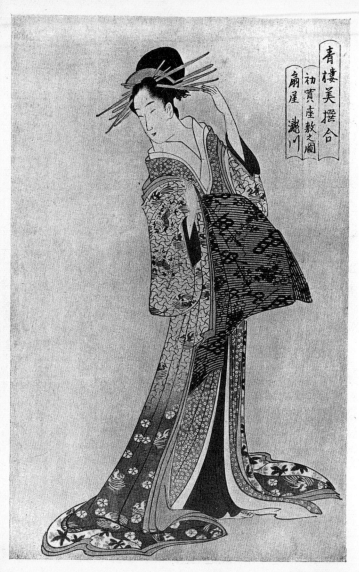

青樓美撰合

初買座敷之圖

扇屋　瀧川

PLATE XIII

PLATE XIV

PLATE XV

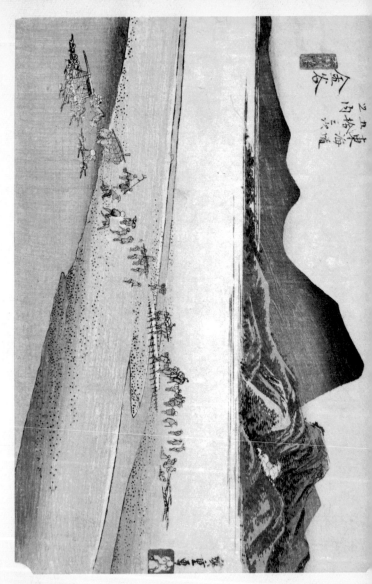

PLATE XVI

PLATE XVII

PLATE XVIII

Fig. 1.

Fig. 2.

PLATE XIX

Fig. 1.                    Fig. 2.                  PLATE XX

Fig. 1.                              Fig. 2.                         PLATE XXI

Fig. 1.                    Fig. 2.                    PLATE XXII

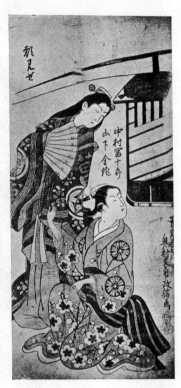

Fig. 1.                    Fig. 2.                PLATE XXIII

PLATE XXIV

PLATE XXV

Fig. 1.  Fig. 2.  PLATE XXVI

PLATE XXVII

Fig. 1.  Fig. 2.  PLATE XXVIII

Fig. 1.

Fig. 2.

PLATE XXIX

PLATE XXX

PLATE XXXI

Fig. 1.

Fig. 2.

PLATE XXXII

春好画

PLATE XXXIII

PLATE XXXIV

PLATE XXXV

PLATE XXXVI

柴田修理進勝家

小谷の方

哥麿筆

PLATE XXXVII

真柴久吉

哥麿筆

PLATE XXXVIII

仁義禮智信

豐
國
畫

PLATE XXXIX

豊

國画

PLATE XL

婦人買初の圖

子興筆

PLATE XLI

okasaki

kanagawa

PLATE XLII

星の霜
當世
風俗

PLATE XLIII

山似屏風帆似章
町版来往月明中

PLATE XLIV

和田新左衛門正朝

PLATE XLV

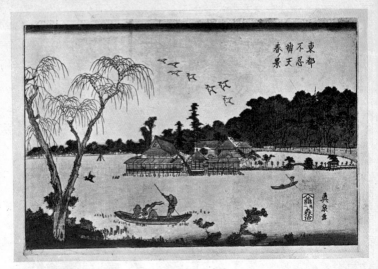

東都不忍辯天春景

奥象寫

Fig. 1.

小林清親畫　　　御茶水螢　　　松木平吉版

Fig. 2.

PLATE XLVI

# TABLES TO FACILITATE THE READING OF DATED BOOKS AND PRINTS

## TABLE I

| Jikkan or "the ten celestial stems." | | | Jūnishi or "the twelve zodiacal signs." | | | | |
|---|---|---|---|---|---|---|---|
| 甲 | 宇 乙 | Ki-no-e | 子 | 孑 | 吊 | Ne | Rat |
| 乙 | | Ki-no-to | 丑 | 丑 | 丑 | Ushi | Ox |
| 丙 | 丙 丙 | Hi-no-e | 寅 | 寅 | 寅 | Tora | Tiger |
| 丁 | | Hi-no-to | 卯 | 卯 | 卯 | U | Hare |
| 戊 | 戌 弓 | Tsuchi-no-e | 辰 | 辰 | 弓 | Tatsu | Dragon |
| 己 | | Tsuchi-no-to | 巳 | 巳 | 朩 | Mi | Snake |
| 庚 | 庚 | Ka-no-e | 午 | 午 | 米 | Uma | Horse |
| 辛 | 辛 | Ka-no-to | 未 | 未 | 月 | Hitsuji | Goat |
| 壬 | 壬 | Mizu-no-e | 申 | 申 | 酉 | Saru | Monkey |
| 癸 | 癸 | Mizu-no-to | 酉 | 酉 | 酉 | Tori | Cock |
| | | | 戌 | 戌 | 㐱 | Inu | Dog |
| | | | 亥 | 豕 | 亥 | I | Boar |

# TABLE II

## SEXAGENARY CYCLE

FORMED BY THE COMBINATION OF THE JIKKAN WITH THE JŪNISHA IN REGULAR ROTATION OF ONE OF EACH

| E-TO | of year. | No. of cycle. | E-TO | of year. | No. of cycle. | E-TO | of year. | No. of cycle. |
|---|---|---|---|---|---|---|---|---|
| 甲 子 | Kinoe Ne | 1 | 甲 申 | Kinoe Saru | 21 | 甲 辰 | Kinoe Tatsu | 41 |
| 乙 丑 | Kinoto Ushi | 2 | 乙 酉 | Kinoto Tori | 22 | 乙 巳 | Kinoto Mi | 42 |
| 丙 寅 | Hinoe Tora | 3 | 丙 戌 | Hinoe Inu | 23 | 丙 午 | Hinoe Uma | 43 |
| 丁 卯 | Hinoto U | 4 | 丁 亥 | Hinoto I | 24 | 丁 未 | Hinoto Hitsuji | 44 |
| 戊 辰 | Tsuchinoe Tatsu | 5 | 戊 子 | Tsuchinoe Ne | 25 | 戊 申 | Tsuchinoe Saru | 45 |
| 己 巳 | Tsuchinoto Mi | 6 | 己 丑 | Tsuchinoto Ushi | 26 | 己 酉 | Tsuchinoto Tori | 46 |
| 庚 午 | Kanoe Uma | 7 | 庚 寅 | Kanoe Tora | 27 | 庚 戌 | Kanoe Inu | 47 |
| 辛 未 | Kanoto Hitsuji | 8 | 辛 卯 | Kanoto U | 28 | 辛 亥 | Kanoto I | 48 |
| 壬 申 | Mizunoe Saru | 9 | 壬 辰 | Mizunoe Tatsu | 29 | 壬 子 | Mizunoe Ne | 49 |
| 癸 酉 | Mizunoto Tori | 10 | 癸 巳 | Mizunoto Mi | 30 | 癸 丑 | Mizunoto Ushi | 50 |
| 甲 戌 | Kinoe Inu | 11 | 甲 午 | Kinoe Ushi | 31 | 甲 寅 | Kinoe Tora | 51 |
| 乙 亥 | Kinoto I | 12 | 乙 未 | Kinoto Hitsuji | 32 | 乙 卯 | Kinoto U | 52 |
| 丙 子 | Hinoe Ne | 13 | 丙 申 | Hinoe Saru | 33 | 丙 辰 | Hinoe Tatsu | 53 |
| 丁 丑 | Hinoto Ushi | 14 | 丁 酉 | Hinoto Tori | 34 | 丁 巳 | Hinoto Mi | 54 |
| 戊 寅 | Tsuchinoe Tora | 15 | 戊 戌 | Tsuchinoe Inu | 35 | 戊 午 | Tsuchinoe Ushi | 55 |
| 己 卯 | Tsuchinoto U | 16 | 己 亥 | Tsuchinoto I | 36 | 己 未 | Tsuchinoto Hitsuji | 56 |
| 庚 辰 | Kanoe Tatsu | 17 | 庚 子 | Kanoe Ne | 37 | 庚 申 | Kanoe Saru | 57 |
| 辛 巳 | Kanoto Mi | 18 | 辛 丑 | Kanoto Ushi | 38 | 辛 酉 | Kanoto Tori | 58 |
| 壬 午 | Mizunoe Uma | 19 | 壬 寅 | Mizunoe Tora | 39 | 壬 戌 | Mizunoe Inu | 59 |
| 癸 未 | Mizunoto Hitsuji | 20 | 癸 卯 | Mizunoto U | 40 | 癸 亥 | Mizunoto I | 60 |

# TABLE III

## COMPARATIVE CHRONOLOGICAL TABLE
## OF JAPANESE DATES

### WITH THOSE OF THE GREGORIAN CALENDAR AS USED IN ENGLAND
### FROM 19TH FEBRUARY, 1861, TO 30TH DECEMBER, 1872

*Note.*—The letter I following a long or short month indicates an Intercalary month.

| Nengō or Name of Period. | | Year of Period. | Year by Cycle. | Year began on | Year ended on | Dai no Tsuki or Long Months. | Shō no Tsuki or Short Months. |
|---|---|---|---|---|---|---|---|
| 'en-na | 天和 | 1 | 58 | 9 Feb., 1681 | 28 Jan., 1682 | 2, 6, 8, 10, 11, 12 | 1, 3, 4, 5, 7, 9 |
| | | 2 | 59 | 29 Jan., 1682 | 17 Jan., 1683 | 2, 3, 7, 9, 11, 12 | 1, 4, 5, 6, 8, 10 |
| | | 3 | 60 | 18 Jan., 1683 | 5 Feb., 1684 | 1, 3, 5, 7, 9, 11 | 2, 4, 5 I, 6, 8, 10, 12 |
| ō-kyō | 貞享 | 1 | 1 | 6 Feb., 1684 | 24 Jan., 1685 | 2, 3, 5, 7, 10, 12 | 1, 4, 6, 8, 9, 11 |
| | | 2 | 2 | 25 Jan., 1685 | 13 Jan., 1686 | 2, 4, 5, 7, 9, 11 | 1, 3, 6, 8, 10, 12 |
| | | 3 | 3 | 14 Jan., 1686 | 1 Feb., 1687 | 1, 3, 4, 6, 7, 9, 11 | 2, 3 I, 5, 8, 10, 12 |
| | | 4 | 4 | 2 Feb., 1687 | 22 Jan., 1688 | 1, 4, 6, 7, 9, 10, 12 | 2, 3, 5, 8, 11 |
| en-roku | 元祿 | 1 | 5 | 23 Jan., 1688 | 10 Jan., 1689 | 2, 5, 7, 9, 10, 11 | 1, 3, 4, 6, 8, 12 |
| | | 2 | 6 | 11 Jan., 1689 | 29 Jan., 1690 | 1, 2, 5, 7, 9, 10, 11 | 1 I, 3, 4, 6, 8, 12 |
| | | 3 | 7 | 30 Jan., 1690 | 18 Jan., 1691 | 1, 3, 6, 9, 10, 12 | 2, 4, 5, 7, 8, 11 |
| | | 4 | 8 | 19 Jan., 1691 | 6 Feb., 1692 | 1, 2, 4, 7, 9, 10, 12 | 3, 5, 6, 8, 8 I, 11 |
| | | 5 | 9 | 7 Feb., 1692 | 25 Jan., 1693 | 1, 3, 4, 7, 10, 12 | 2, 5, 6, 8, 9, 11 |
| | | 6 | 10 | 26 Jan., 1693 | 14 Jan., 1694 | 1, 2, 4, 6, 8, 11 | 3, 5, 7, 9, 10, 12 |
| | | 7 | 11 | 15 Jan., 1694 | 2 Feb., 1695 | 1, 2, 4, 5, 6, 8, 10 | 3, 5 I, 7, 9, 11, 12 |
| | | 8 | 12 | 3 Feb., 1695 | 23 Jan., 1696 | 1, 3, 4, 6, 8, 9, 11 | 2, 5, 7, 10, 12 |
| | | 9 | 13 | 24 Jan., 1696 | 12 Jan., 1697 | 1, 4, 6, 7, 9, 10, 12 | 2, 3, 5, 8, 11 |
| | | 10 | 14 | 13 Jan., 1697 | 31 Jan., 1698 | 2, 4, 6, 8, 9, 11, 12 | 1, 2 I, 3, 5, 7, 10 |
| | | 11 | 15 | 1 Feb., 1698 | 20 Jan., 1699 | 2, 5, 8, 9, 11, 12 | 1, 3, 4, 6, 7, 10 |
| | | 12 | 16 | 21 Jan., 1699 | 8 Feb., 1700 | 1, 3, 6, 9, 10, 11, 12 | 2, 4, 5, 7, 8, 9 I |
| | | 13 | 17 | 9 Feb., 1700 | 27 Jan., 1701 | 1, 3, 6, 9, 11, 12 | 2, 4, 5, 7, 8, 10 |
| | | 14 | 18 | 28 Jan., 1701 | 16 Jan., 1702 | 1, 3, 5, 7, 10, 12 | 2, 4, 6, 8, 9, 11 |
| | | 15 | 19 | 17 Jan., 1702 | 4 Feb., 1703 | 1, 3, 4, 6, 8, 10, 12 | 2, 5, 7, 8 I, 9, 11 |
| | | 16 | 20 | 5 Feb., 1703 | 24 Jan., 1704 | 2, 3, 5, 6, 8, 10 | 1, 4, 7, 9, 11, 12 |
| ō-yei | 寶永 | 1 | 21 | 25 Jan., 1704 | 13 Jan., 1705 | 1, 3, 5, 6, 8, 9, 11 | 2, 4, 7, 10, 12 |
| | | 2 | 22 | 14 Jan., 1705 | 1 Feb., 1706 | 1, 4, 5, 7, 8, 10, 11 | 2, 3, 4 I, 6, 9, 12 |
| | | 3 | 23 | 2 Feb., 1706 | 22 Jan., 1707 | 1, 4, 7, 8, 10, 11, 12 | 2, 3, 5, 6, 9 |
| | | 4 | 24 | 23 Jan., 1707 | 11 Jan., 1708 | 2, 5, 8, 10, 11, 12 | 1, 3, 4, 6, 7, 9 |
| | | 5 | 25 | 12 Jan., 1708 | 29 Jan., 1709 | 1, 3, 5, 8, 10, 11, 12 | 1 I, 2, 4, 6, 7, 9 |
| | | 6 | 26 | 30 Jan., 1709 | 18 Jan., 1710 | 2, 3, 6, 9, 11, 12 | 1, 4, 5, 7, 8, 10 |
| | | 7 | 27 | 19 Jan., 1710 | 5 Feb., 1711 | 2, 3, 5, 7, 9, 11 | 1, 4, 6, 8, 8 I, 10, 12 |
| ō-toku | 正德 | 1 | 28 | 6 Feb., 1711 | 26 Jan., 1712 | 1, 2, 3, 5, 7, 10, 12 | 4, 6, 8, 9, 11 |
| | | 2 | 29 | 27 Jan., 1712 | 14 Jan., 1713 | 2, 5, 7, 8, 10 | 1, 3, 4, 6, 9, 11, 12 |
| | | 3 | 30 | 15 Jan., 1713 | 3 Feb., 1714 | 1, 2, 3, 5, 6, 7, 9, 10, 12 | 4, 5 I, 8, 11 |
| | | 4 | 31 | 4 Feb., 1714 | 23 Jan., 1715 | 3, 5, 7, 8, 10. 11 | 1, 2, 4, 6, 9, 12 |
| | | 5 | 32 | 24 Jan., 1715 | 13 Jan., 1716 | 1, 2, 4, 7, 8, 10, 11, 12 | 3, 5, 6, 9 |

## TABLE III—*continued*

| Nengō or Name of Period. | Year of Period. | Year by Cycle. | Year began on | Year ended on | Dai no Tsuki or Long Months. | Shō no Tsuki or Short Months. |
|---|---|---|---|---|---|---|
| Kyō-hō 享保 | 1 | 33 | 14 Jan., 1716 | 30 Jan., 1717 | 2, 4, 7, 9, 10, 11 | 1, 2 I, 3, 5, 6, 8, 12 |
| | 2 | 34 | 31 Jan., 1717 | 19 Jan., 1718 | 1, 2, 5, 8, 10, 11 | 3, 4, 6, 7, 9, 12 |
| | 3 | 35 | 20 Jan., 1718 | 7 Feb., 1719 | 1, 2, 4, 6, 9, 10 I, 12 | 3, 5, 7, 8, 10, 11 |
| | 4 | 36 | 8 Feb., 1719 | 27 Jan., 1720 | 1, 2, 4, 6, 9, 11 | 3, 5, 7, 8, 10, 12 |
| | 5 | 37 | 28 Jan., 1720 | 16 Jan., 1721 | 1, 2, 4, 5, 7, 10, 12 | 3, 6, 8, 9, 11 |
| | 6 | 38 | 17 Jan., 1721 | 4 Feb., 1722 | 2, 4, 5, 7, 8, 10, 12 | 1, 3, 6, 7 I, 9, 11 |
| | 7 | 39 | 5 Jan., 1722 | 24 Jan., 1723 | 2, 4, 6, 7, 9, 11 | 1, 3, 5, 8, 10, 12 |
| | 8 | 40 | 25 Jan., 1723 | 14 Jan., 1724 | 1, 3, 6, 7, 9, 10, 12 | 2, 4, 5, 8, 11 |
| | 9 | 41 | 15 Jan., 1724 | 1 Feb., 1725 | 1, 4, 6, 8, 9, 10, 12 | 2, 3, 4 I, 5, 7, 11 |
| | 10 | 42 | 2 Feb., 1725 | 21 Jan., 1726 | 1, 4, 7, 9, 10, 12 | 2, 3, 5, 6, 8, 11 |
| | 11 | 43 | 22 Jan., 1726 | 10 Jan., 1727 | 1, 3, 5, 8, 10, 12 | 2, 4, 6, 7, 9, 11 |
| | 12 | 44 | 11 Jan., 1727 | 29 Jan., 1728 | 1, 1 I, 3, 5, 8, 10, 12 | 2, 4, 6, 7, 9, 11 |
| | 13 | 45 | 30 Jan., 1728 | 7 Feb., 1729 | 1, 3, 4, 6, 9, 11 | 2, 5, 7, 8, 10, 12 |
| | 14 | 46 | 8 Jan., 1729 | 5 Feb., 1730 | 1, 3, 4, 6, 8, 9 I, 11 | 2, 5, 7, 9, 10, 12 |
| | 15 | 47 | 6 Feb., 1730 | 26 Jan., 1731 | 1, 3, 5, 6, 8, 10, 12 | 2, 4, 7, 9, 11 |
| | 16 | 48 | 27 Jan., 1731 | 15 Jan., 1732 | 2, 4, 6, 8, 9, 11 | 1, 3, 5, 7, 10, 12 |
| | 17 | 49 | 16 Jan., 1732 | 2 Feb., 1733 | 1, 3, 5 I, 7, 8, 9, 11 | 2, 4, 5, 6, 10, 12 |
| | 18 | 50 | 3 Feb., 1733 | 23 Jan., 1734 | 1, 3, 6, 8, 9, 11, 12 | 2, 4, 5, 7, 10 |
| | 19 | 51 | 24 Jan., 1734 | 12 Jan., 1735 | 2, 4, 7, 9, 11, 12 | 1, 3, 5, 6, 8, 10 |
| | 20 | 52 | 13 Jan., 1735 | 31 Jan., 1736 | 1, 3, 4, 7, 9, 11, 12 | 2, 3 I, 5, 6, 8, 10 |
| Gem-bun 元文 | 1 | 53 | 1 Feb., 1736 | 19 Jan., 1737 | 2, 3, 5, 8, 11, 12 | 1, 4, 6, 7, 9, 10 |
| | 2 | 54 | 20 Jan., 1737 | 7 Feb., 1738 | 2, 3, 4, 6, 9, 11, 12 | 1, 5, 7, 8, 10, 11 I |
| | 3 | 55 | 8 Feb., 1738 | 27 Jan., 1739 | 2, 3, 5, 7, 9, 11 | 1, 4, 6, 8, 10, 12 |
| | 4 | 56 | 28 Jan., 1739 | 17 Jan., 1740 | 1, 3, 5, 6, 8, 10, 12 | 2, 4, 7, 9, 11 |
| | 5 | 57 | 18 Jan., 1740 | 4 Feb., 1741 | 2, 5, 6, 7 I, 8, 10, 12 | 1, 3, 4, 7, 9, 11 |
| Kwampō 寛保 | 1 | 58 | 5 Feb., 1741 | 24 Jan., 1742 | 2, 5, 7, 8, 10, 11 | 1, 3, 4, 6, 9, 12 |
| | 2 | 59 | 25 Jan., 1742 | 14 Jan., 1743 | 1, 3, 6, 8, 10, 11, 12 | 2, 4, 5, 7, 9 |
| | 3 | 60 | 15 Jan., 1743 | 2 Feb., 1744 | 2, 4, 6, 9, 10, 11, 12 | 1, 3, 4 I, 5, 7, 8 |
| Yen-kyō 延享 | 1 | 1 | 3 Feb., 1744 | 20 Jan., 1745 | 2, 4, 7, 10, 11 | 1, 3, 5, 6, 8, 9, 12 |
| | 2 | 2 | 21 Jan., 1745 | 8 Feb., 1746 | 1, 2, 3, 5, 8, 11, 12 | 4, 6, 7, 9, 10, 12 I |
| | 3 | 3 | 9 Feb., 1746 | 29 Jan., 1747 | 1, 2, 4, 6, 8, 11, 12 | 3, 5, 7, 9, 10 |
| | 4 | 4 | 30 Jan., 1747 | 18 Jan., 1748 | 2, 4, 5, 7, 9, 11 | 1, 3, 6, 8, 10, 12 |
| Kwan-yen 寛延 | 1 | 5 | 19 Jan., 1748 | 5 Feb., 1749 | 2, 3, 5, 7, 8, 10, 11 | 1, 4, 6, 9, 10 I, 12 |
| | 2 | 6 | 6 Feb., 1749 | 26 Jan., 1750 | 1, 4, 6, 7, 9, 10, 12 | 2, 3, 5, 8, 11 |
| | 3 | 7 | 27 Jan., 1750 | 15 Jan., 1751 | 2, 5, 7, 9, 10, 11 | 1, 3, 4, 6, 8, 12 |
| Hō-reki 寶曆 | 1 | 8 | 16 Jan., 1751 | 3 Feb., 1752 | 1, 3, 6, 7, 9, 10, 12 | 2, 4, 5, 6 I, 8, 11 |
| | 2 | 9 | 4 Feb., 1752 | 2 Feb., 1753 | 1, 3, 6, 9, 10, 12 | 2, 4, 5, 7, 8, 11 |
| | 3 | 10 | 3 Feb., 1753 | 22 Jan., 1754 | 1, 2, 7, 10, 11 | 3, 4, 5, 6, 8, 9, 12 |
| | 4 | 11 | 23 Jan., 1754 | 10 Feb., 1755 | 1, 2, 3, 4, 7, 10, 12 | 2 I, 5, 6, 8, 9, 11 |
| | 5 | 12 | 11 Feb., 1755 | 30 Jan., 1756 | 1, 2, 4, 6, 8, 11 | 3, 5, 7, 9, 10, 12 |
| | 6 | 13 | 31 Jan., 1756 | 17 Feb., 1757 | 1, 2, 4, 6, 7, 9, 11 | 3, 5, 8, 10, 11 I, 12 |
| | 7 | 14 | 18 Feb., 1757 | 7 Feb., 1758 | 1, 3, 4, 6, 8, 9, 11 | 2, 5, 7, 10, 12 |
| | 8 | 15 | 8 Feb., 1758 | 28 Jan., 1759 | 1, 4, 6, 8, 9, 10, 12 | 2, 3, 5, 7, 11 |

| Nengō or Name of Period. | Year of Period. | Year by Cycle. | Year began on | Year ended on | Dai no Tsuki or Long Months. | Shō no Tsuki or Short Months. |
|---|---|---|---|---|---|---|
| | 9 | 16 | 29 Jan., 1759 | 16 Feb., 1760 | 2, 5, 7, 8, 9, 11, 12 | 1, 3, 4, 6, 7 I, 10 |
| | 10 | 17 | 17 Feb., 1760 | 4 Feb., 1761 | 2, 5, 8, 9, 11, 12 | 1, 3, 4, 6, 7, 10 |
| | 11 | 18 | 5 Feb., 1761 | 24 Jan., 1762 | 1, 3, 6, 9, 11, 12 | 2, 4, 5, 7, 8, 10 |
| | 12 | 19 | 25 Jan., 1762 | 12 Feb., 1763 | 1, 2, 4, 6, 9, 11, 12 | 3, 4 I, 5, 7, 8, 10 |
| | 13 | 20 | 13 Feb., 1763 | 1 Feb., 1764 | 1, 3, 5, 7, 10, 12 | 2, 4, 6, 8, 9, 11 |
| Mei-wa 明和 | 1 | 21 | 2 Feb., 1764 | 19 Feb., 1765 | 1, 3, 4, 6, 8, 11, 12 I | 2, 5, 7, 9, 10, 12 |
| | 2 | 22 | 20 Feb., 1765 | 8 Feb., 1766 | 2, 3, 5, 6, 8, 10 | 1, 4, 7, 9, 11, 12 |
| | 3 | 23 | 9 Feb., 1766 | 29 Jan., 1767 | 1, 3, 5, 6, 8, 9, 11 | 2, 4, 7, 10, 12 |
| | 4 | 24 | 30 Jan., 1767 | 17 Feb., 1768 | 2, 4, 6, 8, 9, 10, 11 | 1, 3, 5, 7, 9 I, 12 |
| | 5 | 25 | 18 Feb., 1768 | 6 Feb., 1769 | 1, 4, 7, 8, 10, 11, 12 | 2, 3, 5, 6, 9 |
| | 6 | 26 | 7 Feb., 1769 | 26 Jan., 1770 | 2, 5, 8, 10, 11, 12 | 1, 3, 4, 6, 7, 9 |
| | 7 | 27 | 27 Jan., 1770 | 14 Feb., 1771 | 1, 3, 6, 8, 10, 11, 12 | 2, 4, 5, 6 I, 7, 9 |
| | 8 | 28 | 15 Feb., 1771 | 3 Feb., 1772 | 2, 4, 6, 9, 11, 12 | 1, 3, 5, 7, 8, 10 |
| An-yei 安永 | 1 | 29 | 4 Feb., 1772 | 27 Jan., 1773 | 2, 3, 5, 7, 10, 12 | 1, 4, 6, 8, 9, 11 |
| | 2 | 30 | 28 Jan., 1773 | 10 Feb., 1774 | 2, 3, 4, 5, 7, 10, 12 | 1, 3 I, 6, 8, 9, 11 |
| | 3 | 31 | 11 Feb., 1774 | 30 Jan., 1775 | 2, 3, 5, 7, 9, 11 | 1, 4, 6, 8, 10, 12 |
| | 4 | 32 | 31 Jan., 1775 | 18 Feb., 1776 | 1, 3, 5, 7, 8, 10, 11 | 2, 4, 6, 9, 12, 12 I |
| | 5 | 33 | 19 Feb., 1776 | 7 Feb., 1777 | 1, 3, 5, 7, 9, 10, 11 | 2, 4, 6, 8, 12 |
| | 6 | 34 | 8 Feb., 1777 | 27 Jan., 1778 | 1, 4, 7, 9, 10, 11 | 2, 3, 5, 6, 8, 12 |
| | 7 | 35 | 28 Jan., 1778 | 15 Feb., 1779 | 2, 5, 7, I, 9, 10, 11 | 3, 4, 6, 7, 8, 12 |
| | 8 | 36 | 16 Feb., 1779 | 4 Feb., 1780 | 1, 3, 5, 8, 10, 11 | 2, 4, 6, 7, 9, 12 |
| | 9 | 37 | 5 Feb., 1780 | 23 Jan., 1781 | 1, 2, 4, 6, 9, 11 | 3, 5, 7, 8, 10, 12 |
| Tem-mei 天明 | 1 | 38 | 24 Jan., 1781 | 11 Feb., 1782 | 1, 2, 3, 5, 6, 9, 11 | 4, 5 I, 7, 8, 10, 12 |
| | 2 | 39 | 12 Feb., 1782 | 1 Feb., 1783 | 1, 2, 4, 6, 8, 10, 12 | 3, 5, 7, 9, 11 |
| | 3 | 40 | 2 Feb., 1783 | 21 Jan., 1784 | 2, 4, 5, 7, 9, 11 | 1, 3, 6, 8, 10, 12 |
| | 4 | 41 | 22 Jan., 1784 | 8 Feb., 1785 | 2, 4, 6, 7, 9, 11 | 1 I, 3, 5, 8, 10, 12 |
| | 5 | 42 | 9 Feb., 1785 | 29 Jan., 1786 | 1, 3, 6, 7, 9, 10, 12 | 2, 4, 5, 8, 11 |
| | 6 | 43 | 30 Jan., 1786 | 17 Feb., 1787 | 2, 4, 7, 9, 10, 10 I, 12 | 1, 3, 5, 6, 8, 11 |
| | 7 | 44 | 18 Feb., 1787 | 6 Feb., 1788 | 1, 4, 7, 9, 10, 12 | 2, 3, 5, 6, 8, 11 |
| | 8 | 45 | 7 Feb., 1788 | 25 Jan., 1789 | 1, 3, 5, 8, 10, 12 | 2, 4, 6, 7, 9, 11 |
| Kwan-sei 寛政 | 1 | 46 | 26 Jan., 1789 | 13 Feb., 1790 | 1, 2, 4, 6, 8, 10, 12 | 3, 5, 6 I, 7, 9, 11 |
| | 2 | 47 | 14 Feb., 1790 | 2 Feb., 1791 | 1, 3, 4, 6, 9, 11 | 2, 5, 7, 8, 10, 12 |
| | 3 | 48 | 3 Feb., 1791 | 23 Jan., 1792 | 1, 3, 4, 6, 8, 10, 12 | 2, 5, 7, 9, 11 |
| | 4 | 49 | 24 Jan., 1792 | 10 Feb., 1793 | 2, 3, 5, 6, 8, 10, 12 | 1, 2 I, 4, 7, 9, 11 |
| | 5 | 50 | 11 Feb., 1793 | 30 Jan., 1794 | 2, 4, 6, 8, 9, 11 | 1, 3, 5, 7, 10, 12 |
| | 6 | 51 | 31 Jan., 1794 | 18 Feb., 1795 | 1, 3, 6, 8, 9, 10, 11 I | 2, 4, 5, 7, 11, 12 |
| | 7 | 52 | 19 Feb., 1795 | 8 Feb., 1796 | 1, 3, 6, 8, 9, 11, 12 | 2, 4, 5, 7, 10 |
| | 8 | 53 | 9 Feb., 1796 | 27 Jan., 1797 | 2, 4, 7, 9, 11, 12 | 1, 3, 5, 6, 8, 10 |
| | 9 | 54 | 28 Jan., 1797 | 15 Feb., 1798 | 1, 3, 5, 8, 10, 11, 12 | 2, 4, 6, 7, 7 I, 9 |
| | 10 | 55 | 16 Feb., 1798 | 4 Feb., 1799 | 2, 3, 5, 8, 11, 12 | 1, 4, 6, 7, 9, 10 |
| | 11 | 56 | 5 Feb., 1799 | 24 Jan., 1800 | 2, 3, 4, 7, 9, 12 | 1, 5, 6, 8, 10, 11 |
| | 12 | 57 | 25 Jan., 1800 | 12 Feb., 1801 | 1, 3, 4, 5, 7, 9, 11 | 2, 4 I, 6, 8, 10, 12 |

| Nengō or Name of Period. | Year of Period. | Year by Cycle. | Year began on | Year ended on | Dai no Tsuki or Long Months. | Shō no Tsuki or Short Months. |
|---|---|---|---|---|---|---|
| Kyō-wa 享和 | 1 | 58 | 13 Feb., 1801 | 2 Feb., 1802 | 1, 3, 5, 7, 8, 10, 12 | 2, 4, 6, 9, 11 |
| | 2 | 59 | 3 Feb., 1802 | 22 Jan., 1803 | 2, 5, 7, 8, 9, 11 | 1, 3, 4, 6, 10, 12 |
| | 3 | 60 | 23 Jan., 1803 | 10 Feb., 1804 | 1, 2, 5, 7, 8, 10, 11 | 1 I, 3, 4, 6, 9, 12 |
| Bun-kwa 文化 | 1 | 1 | 11 Feb., 1804 | 30 Jan., 1805 | 1, 3, 6, 8, 10, 11, 12 | 2, 4, 5, 7, 9 |
| | 2 | 2 | 31 Jan., 1805 | 17 Feb., 1806 | 2, 4, 8, 9, 10, 11 | 1, 3, 5, 6, 7, 8 I, 12 |
| | 3 | 3 | 18 Feb., 1806 | 6 Feb., 1807 | 1, 2, 4, 8, 10, 11 | 3, 5, 6, 7, 9, 12 |
| | 4 | 4 | 7 Feb., 1807 | 27 Jan., 1808 | 1, 2, 3, 5, 8, 11, 12 | 4, 6, 7, 9, 10 |
| | 5 | 5 | 28 Jan., 1808 | 13 Feb., 1809 | 2, 3, 5, 6 I, 8, 11 | 1, 4, 6, 7, 9, 10, 12 |
| | 6 | 6 | 14 Feb., 1809 | 3 Feb., 1810 | 1, 2, 4, 5, 7, 9, 11 | 3, 6, 8, 10, 12 |
| | 7 | 7 | 4 Feb., 1810 | 24 Jan., 1811 | 2, 4, 5, 7, 8, 10, 12 | 1, 3, 6, 9, 11 |
| | 8 | 8 | 25 Jan., 1811 | 12 Feb., 1812 | 2 I, 4, 6, 7, 9, 10, 12 | 1, 2, 3, 5, 8, 11 |
| | 9 | 9 | 13 Feb., 1812 | 31 Jan., 1813 | 2, 5, 7, 9, 10, 11 | 1, 3, 4, 6, 8, 12 |
| | 10 | 10 | 1 Feb., 1813 | 19 Feb., 1814 | 1, 3, 7, 9, 10, 11, 12 | 2, 4, 5, 6, 8, 11 I |
| | 11 | 11 | 20 Feb., 1814 | 8 Feb., 1815 | 1, 3, 7, 9, 10, 12 | 2, 4, 5, 6, 8, 11 |
| | 12 | 12 | 9 Feb., 1815 | 28 Jan., 1816 | 1, 2, 4, 8, 10, 12 | 3, 5, 6, 7, 9, 11 |
| | 13 | 13 | 29 Jan., 1816 | 15 Feb., 1817 | 1, 2, 4, 6, 8, 10, 12 | 3, 5, 7, 8 I, 9, 11 |
| | 14 | 14 | 16 Feb., 1817 | 4 Feb., 1818 | 1, 3, 4, 6, 8, 11 | 2, 5, 7, 9, 10, 12 |
| Bun-sei 文政 | 1 | 15 | 5 Feb., 1818 | 25 Jan., 1819 | 1, 2, 4, 6, 7, 9, 12 | 3, 5, 8, 10, 11 |
| | 2 | 16 | 26 Jan., 1819 | 13 Feb., 1820 | 2, 4, 5, 6, 8, 9, 11 | 1, 3, 4, I, 7, 10, 12 |
| | 3 | 17 | 14 Feb., 1820 | 2 Feb., 1821 | 2, 4, 6, 8, 9, 10, 12 | 1, 3, 5, 7, 11 |
| | 4 | 18 | 3 Feb., 1821 | 22 Jan., 1822 | 2, 5, 7, 9, 10, 12 | 1, 3, 4, 6, 8, 11 |
| | 5 | 19 | 23 Jan., 1822 | 10 Feb., 1823 | 1, 2, 6, 8, 9, 11, 12 | 1 I, 3, 4, 5, 7, 10 |
| | 6 | 20 | 11 Feb., 1823 | 30 Jan., 1824 | 1, 3, 7, 9, 11, 12 | 2, 4, 5, 6, 8, 10 |
| | 7 | 21 | 31 Jan., 1824 | 17 Feb., 1825 | 1, 2, 5, 8, 9, 11, 12 | 3, 4, 6, 7, 8 I, 10 |
| | 8 | 22 | 18 Feb., 1825 | 6 Feb., 1826 | 1, 3, 5, 7, 10, 12 | 2, 4, 6, 8, 9, 11 |
| | 9 | 23 | 7 Feb., 1826 | 26 Jan., 1827 | 1, 3, 4, 6, 8, 11 | 2, 5, 7, 9, 10, 12 |
| | 10 | 24 | 27 Jan., 1827 | 14 Feb., 1828 | 1, 3, 4, 6, 7, 8, 11 | 2, 5, 6 I, 9, 10, 12 |
| | 11 | 25 | 15 Feb., 1828 | 3 Feb., 1829 | 1, 3, 5, 5, 8, 10, 11 | 2, 4, 7, 9, 12 |
| | 12 | 26 | 4 Feb., 1829 | 24 Jan., 1830 | 2, 4, 6, 8, 9, 11, 12 | 1, 3, 5, 7, 10 |
| Tem-pō 天保 | 1 | 27 | 25 Jan., 1830 | 12 Feb., 1831 | 3, 4, 7, 8, 10, 11, 12 | 1, 2, 3 I, 5, 6, 9 |
| | 2 | 28 | 13 Feb., 1831 | 1 Feb., 1832 | 2, 6, 8, 10, 11, 12 | 1, 3, 4, 5, 7, 9 |
| | 3 | 29 | 2 Feb., 1832 | 19 Feb., 1833 | 1, 3, 7, 9, 11, 11 I, 12 | 2, 4, 5, 6, 8, 10 |
| | 4 | 30 | 20 Feb., 1833 | 8 Feb., 1834 | 2, 4, 7, 9, 11, 12 | 1, 3, 5, 6, 8, 10 |
| | 5 | 31 | 9 Feb., 1834 | 28 Jan., 1835 | 2, 3, 5, 8, 10, 12 | 1, 4, 6, 7, 9, 11 |
| | 6 | 32 | 29 Jan., 1835 | 16 Feb., 1836 | 2, 3, 5, 6, 8, 10, 12 | 1, 4, 7, 7 I, 9, 11 |
| | 7 | 33 | 17 Feb., 1836 | 4 Feb., 1837 | 2, 4, 5, 7, 9, 11 | 1, 3, 6, 8, 10, 12 |
| | 8 | 34 | 5 Feb., 1837 | 25 Jan., 1838 | 1, 3, 5, 7, 8, 10, 12 | 2, 4, 6, 9, 11 |
| | 9 | 35 | 26 Jan., 1838 | 13 Feb., 1839 | 2, 4, 7, 9, 10, 12 | 1, 3, 4 I, 5, 6, 8, 11 |
| | 10 | 36 | 14 Feb., 1839 | 2 Feb., 1840 | 2, 5, 7, 9, 10, 11 | 1, 3, 4, 6, 8, 12 |
| | 11 | 37 | 3 Feb., 1840 | 22 Jan., 1841 | 1, 2, 6, 8, 10, 11, 12 | 3, 4, 5, 7, 9 |
| | 12 | 38 | 23 Jan., 1841 | 9 Feb., 1842 | 1 I, 3, 6, 8, 10, 11 | 1, 2, 4, 5, 7, 9, 12 |
| | 13 | 39 | 10 Feb., 1842 | 29 Jan., 1843 | 1, 2, 4, 7, 9, 11 | 3, 5, 6, 8, 10, 12 |
| | 14 | 40 | 30 Jan., 1843 | 17 Feb., 1844 | 1, 2, 3, 5, 8, 9 I, 11 | 4, 6, 7, 9, 10, 12 |

## TABLE III—continued

| Nengō or Name of Period. | | Year of Period. | Year by Cycle. | Year began on | Year ended on | Dai no Tsuki or Long Months. | Shō no Tsuki or Short Months. |
|---|---|---|---|---|---|---|---|
| -kwa | 弘化 | 1 | 41 | 18 Feb., 1844 | 6 Feb., 1845 | 1, 2, 4, 6, 8, 10, 12 | 3, 5, 7, 9, 11 |
| | | 2 | 42 | 7 Feb., 1845 | 26 Jan., 1846 | 2, 4, 5, 7, 9, 11 | 1, 3, 6, 8, 10, 12 |
| | | 3 | 43 | 27 Jan., 1846 | 14 Feb., 1847 | 1, 3, 5, 6, 7, 9, 11 | 2, 4, 5 I, 8, 10, 12 |
| | | 4 | 44 | 15 Feb., 1847 | 4 Feb., 1848 | 1, 3, 6, 7, 9, 10, 12 | 2, 4, 5, 8, 11 |
| -yei | 嘉永 | 1 | 45 | 5 Feb., 1848 | 23 Jan., 1849 | 2, 5, 7, 9, 10, 11 | 1, 3, 4, 6, 8, 12 |
| | | 2 | 46 | 24 Jan., 1849 | 11 Feb., 1850 | 1, 3, 5, 7, 9, 10, 12 | 2, 4, 4 I, 6, 8, 11 |
| | | 3 | 47 | 12 Feb., 1850 | 31 Jan., 1851 | 1, 3, 6, 8, 10, 12 | 2, 4, 5, 7, 9, 11 |
| | | 4 | 48 | 1 Feb., 1851 | 20 Jan., 1852 | 1, 2, 4, 7, 9, 11 | 3, 5, 6, 8, 10, 12 |
| | | 5 | 49 | 21 Jan., 1852 | 7 Feb., 1851 | 1, 2, 3, 4, 7, 9, 11 | 2 I, 5, 6, 8, 10, 12 |
| | | 6 | 50 | 8 Feb., 1853 | 28 Jan., 1854 | 1, 3, 4, 5, 8, 10, 12 | 2, 5, 7, 9, 11 |
| -sei | 安政 | 1 | 51 | 29 Jan., 1854 | 16 Feb., 1855 | 2, 4, 6, 7, 8, 10, 12 | 1, 3, 5, 7 I, 9, 11 |
| | | 2 | 52 | 17 Feb., 1855 | 5 Feb., 1856 | 2, 5, 6, 8, 9, 11 | 1, 3, 4, 7, 10, 12 |
| | | 3 | 53 | 6 Feb., 1856 | 25 Jan., 1857 | 1, 4, 6, 8, 9, 10, 12 | 2, 3, 5, 7, 11 |
| | | 4 | 54 | 26 Jan., 1857 | 13 Feb., 1858 | 2, 5, 6, 8, 9, 11, 12 | 1, 3, 4, 5 I, 7, 10 |
| | | 5 | 55 | 14 Feb., 1858 | 2 Feb., 1859 | 2, 5, 8, 9, 11, 12 | 1, 3, 4, 6, 7, 10 |
| | | 6 | 56 | 3 Feb., 1859 | 22 Jan., 1860 | 1, 3, 6, 9, 11, 12 | 2, 4, 5, 7, 8, 10 |
| n-yen | 萬延 | 1 | 57 | 23 Jan., 1860 | 9 Feb., 1861 | 1, 3, 3 I, 6, 9, 11, 12 | 2, 4, 5, 7, 8, 10 |
| n-kyū | 文久 | 1 | 58 | 10 Feb., 1861 | 29 Jan., 1862 | 2, 3, 5, 7, 9, 12 | 1, 4, 6, 8, 10, 11 |
| | | 2 | 59 | 30 Jan., 1862 | 17 Feb., 1863 | 1, 3, 4, 6, 8, 9, 11 | 2, 5, 7, 8 I, 10, 12 |
| | | 3 | 60 | 18 Feb., 1863 | 7 Feb., 1864 | 2, 3, 5, 7, 8, 10, 12 | 1, 4, 6, 9, 11 |
| n-ji | 元治 | 1 | 1 | 8 Feb., 1864 | 26 Jan., 1865 | 3, 5, 7, 8, 9, 11 | 1, 2, 4, 6, 10, 12 |
| -ō | 慶應 | 1 | 2 | 27 Jan., 1865 | 14 Feb., 1866 | 1, 4, 5 I, 7, 8, 10, 11 | 2, 3, 5, 6, 9, 12 |
| | | 2 | 3 | 15 Feb., 1866 | 4 Feb., 1867 | 1, 3, 7, 8, 10, 11, 12 | 2, 4, 5, 6, 9 |
| | | 3 | 4 | 5 Feb., 1867 | 24 Jan., 1868 | 2, 4, 8, 10, 11, 12 | 1, 3, 5, 6, 7, 9 |
| i-ji | 明治 | 1 | 5 | 25 Jan., 1868 | 10 Feb., 1869 | 2, 3, 5, 8, 10, 11 | 1, 4, 4 I, 6, 7, 9, 12 |
| | | 2 | 6 | 11 Feb., 1869 | 31 Jan., 1870 | 1, 2, 3, 6, 9, 11, 12 | 4, 5, 7, 8, 10 |
| | | 3 | 7 | 1 Feb., 1870 | 18 Feb., 1871 | 2, 3, 5, 7, 9, 11 | 1, 4, 6, 8, 10, 10 I, 12 |
| | | 4 | 8 | 19 Feb., 1871 | 8 Feb., 1872 | 1, 2, 4, 5, 7, 9, 12 | 3, 6, 8, 10, 11 |
| | | 5 | 9 | 9 Feb., 1872 | 31 Dec., 1872 | 2, 4, 5, 7, 8, 10, 12 | 1, 3, 6, 9, 11 |

# TABLE IV

Long and Short months arranged in groups according to the years in which they are identical, together with intervening number of years.

| Group. | Period. | Year. | E-To of Year. | Intervening No. of Years. |
|---|---|---|---|---|
| 1 | Tenna | 1 | Kanoto U | 150 |
|  | Tempō | 2 | Kanoto Tori |  |
| 2 | Jōkyō | 1 | Kinoe Ne | 88 |
|  | Anyei | 1 | Mizunoe Tatsu |  |
| 3 | Jōkyō | 2 | Kinoto Ushi | 62 |
|  | Yenkyō | 4 | Hinoto U | 36 |
|  | Temmei | 3 | Mizunoto U | 53 |
|  | Tempō | 7 | Hinoe Saru | 9 |
|  | Kōkwa | 2 | Kinoto Mi |  |
| 4 | Jōkyō | 4 | Hinoto U | 9 |
|  | Genroku | 2 | Hinoe Ne | 53 |
|  | Kwanyen | 2 | Tsuchinoto Mi |  |
| 5 | Genroku | 1 | Tsuchinoe Ttasu | 62 |
|  | Kwanyen | 3 | Kanoe Uma | 62 |
|  | Bunkwa | 9 | Mizunoe Saru | 9 |
|  | Tempō | 10 | Tsuchinoto I |  |
|  | Kayei | 1 | Tsuchinoe Saru |  |
| 6 | Genroku | 3 | Kanoe Uma | 62 |
|  | Hōreki | 2 | Mizunoe Saru |  |
| 7 | Genroku | 6 | Mizunoto Tori | 62 |
|  | Hōreki | 5 | Kinoto I |  |
| 8 | Genroku | 8 | Hinoto Ushi | 62 |
|  | Hōreki | 7 | Kinoto I |  |
| 9 | Genroku | 11 | Tsuchinoe Tora | 62 |
|  | Hōreki | 10 | Kanoe Tatsu | 98 |
|  | Ansei | 5 | Tsuchinoe Ushi |  |
| 10 | Genroku | 13 | Kanoe Tatsu | 61 |
|  | Hōreki | 11 | Kanoto Mi | 98 |
|  | Ansei | 6 | Tsuchinoto Hitsuji |  |
| 11 | Genroku | 14 | Kinoto Tori | 62 |
|  | Hōreki | 13 | Kanoto Mi | 62 |
|  | Bunsei | 8 | Mizunoto Hitsuji |  |
| 12 | Genroku | 16 | Mizunoto Hitsuji | 62 |
|  | Meiwa | 2 | Kinoto Tori |  |
| 13 | Hōyei | 1 | Hinoe Inu | 62 |
|  | Meiwa | 3 | Kinoe Saru |  |
| 14 | Hōyei | 3 | Hinoe Inu | 62 |
|  | Meiwa | 5 | Tsuchinoe Ne |  |
| 15 | Hōyei | 4 | Hinoto I | 62 |
|  | Meiwa | 6 | Tsuchinoto Ushi |  |
| 16 | Kyōhō | 2 | Hinoto Tori | 62 |
|  | Anyei | 8 | Tsuchinoto I |  |

| Group. | Period. | Year. | E-To of Years. | Intervening No. of Years. |
|---|---|---|---|---|
| 17 | Kyōhō | 4 | Tsuchinoto I | 6 |
|  | Anyei | 9 | Kanoe Ne |  |
| 18 | Kyōhō | 8 | Mizunoto U | 6 |
|  | Temmei | 5 | Kinoto Mi | 6 |
|  | Kōkwa | 4 | Hinoto Hitsuji |  |
| 19 | Kyōhō | 10 | Kinoto Mi | 6 |
|  | Temmei | 7 | Hinoto Hitsuji |  |
| 20 | Kyōhō | 11 | Hinoe Uma | 6 |
|  | Temmei | 8 | Tsuchinoe Saru |  |
| 21 | Kyōhō | 13 | Tsuchinoe Saru | 6 |
|  | Kwansei | 2 | Kanoe Inu |  |
| 22 | Kyōhō | 15 | Kanoe Inu |  |
|  | Gembun | 4 | Tsuchinoto Hitsuji |  |
| 23 | Kyōhō | 16 | Kanoto I | 6 |
|  | Kwansci | 5 | Mizunoe Ushi |  |
| 24 | Kyōhō | 18 | Mizunoe Ushi | 6 |
|  | Kwansei | 7 | Kinoto U |  |
| 25 | Kyōhō | 19 | Kinoe Tora | 6 |
|  | Kwansei | 8 | Hinoe Tatsu | 3 |
| 26 | Tempō | 4 | Mizunoto Mi | 6 |
|  | Gembun | 1 | Hinoe Tatsu |  |
|  | Kwansei | 10 | Tsuchineo Ushi |  |
| 27 | Gembun | 3 | Tsuchinoe Ushi | 3 |
|  | Anye | 3 | Kinoe Usihi |  |
| 28 | Kwampō | 2 | Mizunoe Inu | 6 |
|  | Bunkwa | 1 | Kinoe Ne |  |
| 29 | Hōreki | 8 | Tsuchinoe Tora | 9 |
|  | Ansei | 3 | Hinoe Tatsu |  |
| 30 | Temmei | 2 | Mizunoe Tora | 6 |
|  | Kōkwa | 1 | Kinoe Tatsu |  |
| 31 | Kwansei | 3 | Kanoto I | 6 |
|  | Kayei | 6 | Mizunoe Ushi |  |
| 32 | Kyōwa | 1 | Hinoto Tori | 3 |
|  | Tempō | 8 | Kanoto Tori |  |
| 33 | Bunkwa | 7 | Kanoe Uma | 6 |
|  | Meiji | 5 | Mizunoe Saru |  |
| 34 | Bunkwa | 14 | Hinoto Ushi |  |
|  | Bunsei | 9 | Hinoe Inu | 6 |
| 35 | Tempō | 13 | Mizunoe Tora |  |
|  | Kayei | 4 | Kanoto I |  |

For first day of each month, consult Bramsen's[1] chronological tables; taking care to adjust dates given therein to the English calendar by deducting 10 days between 15th October, 1582, and 10th March, 1700, and 11 days between 12th March, 1700, and 13th September 1752.

[1] Published in 1910 as the Supplement of Vol. XXXVI, *Transactions of the Asiatic Society of Japan.*

## TABLE IV—*continued*

### REMARKS UPON THE ABOVE GROUPS

Except in the last two years of groups 3 and 5, in the first two years of group 4, and in the two years of groups 22, 34, and 35, when the intervening number of years is but nine, there is no difficulty in determining which years are meant when only the long or short months or both appear on a print.

The following examples of such extreme cases, taken from *surimono*, will explain the application of determining factors.

A. On a *surimono* by Hokkei are the long months 2, 4, 7, 9, 11, 12, which of themselves may indicate Tempō 17 or Kōkwa 2 ; but as the picture represents a monkey dancing at the instigation of his trainer, it is clear that the Monkey year of 1836 is meant.

B. On a *surimono* by Yeisen are the short months 3, 5, 6, 8, 10, 12, which of themselves may indicate Tempō 13 or Kayei 4 ; but as Yeisen died in Kayei 1 (1848) it is clear that the former year is meant.

In most cases the E-To of the year also appears on the print, e.g. Hinoto Ushi, Hinoe Inu, etc., when no confusion can arise, for in no single case in the above-mentioned groups are these identical. In a case when the celestial stem is omitted and the zodiacal sign and long or short months given, as for instance, Inu and short months 2, 4, 7, 9, 11, it is clear that Kyōhō 15 is meant, despite the fact that these months are also common to Gembun 4, because the former is a Dog year, whereas the latter is a Goat year.

The months are apportioned to the seasons as follows :—

> Haru, Spring, 1st, 2nd, and 3rd months.
> Natsu, Summer, 4th, 5th, and 6th months.
> Aki, Autumn, 7th, 8th, and 9th months.
> Fuyu, Winter, 10th, 11th, and 12th months.

### VARIOUS FORMS OF NUMERALS USED TO INDICATE THE MONTHS

| | | | | |
|---|---|---|---|---|
| 正 武 | Shō | First | 九 | Ku | Ninth |
| 二 青 | Ni | Second | 十 | Jū | Tenth |
| 三 二 春 | San | Third | 十一 霜月 | Jū-ichi | Eleventh |
| 四 R | Shi | Fourth | 土 | Jū-ni | Twelfth |
| 五 R X | Go | Fifth | 閏 壬 壬 | Urū | Intercalary |
| 六 央 | Roku | Sixth | 月 | Gwatsu or Tsuki | } Month |
| 七 | Shichi | Seventh | | | |
| 八 門 | Hachi | Eighth | | | |

Gwatsu is understood after each numeral, except the second form of 11th month pronounced Shimotsuki.

# THE CENSORSHIP OF PRINTS

A censorship of printed matter in general was instituted by the Bakufu or Shōgun's Government during the last quarter of the 18th century. In Yedo the administration and control was vested in one of the two Machi-bugyō (Governors and City Magistrates), who were responsible to the Bakufu that nothing calculated to throw discredit upon the Government or subversive of public morality was published, and that copyright was not infringed.

They were empowered to inflict upon anyone who contravened the laws various punishments, the most common of which were reprimand, severe reprimand, fines, confiscation of unauthorized matter and of the wood-blocks, confinement to his house with or without handcuffs, imprisonment, and banishment from Yedo for a specified period. The culprits were usually authors, artists, engravers, printers, and publishers, who were each and all severally held responsible for infraction of the regulations. Censors, too, were liable to punishment when such infraction was due to negligence in the proper performance of their duties. The procedure adopted was briefly as follows. The artist's original sketch had to be submitted by the publisher to the nearest censor, who, if satisfied that it fulfilled the statutes of the law, passed and returned it to the publisher, who was then at liberty to have the blocks engraved and to print off the desired number of copies for sale.

If in doubt, the censor had to forward it to the censorship department in the Machi-bugyō's office, where the matter was decided. If publication was sanctioned, the censor was so informed, and he then returned it with his approval to the publisher. In spite of the apparent thoroughness of the system, abuses crept in owing to evasion on the part of publishers or slackness on that of censors ; and the authorities found it necessary to issue proclamations from time to time directing attention to such abuses and warning censors to exercise a more vigilant inspection in future, and to bring offenders to book. In the 7th month of Kyōhō 6 (1721) an edict was promulgated suspending, amongst other matters, the printing and sale for the time being of single-sheet pictures (ichimai-ye). Again, in the 5th month of Kwansei 2 (1790), a similar injunction was issued, which was modified in the 9th month of that year as follows : " Despite all previous warnings, books have assumed an improper tone. You, Gyōji, must censor all matter intended for publication, including picture-books, readers, novels, etc. ; and any that are harmful to morals or in any way indecent must be forbidden. Those already published must be suppressed. As regards single-sheet pictures, those with pictures only may, as a rule, be passed ; but if there is any inscription on them, you must inspect it most carefully ; and no doubtful matter must in any case be allowed to be published. Persons who disregard this order must be accused by you in court. Moreover, if your censoring is imperfectly carried out, or if you neglect to censor at all, you shall be held personally responsible.

Those whom these instructions concern, must bear them well in mind, as well as those issued in the Kyōhō period, which will be embodied in this proclamation. Remember, therefore, this injunction as also all previous ones, and see to it that you carry out your examination in a proper and vigilant manner.

The above addressed to the Gyōji of the Wholesale Publishers' Guild in the 9th month of the 2nd year of Kwansei."

The censors referred to as " Gyōji " were wholesale publishers selected periodically to carry out the duties of examining all matter for publication. They were of proved probity and well connected ; but, owing to carelessness or negligence, had frequently to be censured. Sometimes headmen of wards (Nanushi) were appointed in their stead ; in both cases the appointments took effect from the commencement of each year, and were for a certain term of office which was fixed by roster. The following example of a roster for 1840, when Nanushi were appointed, will explain the system.[1]

" Monthly Roster of Duties for the superintending Nanushi in charge, revised in the 1st month of Tempō 11, the year of the Rat.

| | | |
|---|---|---|
| Fifth and twelfth months | . . | Taruya Saburoyemon. |
| Sixth month | . . . | Wada Genshichi. |
| Seventh month | . . . | Takeguchi Shōyemon. |
| Second and ninth months | . . | Ōtsuka Gorobei. |
| First and eighth months | . . | Takano Shinyemon. |
| Third and tenth months | . . | Watanabe Shōyemon. |
| Fourth and eleventh months | . . | Fukatsu Ihei." |

Immediately following the edict of the 9th month of 1790, official censors impressed, apparently for the first time, a seal of approval (ken-in) upon prints. Prior to this, no such seal seems to have been in use. This took the form of a round seal enclosing the character " Kiwame," as reproduced

Taken from a document in the possession of the writer, in which also are set forth the names of 30 gyōji of the Old division, 23 of the New division, and 24 of the Supplementary division held in waiting in cases of necessity. In addition is a Notice warning the public against the illegal sale of prints by engravers.

in the accompanying table, No. 1. This seal was in use alone till the end of Kwansei 11, which expired on January 24th, 1800; and continued to be used either singly or accompanied by or in combination with other seals till about 1845. It is shown in 1a in combination with seal 4, meaning " approved " in 2nd (month = 1806); a combination found on a print by Kiyomine, but not so far elsewhere. For other combinations, see Nos. 65 to 67. For its use in square form, see Nos. 28 to 30. It has nothing to do with the quality of a print, nor with its authenticity, except indirectly on the presumption that the censor was aware of the artist's identity. It is often absent, especially between 1790 and 1800. This may have been due partly to evasion by publishers or to negligence of censors; but more generally infringement of copyright was the cause. Its absence, therefore, is of itself no proof that a print antedates 1790; though, taken with other factors, it often affords valuable evidence that such was the case. As regards infringement of copyright, we have proof of such in the document of 1840 already mentioned. Briefly it reads as follows:

" *Notice to the Public.* ' *All printed matter was of old authorized to be sold by recognized wholesale publishers; but recently block-cutters have been placing on the market printed matter without authority. We, therefore. instituted proceedings in the Appeal Court, which decided that block-cutters were only allowed to cut blocks; but that printing and the sale of printed matter was entirely in the hands of authorized publishers. In consequence of this decision, we, the undersigned, beg to acquaint the public that henceforth all printed matter for sale by authorized publishers will bear such names or seals as are affixed hereto* (*which here follow*) : *Printers' Guild of Wholesale Publishers.*' *Dated* 10*th Month,* 1840."

Okumura Masanobu and Kitagawa Utamaro were both compelled to attach the words Shōmei, i.e. " genuine name," to their signatures to protect themselves from contemporary forgeries; and there is little doubt that in their time, too, engravers were responsible for most of the counterfeits.

The following notes will explain the remaining seals in the accompanying table, which includes the greater majority of censor and date seals and are typical of the few omitted.

No. 2. Saru shō, i.e. Monkey (year) 1st (month), corresponding to 1800. Found on prints by Shikō (II ?) and Toyokuni I. The same seal, but for the 2nd month, occurs on a print by the latter.

A to M inclusive contain the names in abbreviated form of some whole-sale publishers who acted as *gyōji*. They are usually accompanied by Kiwame seal No. 1. Detailed explanation as below.

A. Tsū-ji; full name uncertain. Perhaps Tsūmura Ji ?
B. Yama-guchi, i.e. Yamaguchiya Tōbei.
C. Another form of Yama-guchi; perhaps Yamaguchiya Chūsuke.
D. Mura-ji, i.e. Murataya Jirobei.
E. Nishi-miya, i.e. Nishinomiya Shinroku.
F. Mori-ji, i.e. Mori-ya Jihei.
G. Kami-mura, i.e. Kami- (or Uye-) mura Kichiyemon.
H. Gyōji aratame. This means " examined by a Gyōji," whose name is not given. It affords interesting evidence of what has been said. Found on a print by Toyokuni I, dated 1813.
I. Yama-tō, i.e. Yamaguchiya Tōbei. Compare B above.
J. Iwa-to, i.e. Iwatoya Kisaburō.
K. Tai-hō. This publisher has not been identified.
L. Tsuru-kin, i.e. Tsuruya Kinsuke.
M. Ryū-sa-burō. Not identified. Found on one print only by Yeizan.

The first of these, Tsū-ji, is found on prints by most artists working from 1804 to 1817. It is interesting to note that it occurs on a print by Kiyonaga of a Kintoki series dating from about 1804. Another of this artist's prints—children's amusements—is dated 1799, but not with a date-seal.

These two instances are given to show that, though Kiyonaga practically gave up print-designing in the beginning of Kwansei, he occasionally returned to work. One of his *surimono* is dated 2nd month of Bunkwa 2.

No. 3. *a = hachi*, eight; *b = jū*, ten; *c* also *= jū*, ten; *d = jūni*, twelve. These four stand respectively for the 8th, 10th, and 12th months of 1805.

Nos. 3*e*, 4 and 4*a*. 3*e = shō*, first; 4 = *ni*, two; 4*a = shi*, four. These three stand for the 1st, 2nd, and 4th months of 1806.

Nos. 5 to 10 read in rotation : Tora go, roku, shichi, jū, jū ichi, jū ni ; i.e. Tiger (year), 5, 6, 7, 10, 11, 12 (months) of Bunkwa 3. For corresponding dates, see Chronological Table. Also for those below.

Nos. 11 to 17 read in rotation : U san, go, roku, hachi, ku, jū ichi (two forms) ; i.e. Hare (year), 3, 5, 6, 8, 9, 11 (months) of Bunkwa 4.

Nos. 18 to 20 read in rotation : Tatsu shi, go, jū ; i.e. Dragon (year) 4, 5, 10 (months) of Bunkwa 5.

No. 21.  Mi ni, i.e. Snake (year) 2 (month) of Bunkwa 6.

No. 22.  Uma hachi, i.e. Horse (year) 8 (month) of Bunkwa 7.

No. 23.  Hitsuji ni, i.e. Goat (year) 2 (month) of Bunkwa 8.

No. 24.  Inu hachi, i.e. Dog (year) 8 (month) of Bunkwa 11.

No. 25.  Inu shichi, i.e. Dog (year) 7 (month) of Bunkwa 11.

Nos. 26 to 35 inclusive are found on Uchiwa-ye or fan pictures.

No. 26.  Tora aratame, i.e. examined in Tiger (year) = 1818.

No. 27.  U aratame, i.e. examined in Hare (year) = 1819.

No. 28.  Saru kiwame, i.e. approved in Monkey (year) = 1824.

No. 29.  Inu kiwame, i.e. approved in Dog (year) = 1826.

No. 30.  I and I kiwame, i.e. Boar (year) and Boar (year) approved. Both equal 1827 ; the kiwame being omitted in the first, perhaps by mistake of engraver.

No. 31.  Ne, i.e. Rat (year) = 1828.  } Kiwame omitted as in 30 (1)
No. 32.  Ushi, i.e. Ox (year) = 1829.  } above.

No. 33.  Tora aratame, i.e. Tiger (year) examined = 1830.

No. 34.  U aratame, i.e. Hare (year) examined = 1831.

No. 35.  Tatsu aratame, i.e. Dragon (year) examined = 1832.

Nos. 36 to 49 inclusive read in rotation : Fu, Take, Mura, Watari, Watanabe, Mura-matsu, Ta-naka (two forms), Magomi, Fuku, Mura-ta, Yoshi-mura, Me-ra, Kinu-gasa, and Hama.  These are the abbreviated names of Nanushi, three of whom are found with their full names in the roster above-quoted ; viz. Fu (-katsu Ihei), Take (-guchi Shōyemon), and Wata or Watanabe (Shōyemon).

No. 50.  (a) The oval aratame seal ; (b) the round aratame seal ; each meaning " examined."  The first in use from 1848 to 1851, and the last from Dec. 1853 to 1857 inclusive.

Nos. 51 to 58 read in rotation : Ne roku, i.e. Rat (year) 6th (month) = 1852 ; Ushi jū ichi, i.e. Ox (year) 11th (month) = 1853 ; Tora ni, i.e. Tiger (year) 2nd (month) = 1854 ; Ne urū, i.e. Rat (year) intercalary (month) = 1852, 2nd month extra ; U jū ni, i.e. Hare (year) 12th (month), began 8th January, 1856 ; Tatsu ku, i.e. Dragon (year) 9th (month) = 1856 ; Mi hachi, i.e. Snake (year) eighth (month) = 1857 ; Uma ni, i.e. Horse 2 = 1858.  After the 11th month of Ox year, which began on 30th December, 1853, the round aratame seal accompanies these seals, except during the Horse year of 1858, when for some unknown reason it was omitted.

Nos. 59 and 60 read respectively Ne uru, i.e. Rat (year), intercalary (2nd month) = 1852 ; and Ushi shō, i.e. Ox (year) 1st (month) = 1853. These are usually accompanied by one or other of the Nanushi seals 40 to 49, and are seen only on Fan prints, as also are Nos. 61 to 67.

Nos. 61 to 64 read in rotation : Tiger 5 = 1854 ; Hare 2 = 1855 ; Dragon 2 = 1856 ; Snake 2 = 1857.

Nos. 65 to 67 read in rotation : Horse (1858) approved ; Goat (1859) approved ; Monkey (1860) approved.

Nos. 68 to 82 are incorporated with the aratame seal, and read in rotation as follows. (To avoid repetition, the transliteration from the vernacular is here omitted, as in the two previous categories 61 to 67.) Nos. 68 and 69 Goat 1 = 1859, examined ; Monkey 3rd intercalary = 1860, examined ; Cock 8 = 1861, examined ; Dog 1 = 1862, examined ; Boar 4 = 1863, examined ; Gen-ji, i.e. Genji (period) = 1864 ; Rat 1 = 1864, examined ; Ox 12 examined, began January 17th, 1866 ; Tiger 4 = 1866, examined ; Hare 5 = 1867, examined ; Dragon 10 = 1868, examined ; Snake 1 = 1869, examined ; Horse intercalary (10th month) = 1870, examined ; Horse 11 = 1870, examined.

No. 83 reads Cock 9 = 1872.

No. 84 reads Dog 11 = 1874.

Several of these date-seals found on prints of actors in character from some particular play have been checked with the date upon which the play in question was produced, and in each case the dates correspond. This proves that the artist's design practically coincided with the date of production of a play ; and this was probably the case during the years before date-seals were used. Consequently a print identified from the stage records as representing a scene from a certain play may be confidently dated as having been designed on or about the date upon which the play was produced.

# SPECIMENS OF SOME CENSOR SEALS FROM NOV., 1790, TO DEC., 1874

## INCLUSIVE APPROXIMATE DATES BETWEEN WHICH CENSOR SEALS OF THE TYPE SHOWN ON THE OPPOSITE PAGE WERE IN USE

| Number of Seal. | Dates. | Number of Seal. | Dates. |
|---|---|---|---|
| 1 | Kiwame seal, November, 1790, to January, 1845, either singly or accompanied by other seals. | 27 | 1819 |
| | | 28 | 1824 |
| | | 29 | 1826 |
| 1a | | 30 | 1827 |
| 2 | 1800 | 31 | 1828 |
| 3a, b, c, d | 8–12 mo. 1805–6 | 32 | 1829 |
| 3e, 4, 4a | 1–4 mo. 1806 | 33 | 1830 |
| 5–10 | 5–12 mo. 1806–7 | 34 | 1831 |
| 11–17 | 1807–1808 | 35 | 1832 |
| 18–20 | 1808 | 36–49 | 1840–1853 |
| 21 | 1809 | 50–58 | 1848–1858 |
| 22 | 1810 | 59–60 | 1852–1853, with seals 40–49 |
| 23 | 1811 | 61–64 | 1854–1857, with seal 50 |
| 24–25 | 1814 | 65–67 | 1858–1860 |
| 26 | 1818 | 68–84 | 1859–1874 |

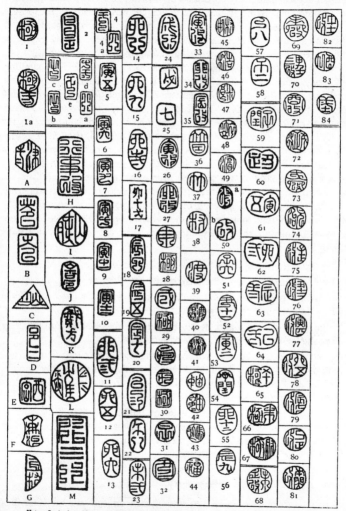

*Note.*—Seals A to M are abbreviations of Censors' names, and were in use from 1804 to 1817.

# ACTORS' MON

When an actor's name was inscribed on a print, it usually took the form of his professional name (*geimei*) by which he was known to the public, e.g. Segawa Kikunojō. Sometimes his *haimyō* or literary name, which in the above example was Rokō, was added or substituted. More rarely he was indicated by his *ya-gō* (or *ka-mei*) and *haimyō*, e.g. Sakai-ya Shūkwaku, the actor whose *geimei* was Nakamura Nakazō II; or by his *ya-gō* alone, e.g. Kōrai-ya, the actor whose *geimei* was Ichikawa Kōmazō II and whose *haimyō* was Kinshō. Each actor used two *Mon* called *Jō* and *Kae*, meaning "Fixed" and "Alternative" respectively. The *Jō-mon* was used when in stage costume, and was frequently common to actors belonging to the same *Ke* or Line. The *Kae-mon* was more personal and, though occasionally found on prints of actors in character, was generally reserved for private attire. In exceptional cases both *Mon* appear on a print.

In the following table of 111 selected *Mon* of actors who appeared on the Yedo stage during the 18th century, it has been necessary, in order to permit of the explanatory text appearing on the same page and opposite to the *Mon* to which it refers, to make the same as brief as possible. The following remarks will elucidate the system adopted and the abbreviations that have been employed.

1. The serial numbers in the text correspond to those of the *Mon*.

2. The *Mon*, except when otherwise stated, are *Jō-mon*.

3. An actor's *geimei* is printed in larger type than his *yagō* or *haimyō* which follow and are printed in italics.

4. When dates of birth and death are known they follow immediately after the *geimei* or *haimyō*, as the case may be.

5. In recording changes of *geimei* and the dates of such changes the letters FN stand for the first *geimei* by which an actor was known. The letters PN stand for Present Name, and refer to the *geimei* immediately following the serial number.

6. The letters M or F, meaning male or female, represent the rôle in which an actor specialized. In cases where he played both male and female parts, M precedes F, or vice versa, according to which of the two rôles he mostly impersonated.

7. The word Act, followed by dates, represent an actor's activity on the Yedo stage during the 18th century.

A more or less chronological sequence based on the year of birth has been preserved.

The reproductions of the *Mon* on white or on black ground have no special significance, as such was dependent on whether dark or light garments were worn by the actor depicted on the print from which the particular *Mon* was traced.

There is no exact foreign equivalent to the *Mon*. Hence the Japanese word has been used throughout. Its nature is that of a badge or design dyed or wrought in cloth. In the case of an actor, his *Jō-mon* indicates the *Ke* or Line of Actors to which he belongs ; his *Kae-mon* identifies the actor himself.

# TABLE OF ACTORS' MON

## WITH DATES OF BIRTH AND DEATH WHEN KNOWN

### AND ACTUAL OR APPROXIMATE DATES OF THEIR ACTIVITY AT YEDO DURING THE EIGHTEENTH CENTURY

*Note.*—Mon 1 to 21 are those of Actors whose activity ceased prior to 1730. The first 12 specialized in female roles, the remaining 9 in male roles.

1. SAWAMURA KODENJI. Act.: 1700–1702.

2. KAMIMURA KICHISABURŌ. Act.: 1700–1708.

3. SODEZAKI NUINOSUKE. Act.: 1702–1711.

4. NISHIKAWA KŌNOSUKE. Act.: 1700–1702.

5. NAKAMURA SENYA. Act.: Dec. 1716–Oct. 1718.

6. IWAI SAGENDA. Act.: 1700–1712.

7. MATSUSHIMA HYŌTARŌ. Act.: 1700–1702; Dec., 1724–Oct., 1725.

8. YOSHIZAWA AYAME I. 1673–1729. Act.: Dec. 1713–Oct. 1714.

9. NAKAMURA TAKESABURŌ. Died, 1724. Act.: 1700–1720.

10. TSUTSUI KICHIJURŌ. Died, 1727. Act.: 1704–1715.

11. ARASHI KIYOSABURŌ. Died, 1713. Act.: Dec. 1707–Oct. 1709; Dec. 1711–April 1713. *Note.*—This actor was the first to play the part of O Shichi when that character was introduced into the play "Arashi Soga," produced at the Nakamura Theatre in the spring of Hōyei 5 (began on January 12, 1708). His success was such that his *Mon* was used in future (as an indication of the rôle) by actors playing O Shichi, in addition to their own *Mon.*

12. HAYAKAWA HASSE. Act.: Dec. 1703–Dec. 1713; Aug. 1727–Dec. 1728.

13. ICHIKAWA DANJŪRŌ I, *Naritaya Saigyū.* 1660–1704. Act.: 1700–Feb. 1704.

14. NAKAMURA SHICHISABURŌ I. Died, 1708. Act.: Nov. 1700–Mar. 1707.

15. NAKAMURA DENKURŌ I, *Maizuru.* Died, 1713. Act.: 1700–Mar. 1713.

16. YAMANAKA HEIKURŌ, *Senka.* 1632–1724. Act.: 1700–1722.

17. ICHIKAWA MONNOSUKE I. Died, 1729. Act.: 1700–Dec. 1727.

18. KATSUYAMA MATAGORŌ. Act.: 1707–1723.

19. IWAI HANSHIRŌ II. M. Act.: 1700–1710. *Note.*—Hanshirō III. 1703–1759. M. F. Act.: 1722–1756 at irregular intervals; used a similar *Mon.*

20. TOMIZAWA HANSABURŌ. M. Act.: 1710–1718.

21. NAKAJIMA KANZAYEMON I. 1662–1716. M. Act.: 1700–1710. *Note.*—Nakajima Mioyemon I. 1702–1764. M. Act.: Dec. 1714–Mar. 1762 used a similar *Mon*; as did Mioyemon II, M. F. N. Miozō. Act.: 1755–1782.

22.    23.    24.

22. MATSUMOTO KŌSHIRŌ I. 1674–1730. M. Act.: Feb. 1700–Dec. 1729.

23. OGAWA ZENGORŌ. M. Act.: *c.* 1711–1732.

24. ICHIKAWA DANZŌ I, *Shikō.* 1684–1740. M. Act.: 1695–Feb. 1740. Used this *Mon* from Dec. 1715 to Dec. 1731, when he removed the ideograph "Ichi."

25. NAKAMURA KICHIBEI. 1684–1765. M. Act.: *c.* Feb. 1716–March, 1739.

26. SODEOKA SHŌTARŌ. F. Act.: *c.* 1716–1733.

27. BANDŌ HIKOSABURŌ I, *Shinsui.* Died, 1751. M. Act.: Dec. 1729–Nov. 1734; Feb. 1738–Dec. 1749.

28. ARASHI SANGORŌ, *Raishi.* 1687–1739. M. Act.: Dec. 1726–Oct. 1729.

29. ŌTANI HIROYEMON II. Died, 1748. F.N.: Ryūzayemon. P.N.: Dec. 1745. M. Act.: *c.* 1725–Dec. 1747.

30. ICHIKAWA SŌSABURŌ. 1687–1754. M. Act.: July, 1731–Dec. 1753.

31. ICHIKAWA DANJŪRŌ II, *Sanshō and Hakuyen.* 1688–1758. F.N.: Kuzō. P.N.: Aug. 1703; Yebizō, Dec. 1735. M. Act.: 1697–Oct. 1741; Dec. 1742–Sept. 1756.

32. SAWAMURA SŌJŪRŌ I, *Tosshi.* 1689–1756. Changed to Chōjūrō, Dec. 1747; to Suketakaya Takasuke, Dec. 1753. M. Act.: Dec. 1718–Sep. 1743; Dec. 1744–Nov. 1746; Dec. 1747–Dec. 1755.

33. SANOGAWA MANGIKU. 1690–1747. F. and M. Act.: Dec. 1718–Sep. 1724; Dec. 1729–Oct. 1731; Dec. 1741–Mar. 1743.

34. SODEZAKI MIWANO. F. Act.: *c.* 1725–Dec. 1735.

35. HAYAKAWA SHINKATSU. F. Act.: *c.* 1703–Dec. 1707; Dec. 1711–Oct. 1738.

36. YAMASHITA KINSAKU I. Died, 1750. F. Act.: Dec. 1711–Dec. 1717; 1723–1727; Dec. 1741–Mar. 1742.

37. ANEGAWA SHINSHIRŌ. 1690–1749. M. Act.: Dec. 1732–Nov. 1734. Kaemon.

38. FUJIMURA HANJŪRŌ. F.N.: Handayū. P.N.: Dec. 1729. M. F. Act.; *c.* 1714–1758.

39. SEGAWA KIKUNOJŌ I, *Rokō.* 1690–1749. F. Act.: Dec. 1730–Oct. 1737; Dec. 1741–Mar. 1748.

40. OGINO ISABURŌ. 1694–1748. M. and F. Act.: *c.* 1724–July, 1747. Kaemon.

41. Jōmon of the above, and of the Ogino Ke in general.

42. SODEZAKI ISENO. F. Act.: *c.* 1726–Dec. 1745.

43. SANJŌ KANTARŌ. 1697–1763. Changed to Hanai Saisaburō II in Dec. 1746. M. F. Act.: Aug. 1714–July, 1749.

44. ARASHI OTOHACHI, *Wakō.* 1695–1769. F.N.: Otanosuke. M. Act.: 1732–Dec. 1768.

45. ŌTANI HIROJI I, *Jitchō.* 1699–1747. M. Act.: Dec. 1701–Oct. 1723; Dec. 1727–Oct. 1737; Dec. 1741–Dec. 1743. Same *Mon* was used by Hiroji II, died, 1757. F.N.: Bunzō; Dec. 1736 changed to Bandō Matatarō; Dec. 1743 to Ōtani Oniji I. P.N.: Dec. 1748. M. Act.: Dec. 1735–Feb. 1756.

46. ICHIMURA UZAYEMON VIII, *Kakō.* 1699–1762. F.N.: Takenojō; Dec. 1737, Uzayemon; P.N. with U written differently, 1751. M. Act.: 1709–1759.

47. YOSHIZAWA AYAME II, *Shunsui.* 1702–1754. F.N.: Sakinosuke II. P.N. Dec. 1729. F. Act.: Dec. 1745–Oct. 1752. *Note.*—Ayame III did not act at Yedo. Ayame IV, *Tachibanaya Shunsui*, 1739–1792, used same *Mon*. F.N. Yamashita Koshikibu and Ichigorō; 1755, Yoshizawa Goroichi; 1764 Sakinosuke III; P.N. Dec. 1778.

48. ARASHI WAKANO. F.M. Act.: 1722–1726; Dec. 1752–1758.

49. NAKAMURA SHICHISABURŌ II, *Shōchō.* 1703–1774. In Dec. 1770 became Nakamura Shōchō. M. Act.: Feb. 1711–Dec. 1773.

50. The *Kae-mon* of the above.

51. TSU-UCHI MONSABURŌ, *Shōkō.* 1703–1753. F.N. Ōtani Rokuzō. P.N. 1730. Changed to Tsuyama Tomozō, Dec. 1751. M. Act.: 1734–Oct. 1738; Dec. 1740–April, 1742. Dec. 1747–Dec. 1751.

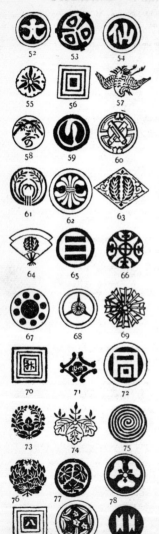

52. TSURUYA NAMBOKU. 1708–1763. M. Act.: Dec. 1732–July 1752.
53. ARASHI KOROKU I, *Sanchō*. 1708–1786. F. Act.: Dec. 1746–Dec. 1755. *Note.*—The same *Mon* was used by Arashi Hinaji. Act.: 1763–Dec. 1774. M. F.
54. NAKAMURA SUKEGORŌ I, *Gyoraku*. 1711–1763. F. N.: Kumetarō Dec. 1736 changed to Sengoku Sukegorō; P. N.: Dec. 1739. M. Act.: Dec. 1725–Mar. 1763.
55. MATSUMOTO KŌSHIRŌ II, *Goryū*. 1711–1778. F. N.: Shichizō; P. N.: Dec. 1735; became Danjūrō IV in Dec. 1754, changing *Jō-mon* to No. 56 and taking No. 57 as *Kae-mon*. Reverted to Kōshirō II in Dec. 1770; became Ichikawa Yebizō II in Dec. 1772. M. Act.: 1719–Mar. 1774; Dec. 1775–Sep. 1776.
58. TAKINAKA KASEN. 1713–1770. F. N.: Takenaka Kasen; P. N.: Feb. 1739; changed to Utagawa Shirogorō in Dec. 1743; to Sawamura Sōjūrō II in Oct. 1749, taking *Mon* No. 59. M. Act.: 1734–Nov. 1769. Hamyō when Sōjūrō, *Tosshi*.
60. NAKAMURA UTAYEMON I, *Kagaya Issen*. 1714–1791. M. Act.: April 1757–Dec. 1761; Dec. 1768–Dec. 1770. *Note.*—Was first called Utanosuke, but not at Yedo.

61. The *Kae-mon* of the above.
62. SEGAWA KIKUJIRŌ, *Sengyo*. 1715–1756. F. Act.: Dec. 1731–Oct. 1737; Dec. 1739–April 1742; Dec. 1743–Dec. 1755.
63. ONOYE KIKUGORŌ I, *Baikō*. 1717–1783. F. M. Act.: Dec. 1742–Sep. 1766; Dec. 1769–Dec. 1773.

64. *Jō-mon* of the above from and including Dec. 1752.
65. ICHIKAWA DANZŌ III, *Mikawaya Shikō*. 1719–1792. F. N.: Bandō Jirosaburō; then Ichikawa Jirosa(-burō); Dec. 1739. Ichikawa Dansaburō II; P. N.: Dec. 1740. M. Act.: 1739–Dec. 1744; Dec. 1761–Dec. 1765; Dec. 1766–Feb. 1772. *Note.*—The *Mon* shown in his *Kae-mon*. His *Jō-mon* is the same as No. 56.
66. NAKAMURA DENKURŌ II, *Maizuru*. 1719–1777. F. N.: Katsujūrō; P. N.: Nov. 1745. Changed to Kansaburō VIII in Dec. 1775. M. Act.: Dec. 1733–Dec. 1775.

67. TOMIZAWA MONTARŌ. F. Act.: c. 1730–c. 1749.
68. TAMAZAWA SAIJIRŌ. F. M. Act.: c. 1733–c. 1751.
69. NAKAMURA TOMIJŪRŌ I, *Keishi*. 1719–1786. F. M. Act.: July to Nov. 1731; April 1742–July 1743; Dec. 1752–Oct. 1757; Dec. 1770–Dec. 1778.

70. ICHIKAWA MASUGORŌ, *Sanshō*. 1721–1742. In Dec. 1735 became Danjūrō III. M. F. Act.: Dec. 1727–April 1741. *Note.*—Sometimes used same *Mon* without the "*masu*" in the centre.
71. NAKAMURA KIYOSABURŌ. 1721–1777. F. Act.: Dec. 1749–Nov. 1752; Dec. 1754–Oct. 1758.
72. SANOGAWA ICHIMATSU I, *Seifu*. 1722–1763. M. F. Act.: Feb. 1741–Aug. 1744; Dec. 1744–April 1762.
73. AZUMA TŌZŌ I, 1723–1776. F. N.: Ikujima Daikichi; P. N.: Nov. 1747. Changed to Agemaki Rinya in Dec. 1756. Reverted to Tōzō in Oct. 1760. F. Act.: 1730–Dec. 1774.
74. NAKAMURA KUMETARŌ I, *Richō*. 1724–1777. F. Act.: Dec. 1748–Aug. 1755.
75. ICHIMURA UZAYEMON IX, *Kakitsu*. 1724–1785. F. N.: Manzō; Feb. 1745, Kamezō; P. N.: Oct. 1762. M. Act.: Dec. 1731–July 1761; Dec. 1761–Mar. 1785. This is his *Kae-mon*; his *Jō-mon* as for No. 46.
76. ICHIKAWA RAIZŌ I, *Tokaiya Gempei*. 1724–1767. F. N.: Arashi Tamagashiwa; Dec. 1753, Ichikawa Masuzō; Dec. 1761. M. F. Act.: Feb.–Aug. 1743; June 1748; Dec. 1750; Feb. 1753–Dec. 1761. *The Mon* shown is his *Kae-mon*. His *Jō-mon* as for No. 56, sometimes with "*Rai*" in centre.
77. OSAGAWA TSUNEYO I. 1724–1766. F. Act.: Dec. 1750–1766.
78. MORITA KANYA VI, *Zankyō*. 1725–1780. F. N.: Takinaka Shigenoi; 1740, Sawamura Shigenoi; Dec. 1746, Sawamura Kodenji; P. N.: Dec. 1747. M. F. Act.: c. 1736–Dec. 1770.
79. ICHIKAWA YAOZŌ I. 1730–1750. P. N.: Matsujima Yaozō; P. N.: Aug. 1749. M. Act.: 1747–July 1759.
80. YAMASHITA KINSAKU II, *Tennōjiya Rikō*. 1733–1799. F. N.: Nakamura Handayū; P. N.: Dec. 1749. F. Act.: Dec. 1752–Dec. 1758; Feb. 1770–Dec. 1780; Dec. 1794.
81. SAKATA HANGORŌ II. 1764–1782. F. N. Sengoku Sajūrō; P. N.: Aug. 1749. M. Act.: 1742–Oct. 1771, April 1773–May 1782. *Note.*—Hangorō III, 1756–1795, used same *Jō-mon*. F. N.: Bandō Kumajirō, then Kumajurō, and later Sakata Hanjūrō. P. N. in 1783.

xli

82.  The *Kae-mon* of Hangorō II.

83.  ICHIKAWA YAOZŌ II, *Chūsha*. 1735–1777. F.N. : Nakamura Denzō ; P.N. : Dec. 1763. M. Act. : 1751–June 1777. *Note.*—Mon shown is his *Kae-mon* ; for *Jō-mon* he used No. 79.

84.  NAKAMURA NAKAZŌ I, *Sakaeya Shūkwaku*. 1736–1790. F.N. : Ichi-jurō ; soon after took P.N. M. Act. : Dec. 1745 ; May 20, 1748 ; Dec. 1754–Aug. 1789. *Mon* 84 was his *Kae-mon*. Mon B was in use from Dec. 1785 to Dec. 1786, when he called himself Nakayama Kojūrō, afterwards reverting to P. N. As *Jō-mon*, he used No. 15, generally with ideograph "*naka*" in centre, to which he added the "*nimben*," as seen in No. 107, from Dec. 1760.

85.  MATSUMOTO KŌSHIRŌ IV, *Kōraiya Kinkō*. 1737–1802. F.N. : Segawa Kinji ; Dec. 1757, Ichikawa Takejūrō ; Feb. 1763, Somegorō ; Dec. 1763, Komazō I ; P. N. : Dec. 1772. M. Act. : Dec. 1754–Oct. 1758 ; Dec. 1760–Sep. 1784 ; Feb. 1786–Oct. 1801. *Jō-mon* No. 55. *Mon* shown is his *Kae-mon*.

86.  BANDŌ HIKOSABURŌ II. 1741–1768. F.N. : Kikumatsu. P.N. : Feb. 1754. M. Act. : Dec. 1756. F. Act. : Dec. 1768.

87.  SEGAWA KIKUNOJŌ II, *Hamamuraya Rokō*. 1741–1773. F.N. : Kichiji ; P.N. : Dec. 1756. F. Act. : 1759–Mar. 1772. *Mon* is his *Kae-mon* ; *Jō-mon* as for No. 39.

88.  ICHIKAWA DANJŪRŌ V, *Naritaya Sanshō*, later Hakuyen. 1741–1806. F.N. : Matsumoto Kōzō ; Dec. 1754, Kōshirō III ; P.N. : Dec. 1770 ; Dec. 1791, Yebizō III. M. Act. : Feb. 1754–Dec. 1796 ; Dec. 1800–1 ; March 1802.

89.  NAKAMURA MATSUYE, *Rikō*. 1742–1786. F.N. : Matsuyemon ; P. N. : Dec. 1761 ; Dec. 1773, *Rikō* (his *haimyō*). F. Act. : Dec. 1761–Sep. 1785. Used No. 90 *Jō-mon* from c. 1769.

91.  ICHIKAWA MONNOSUKE II, *Takinoya Shinsha*. 1743–1794. F.N. : Takinaka Tsiuruzō ; 1759, Hidematsu ; 1764, Benzō ; P. N. : Dec. 1770. M. Act. : 1756–Sep. 1794. *Mon* shown is his *Kae-mon*. When Benzō used No. 70 with ideograph "Ben" in centre ; when Monnosuke, No. 17 ; and later No. 93 with "Mon" in centre for his *Jō-mon* in each case.

92.  ONOYE MATSUSUKE, *Otowaya Sanchō*. 1744–1815. M. F. Act. : Dec. 1756–Sep. 1774 ; Feb. 1778–Oct. 1791 ; Feb. 1794–Aug. 1814. Sometimes used *Mon* No. 64, but with ideograph "*matsu*" within a circle in centre.

93.  ICHIKAWA DANZŌ IV, *Mikawaya Shikō*. 1745–1808. F.N. : Kameya Torazō ; in 1763, Nakamura Torazō ; 1768, Ichikawa Tomozō ; Dec. 1772, Dansaburō ; P. N. : Dec. 1773. M. Act. : Dec. 1769 ; Dec. 1772–Oct. 1783 ; Feb. 1799–Dec. 1801.

94.  BANDŌ MITSUGORŌ I, *Yamatoya Zegyo*. 1745–1782. M. Act. : Dec. 1766–April 1782.

95.  NAKAMURA SUKEGORŌ II, *Sengokuya Gyoraku*. 1745–1806. F.N. : Sengoku Sukeji ; P. N. : Aug. 1763. M. Act. : Dec. 1763–May 1802. *Note.*—Mon shown is his *Kae-mon*. *Jō-mon* same as No. 54.

96.  ŌTANI HIROJI III, *Moraya Jitchō*. 1746–1802. F.N. : Haruji ; Dec. 1758, Oniji II ; P. N. : Dec. 1762. M. Act. : Aug. 1755–May 1780 ; Dec. 1781 ; April 1783–Sep. 1798. *Mon* shown in his *Kae-mon*. *Jō-mon* as No. 45.

97.  BANDŌ MITSUGORŌ II, *Yamatoya Zegyo*. 1746–1829. F.N. : Onoye Monsaburō ; P.N. : Dec. 1785 ; Dec. 1799, Ogino Isaburō II. M. Act. : Dec. 1774–1829. *Mon* shown is his *Kae-mon*. *Jō-mon* as for No. 94.

98.  SEGAWA YŪJIRŌ, *Kinokuni-ya Ki-in*. 1747–1818. F.N. : Sawamura Kimbei ; 1767, Shirogorō ; 1769, Segawa Yūjirō. In 1777, reverted to Shirogorō. In 1779, became Ichikawa Yaozō III ; in 1809, Suketaka-ya Takasuke. M. F. Act. : Dec. 1764–1808. *Mon* shown in *Kae-mon* as Yūjirō. When of Sawamura Line used No. 32 as *Jō-mon* ; when of Segawa No. 39 ; when Yaozō No. 79 with No. 99 as *Kae-mon*, and Chūsha as Haimyō.

100 and 101.  *Jō-* and *Kae-mon* of IWAI HANSHIRŌ V, *Yamatoya Tojaku*. 1747–1800. F.N. : Matsumoto Chōmatsu ; Dec. 1762, Shichizō ; P.N. : Dec. 1765. M. F. Act. : Dec. 1753–Oct. 1784 ; Dec. 1786–Dec. 1796 ; Feb. 1800.

102.  SEGAWA KIKUNOJŌ III, *Hamamuraya Rokō*. 1750–1810. F.N. : Tomisaburō ; P. N. : Dec. 1774 ; Rokō in 1801 ; Dec. 1807, Senjō. F. Act. : 1774–Oct. 1802 ; Dec. 1804–Oct. 1810. *Mon* shown is the *Kae-mon*. *Jō-mon* as for No. 39.

103.  NAKAMURA NOSHIO I. 1752–1777. F. Act. : Dec. 1770–Oct. 1777.

104.  SAWAMURA SŌJŪRŌ III, *Kinokuniya Tosshi*. 1753–1801. F.N. : Tanosuke ; P. N. : Dec. 1771. M. Act. : Dec. 1759–Oct. 1769 ; Dec. 1771–Oct. 1791 ; Dec. 1772 ; Feb. to Oct. 1773 ; Feb. 1794–Dec. 1798 ; Dec. 1800. His *Kae-mon* ; *Jō-mon* as for No. 32.

105.  OSAGAWA TSUNEYO III, *Wataya Kyosen*. 1753–1808. F.N. : Shichizō ; P.N. 1768. F. Act. : 1769–1808.

106.  BANDŌ HIKOSABURŌ III, *Otowaya Shintsui*. 1755–1828. F.N. : Ichimura Kichigorō ; P.N. : Dec. 1770. M. Act. : Dec. 1759–Oct. 1803 ; Dec. 1806–Oct. 1811. His *Kae-mon*. *Jō-mon* as for No. 86.

107.  NAKAMURA NAKAZŌ II, *Sakaiya Shūkwaku*. 1761–1796. F.N. : Ōtani Nagasuke ; Dec. 1778, Haruji II ; 1787, Oniji III ; P. N. : Dec. 1794. M. Act. : 1778–1796. As Oniji used *Mon* No. 29 with ideograph "*Oni*" in centre.

108.  ICHIKAWA KŌMAZŌ II, *Kōraiya Kinkō*. 1764–1838. F.N. : Donzō ; P.N. : Dec. 1772. M. Act. : Feb. 1770–1801, from Dec. of which he became Matsumoto Kōshirō V.

109.  IWAI KUMESABURŌ, *Baiga*, then *Tojaku*. 1736–1847. F. Act. : Dec. 1787–Oct. 1804, changing to Hanshirō V in Dec. His *Kae-mon*. *Jō-mon* as for No. 100.

110.  ICHIKAWA DANJŪRŌ VI, *Naritaya Sanshō*. 1778–1799. F.N. : Tokuzō ; Dec. 1782, Yebizō IV ; P. N. : Dec. 1791. M. Act. : Feb. 1782–April 1799. His *Kae-mon*. *Jō-mon* No. 88.

111.  ICHIKAWA OMEZŌ, *Takinoya Shinsha*. Died, 1833. F.N. : Bennosuke ; P. N. : Dec. 1789. M. Act. : Dec. 1776–1800 ; 1804–1824. His *Kae-mon* ; *Jō-mon* as for No. 108, but with ideograph "O" in the centre.

# YEDO PUBLISHERS
# THEIR TRADE-MARKS AND SEALS

The system of *Nakama* or Guilds was common to all commercial enterprise during the Feudal regime. Wholesale publishers were organized into a guild known as Jihondoiya no Nakama ; and, as we have explained elsewhere, were appointed in rotation as censors of printed matter under the supervision of the Machi-bugyō. Each publisher ordinarily carried on business under three names, viz. his *dō-gō*, his *ya-gō*, and his personal name, e.g. Kōsho-dō Tsuta-ya Jūsaburō. Sometimes he used his family or surname as an alternative designation ; e.g. Uyemura, the surname of Yemiya Kichiyemon. In one case only do we find a fourth name used on prints, viz. that of Karamaro, the *gō* as a humorous poet of Tsutaya Jusaburō.

Each publisher also possessed a trade-mark or shop sign (*iye no shirushi*), which he used to stamp either on the artist's original design with or without one or other or all of his names, when it was engraved along with the design, or on the finished print. In the following tables each of the names of some prominent Yedo print publishers when fully known are recorded, together with the approximate dates of the firm's activity.

The importance of clearly differentiating between the various publishers, more especially in regard to their *dō-gō*, and in cases where the *ya-gō* is identical, will be seen from the following remarks embodying errors that have been noticed in catalogues.

1. Yamaguchiya Tōbei, *dō-gō* Kinkōdō, is frequently confused with Yamaguchiya Chūsuke (*dō-gō* not yet ascertained) and Takatsuya Isuke on account of the similarity of their trade-marks. The latter should not be confused with Takasu Sōshichi.

2. Yamamoto, who is often given as a separate publisher, is really identical with Maruya Kohei, whose family name was Yamamoto. Some prints bear the name of Yamamoto Kohei, Hōsendō Maruya. His shop was at first in Ōdemma-chō, and afterwards in Tōri Abura-chō.

3. Yeisendō is invariably described as Yamaguchiya Shōzō ; and the Ōmi, Naniwa, and Kyōtō series of oblong prints by Hiroshige I are declared to be this latter's publication. As a matter of fact, Shōzō's *gō* was not Yeisendō but Shōyeidō. Yeisendō was the *dō-gō* of Mitaya Kihachi, whose trade-mark has not yet been discovered. The Kyōtō Meishō set was the joint publication of Yeisendō (i.e. Mitaya Kihachi) and of Kawaguchi Uhei (not Shōzō), whose *dō-gō* was Fukusendō and

whose trade-mark is to be seen on the lanterns of the tea-house to the right of the print with the sub-title Shijō kawara yū-suzumi, " Summer evening cooling in the river-bed at Shijō."

Shoyeidō's seal is found on some of Hiroshige's Kwachō or " Flowers and Birds " series ; that of Fukusendō on some of Yeisen's landscapes (*vide* page 482, *Catalogue of Japanese and Chinese Woodcuts in the British Museum*) and elsewhere.

4. Tsutaya Jūsaburō is a different publisher from Tsutaya Kichizō.

5. Iwatoya Kisaburō is a different publisher from Iwatoya Gempachi.

6. Jakurindō was the *dō-gō* of Wakasaya Yoichi, not of Fujiokaya Keijirō ; and this latter is different from Fujiokaya Hikotarō, whose *dō-gō* was Shōgendō, which may but should not be pronounced Matsubaradō. Keijirō's *dō-gō* was Shorindō.

7. Yeiyūdō, often confused with Yeijudō the *dō-gō* of Nishimuraya Yohachi, is the *dō-gō* of Murataya Jirobei. The personal name of Moriji is Jihei not Jirobei, and that of Fuji Kei is Keijirō not Keisuke.

Publishers' seals vary considerably in shape and size. Those here reproduced will suffice to give a general idea of the ideographs which they used, no matter what size or shape the seals may be. It was a common practice for publishers to contract their *ya-gō* and personal names, and these are often a convenient way of differentiating between those whose *ya-gō* is identical. For example : Waka(-saya) Yo(-ichi) ; Mori(-ya) Ji(-hei) ; Ise(-ya) Kim(bei) ; Maru(-ya) Ko(hei) ; and, in the case of the same *ya-gō*, Tsuta(-ya) Jū(-saburō) and Tsuta(-ya) Kichi(-zō) ; Ye(-zakiya) Kichi(-bei) and Ye(-zakiya) Tatsu(-kura) ; Fuji(-okaya) Kei(-jirō) and Fuji(-okaya) Hiko(-tarō).

# A SELECTION OF
# YEDO PUBLISHERS' TRADE-MARKS

## TABLE A

Kinoshita Jinyemon, 1690–1730

Komatsuya Dembei, 1700–1750

*Rikwakudō*
Urokogataya Magobei, 1700–1784

*Seisuidō*
Izutsuya Chūzayemon, 1688–1754

Izutsuya Sanyemon, 1705–1750

Nakajimaya Risuke, 1710–1756

*Kwakujudō*
Okumuraya Genroku, 1715–1780

*Aikindō*
Hiranoya Kichibei, 1720–1736

*Senkwakudō*
Tsuruya Kiyemon, 1675–1867

Izumiya Gonshirō, 1716–1735
(of Dobo-chō, Barrier Gate,
Asakusa ; originator of *beni-ye*)

Yamatoya, 1716–1735

*Bunkidō*
Igaya Kanyemon, 1711–1748

Ōgawa Shichirobei, 1720–1735
Yenomoto Kichibei, 1785–1810

*Shōkwakudō*
Yamashiroya, 1730–1760

Yedoya, 1730–1754

Iwaiya, 1730–1750

Omiya Kuhei, 1730–1750

Sagamiya, 1720–1735

Surugaya, 1740–1760

Tomita, 1745–1763

*Sanrindō*
Yamadaya Sanshiro, 1688–1812

Maruya Kuzayemon, 1730–1744

Kiriya, 1730–1755

*Yeiyūdō*
Murataya Jirobei, 1720–1848

Yenami, 1750–1768

Masuya, 1739–1780

*Hōsendō*
Maruya Kohei, 1720–1783

Mikawaya Rihei, 1741–1770

Iseya Kimbei, 1725–1804

*Yeijudō*
Nishimuraya Yohachi, 1738–1848

*Kōshodō*
Tsutaya Jūsaburō, 1772–1848

*Daikwandō*
Fushimiya Zenroku
1767–present day

Nishimuraya Genroku, 1744–1778

Sakaiya Kurobei, 1751–1768

*Fuyōdō*
Takasu Sōshichi, 1787–1801

xlv

| | |
|---|---|
| *Kinkōdō*<br>Yamaguchiya Tōbei, 1784–1868 | *Kansendō*<br>Izumiya Ichibei, 1785–1868 |
| *Yeirindō*<br>Iwatoya Kisaburō, 1790–1830 | *Yeikyūdō*<br>Yamamotoya Heikichi, 1804–1860 |
| Iwatoya Gempachi, 1760–1781 | Isemago, 1796–1812 |
| Matsumura Yahei<br>(Probably the earlier trade-mark of next) | Takatsuya Isuke, 1789–1817 |
| Matsumura Yahei, 1738–1818 | *Yenjudō*<br>Maruya Jimpachi, 1766–1861 |
| Yamaguchiya Chūsuke, 1790–1820 | Mikawaya Rihei II, 1789–1826 |
| *Rankōdō*<br>Yemiya Kichiyemon, 1711–1818 | Yamaden, 1794–1812 |
| *Bunjudō*<br>Maruya Bunyemon, 1794–1820 | |
| Iseya Jisuke, 1795–1810 | *Gwangetsudō*<br>Nishimiya Shinroku, 1785–1818 |
| *Shōjudō*<br>Daikokuya Heikichi<br>1818–present day | *Taiyeidō*<br>Iseya Sōyemon, 1789–present day |
| Kagaya Kichibei, 1810–1854 | Kinshodō, 1801–1835<br>N.B.—Full style of this publisher has not yet been ascertained. |
| *Bunkindō*<br>Toyojimaya Bunjiyemon<br>1773–1806 | *Kinshūdō*<br>Azumaya Daisuke, 1815–1830 |
| Wakamatsuya Gensuke, 1750–1770 | Akamatsu Shōtarō, 1830–1850 |
| *Sōkwakudō*<br>Tsuruya Kinsuke, 1798–1836 | Iseya Sanjiro, 1795–1850 |
| *Kinshindō*<br>Moriya Jihei, 1800–1853 | *Fukusendō*<br>Kawaguchiya Uhei, 1790–1849 |
| *Tenjudō*<br>Yezakiya Kichibei, 1794–1848 | Soshūya Yohei, 1792–1854 |
| *Jakurindō*<br>Wakasaya Yoichi, 1794–1861 | Tsutaya Kichizō, 1801–1868 |
| Igaya Kanyemon II, 1810–1854 | *Shōyeidō*<br>Kawaguchiya Shōzō, 1818–1848 |
| Matsumoto Sahei, 1800–1855 | Omiya Yohei, 1790–1815 |
| Yamadaya Sasuke, 1795–1812 | *Kikwakudō*<br>Sanoya Kihei, 1790–1865 |
| Yamashiroya Tōkei, 1794–1830 | |

# SELECTION OF YEDO PUBLISHERS' TRADE-MARKS

## TABLE A—*continued*

*Jukwakudō*
Maruya Seijirō, 1818–1853

Nakamuraya Katsugorō
1815–1848

Ōsakaya Shōsuke, 1807–1850

*Sankindō*
Yamazakiya Kimbei, 1762–1823

Sumimaruya Jinsuke, 1804–1830

Yezakiya Tatsukura, 1810–1853

Yedoya Matsugoro, 1812–1852

*Kinchōdō*
Jōshūya Jūzō, 1840–1850

*Kinshōdō*
Yebisuya Shōshichi, 1848–1861

*Kinjudō*
Iseya Rihei, 1804–1848

Iseya Heibei, 1830–1852

Yorozuya Kichibei, 1838–1854

Jōshūya Kinzō, 1830–1852

Kikuya Ichibei, 1832–1854

Echizenya Heisaburo, 1833–1855

Kawaguchiya Chōzō, 1830–1850

Fujiwaraya Bunjiro, 1830–1854

Wakamatsuya Yoshiro
1832–1855

*Yūsuidō*
Aridaya Seiyemon, 1840–1858

*Dansendō*
Ibaya Sensaburo, 1840–1853

Hamadaya Tokubei, 1818–1852

Yamadaya Shōbei, 1852–1863

*Shorindō*
Fujiokaya Keijirō, 1840–1865

Yebiya Rinnosuke, 1838–1855

Echigoya Chōhachi, 1789–1854

Ibaya Kyūbei, 1843–1858

*Shōgendō*
Fujiokaya Hikotaro, 1825–1854

Isekane, 1848–1860

*Bunkwadō*
Shioya Shōsaburō, 1830–1848

*Kinshōdō*
Tsujiokaya Bunsuke, 1828–1858

Ningyōya Takichi, 1836–1854

Moritaya Hanjirō, 1834–1856

Omiya Heihachi, 1832–1852

Shin Iseya Kohei, 1840–1858

Yenhiko, 1840–1860

Yamadaya Jūhei, 1830–1852

Sawamuraya Rihei, 1834–1856

Uyedaya Kyūjirō, 1833–1850

Daikokuya Kyūbei, 1832–1856

*Hōraidō*
Sumiyoshiya Masagorō, 1804–1848

*Hōyeidō*
Take (no) Uchi Magohachi
1830–1840

Maruya Kyūshirō, 1829–1859

# A SELECTION OF
# YEDO PUBLISHERS' SEALS

## TABLE B

HANGIYA
SHICHIROBEI
Nemoto ye-dokoro
(Original bureau of
Pictures).
1680–1710.

NAKAJIMAYA
Sakai chō
Hammoto (Publisher)
1711–1744.
SAKAIYA ⎫
Hammoto ⎬ 1725–1779.

Hammoto IGAYA
Motohama chō.
IGAYA
1711–1848.

SURUGAYA
1740–1760.
IZUTSUYA
Shimmei-mae
Yoko chō
1688–1751.
Ise(ya) Kim(bei)
1725–1804.

YEMIYA
Shiba Shimmei-mae
1711–1818.
KAMI- (or UYE-) MURA
1744–1818.
Later style of
Yemiya (Kichiyemon).

KIKUYA
Bussō(ʔ)chō Asakusa
1720–1738.
YAMATOYA
Shimmei-mae, 1711–1740.

IWAIYA, 1730–1750.
SAGAMIYA, 1720–1735.
KOMATSUYA, 1700–1750.

KOMATSUYA (Dembei)
Yushima Tenjin
onna-zaka no shita
(his address) 1700–1750.
MASUYA, 1741–1780.

Trade-mark
of
MURATA Han
Abura chō
(abbr. of
Murataya Jirobei
1720–1848).

MURATA han
1720–1848 ;
YEIYŪDŌ
(dō-gō of above).

MARUKO
1720–1783.
YAMAMOTO
Han
(Same firm as
Maruya Kohei).

MARUYA han.
MIKAWA(YA)
Ai (hei) han
1741–1770.

ISERI
Ikenokata
Naka chō
1804–1848.
KINJUDŌ
(dō-gō of above).

TSURU
(abbr. for Tsuruya
Kiyemon)
Shimpan, i.e.
new publication.
IWATOYA
(Gempachi)
1760–1781.

(N.B.—Same mark was
used later by Senichi
Izumiya Ichibei).

TSURUSHIN
1751–1768.

(N.B.—Same mark was
used later by Moriji).

JAKURINDŌ
(dō-gō of
Wakasaya Yoichi).

WAKASAYA
(Yoichi), 1794–1861.

## TABLE B—*continued*

Two forms
of
YEIJU han
(abbr. of YEIJUDŌ).

NISHIMURA
YEIJUDŌ
(*Dō-gō* of Nishi-
muraya Yohachi).
(N.B.—Often confused with
Yeiyūdō.)

KŌSHODŌ.
KARAMARO
Han
(i.e. Tsutaya Jusaburō).
Shi(ba)
TAKASU.

TAKATSU (YA
ISUKE) han.
SENICHI han.

SANOKI
1790–1865.

TAKE-MAGO
TSURU-KI.

HŌYEIDŌ.
TAKE(no)UCHI.
KIKWAKU
(abbr. of Kikwakudō),
*dō-gō* of Sanoya Kihei
1790–1865.

KAWASHŌ(-zō)
1818–1848.
SHŌYEIDŌ
(*dō-gō* of above).

SHŌGENDŌ
(*dō-gō* of)
FUJIOKA (ya)
(Hikotarō).

JŌKIN
(abbr. of Jōshūya
Kinzō), 1830–1852.
ISEKANE, 1848–1860.
KAWAGUCHI han
(i.e. Kawaguchiya
Uhei 1790–1849).

SANOKI han, 1790–1865.
YEISENDŌ
(*dō-gō* of
Mitaya Kihachi).

# ARTISTS' SIGNATURES

| NAME | SIGNATURE | NAME | SIGNATURE | NAME | SIGNATURE |
|------|-----------|------|-----------|------|-----------|
| BUNCHO | | HIROSHIGE (early period) | | HOKUSAI | |
| CHŌKI (See also SHIKO and YEISHŌSAI) | | | | also signed :— I-ITSU (2 forms) | |
| GAKUTEI | | (middle period) | | KAKO (e.g. early "Chushingura" series, c. 1798) | |
| GŌKYO | | (late period) | | SORI | |
| HARUNOBU | | | | TAITO | |
| | | HOKKEI | | KIKUMARO (early form) = Kiku-maro | |
| HIROSHIGE | "Ichiryusai" seal Diamond seal ("Hiro") | HOKUJIU | | (late form) = Ki-ku-maro | |

# ARTISTS' SIGNATURES

| NAME | SIGNATURE | NAME | SIGNATURE | NAME | SIGNATURE |
|---|---|---|---|---|---|
| KIYOHIRO | 清廣 | KORIUSAI | 湖龍齋 | KUNIYOSHI | 國芳 |
| KIYOMASU | 清倍 | KUNIMASA | 國政 | MASANOBU (Kitao) | 北尾政演 |
| KIYOMINE | 清峯 | KUNINAGA | 國長 | MASANOBU (Okumura) | 奥村政信 |
| KIYOMITSU | 清滿 | KUNINAO | 國直 | MASAYOSHI | 政美 |
| KIYONAGA | 清長 | KUNISADA | 國貞 | MORONOBU | 師宣 |
| KIYONOBU | 清信 | KUNISADA (also signed TOYOKUNI after 1844) | 豐國 | RYUKŌKU | 柳谷 |
| KIYOTADA | 清忠 | KUNIYASU | 國安 | SADAHIDE | 貞秀 |

# JAPANESE COLOUR-PRINTS

| NAME | SIGNATURE | NAME | SIGNATURE | NAME | SIGNATURE |
|---|---|---|---|---|---|
| SHARAKU | 寫樂 | SHUNCHO (Katsukawa) | 勝川春潮 | SHUNTEI | 春亭 |
| SHIGEMASA | 重政 | SHUNKŌ (Pupil of Shunsho) | 春好 | SHUNYEI | 春英 |
| SHIGENAGA | 重長 | SHUNKŌ (=Shunbeni) (Pupil of Shunyei) | 春紅 | SHUNZAN | 春山 |
| SHIGENOBU (Yanagawa) | 柳川重信 | SHUNMAN | 後滿 | SORI | 宗理 |
| SHIGENOBU (Hiroshige II) | 重宜 | SHUNSEN (Pupil of Shunyei) | 春扇 | SUGAKU | 高岳 |
| SHIKIMARO | 式麿 | SHUNSEN (=Shun-Izumi) (Pupil of Shunsho) | 春泉 | TOYOHARU | 豐春 |
| SHIKO (See also CHŌKI and YEISHŌSAI) | 子興 | SHUNSHO | 春章 | TOYOHIRO | 豐廣 |

# ARTISTS' SIGNATURES

| NAME | SIGNATURE | NAME | SIGNATURE | NAME | SIGNATURE |
|---|---|---|---|---|---|
| TOYONOBU (Ishikawa) | 石川豊信 | TSUKIMARO | 月麿 | YEISHO | 栄昌栄松斎 |
| TOYOKUNI (early form) | 豊國 | UTAMARO (early form) | 歌麿 | YEISHŌSAI (= Choki or Shiko) | |
| (middle period) | 豊國 | (late form) | 哥麿 | YEIZAN (Kikugawa) | 菊川英山 |
| (late period) | 豊國 | YEIRI (Hosoda) | 栄里 | YOSHINOBU | 義信 |
| TOYOKUNI (Gosotei) (Pupil of Toyokuni) | 後素亭豊国 | YEIRI (Rekisentei) | 礫川亭永理 | fudè (" with brush ") in kaisho (capital script) | 筆 |
| | | | | fudè in semi-kaisho script (as written by Utamaro) | 筆 |
| | | YEISEN (Keisai) | 渓斉英泉 | fudè in Sōsho script as written by Hiroshige (late) | 筆 |
| | | | | gwa (" drew ") | 画 |
| TOYOMASA (Ishikawa) | 石川豊雅 | YEISHI (two forms) | 栄之 | ōju (" to order ") | 應需 |
| | | | | utsusu (" copied ") | 寫 |
| | | | | zu (" picture ") | 圖 |

# SELECT BIBLIOGRAPHY

## (A) JAPANESE WORKS CONSULTED

### I. WORKS ON UKIYO-YE AND THE COLOUR-PRINT

Ukiyoye ruikō in its various editions. Yedo, c. 1799–1901.
Ukiyoye-shi benran. Tōkyō, 1893.
Ukiyoye bikō. Tōkyō, 1897.
Honchō ukiyo gwajin den. Tōkyō, 1899.
Ukiyoye hennenshi. Tōkyō, 1912.
Ukiyoye taika gwa-shú. Tōkyō, 1912.
Ukiyo-ye to Fúkei gwa. Tōkyō, 1914.
Ukiyo-ye. Tōkyō, 1915-1920.
Ukiyo-ye no kenkyú. Tōkyō, 1921-1923.

### II. WORKS ON PARTICULAR MASTERS

Hishikawa Moronobu gwafu. Ōsaka, 1909.
Okumura Masanobu gwafu. Ōsaka, 1910.
Nishikawa Sukenobu gwafu. Ōsaka, 1911.

### III. WORKS ON THE THEATRE

Yehon sakae-gusa. Yedo, N.D. (1771).
Gekijō gaku-ya zu-ye. Ōsaka, 1800.
Shibai kummō zu-i. Yedo, 1806.
Hana Yedo kabuki nendai-ki. Yedo, 1811.
Kabuki shimpō. Tōkyō, 1896.
Nippon engeki-shi. Tōkyō, 1904.
Kinsei Nippon engeki-shi. Tōkyō, 1914.

### IV. GENERAL

Kottōshú. Yedo, 1815.
Kwankon shiryō. Yedo, 1826.
Kono Hana. Ōsaka. 1910-1912.
Kono Hana. Tōkyō, 1912-1913.
Hikkwa-shi. Ōsaka, 1911.
Nippon dai jiten kotoba no izumi. Tōkyō, 1921.

## (B) WORKS IN EUROPEAN LANGUAGES.

### I. GENERAL

Anderson, W. Japanese Wood Engravings. London, 1895.
Aubert, Louis. Les Maîtres de l'Estampe japonaise. Paris, 1914.
Bramsen, William. Japanese Chronology and Calendars, etc.
British Museum. Catalogue of Japanese and Chinese Woodcuts. By L. Binyon. 1916.
Duret, Th. Livres et Albums illustrés du Japon. Paris, 1900.
Einstein, Carl. Der frühere Japanische Holzschnitt. Berlin, N.D.

# SELECT BIBLIOGRAPHY

Fenollosa, E. F.  An outline of the history of Ukiyo-yé.  Tōkyō, 1901.

Gookin, F. W.  Japanese Colour-Prints and their Designers.  The Japan Society, New York, 1913.

Kurth, Julius.  Der Japanische Holzschnitt.  Munich, 1911.  New edition, 1922.

Kurth, Julius.  Die Primitiven des Japanholzschnitts.  Dresden, 1922.

Kurth, Julius.  Der Chinisische Farbendruck.  Plauen, 1922.

Lemoisne, P. A.  L'Estampe japonaise.  Paris, 1914.

Morrison, Arthur.  Painters of Japan.  (Vol. II.  Chapter on Ukiyo-ye.)

Seidlitz, W. von.  Geschichte des Japanischen Farbenholzschnitts.  Dresden, 1897  Revised edition, 1910.  English edition, 1910.

Strange, E. F.  Japanese Illustration.  London, 1897.  New edition, 1904.

Strange, E. F.  Japanese Colour-Prints.  London, 1904.  4th edition, 1913.

Strange, E. F.  Colour-Prints of Japan.  London, 1904.

Tajima, S.  Masterpieces selected from the Ukiyo-ye School.  Tōkyō.  5 vols.  1906–1909.

Tressan, Le Marquis de.  Documents japonais relatifs à l'histoire de l'estampe in Bulletin de la Société franco-japonaise de Paris, January, 1914.

## 2. WORKS ON PARTICULAR MASTERS

De Goncourt, E.  Outamaro.  Paris, 1891.

De Goncourt, E.  Hokusai.  Paris, 1896.

Field, H. E.  Kiyonaga.  Burlington Magazine, Vol. XIII, p. 241.

Holmes, C. J.  Hokusai.  London, 1899.

Kurth, J.  Utamaro.  Leipzig, 1907.

Kurth, J.  Suzuki Harunobu.  Munich and Liepzig, 1910.

Kurth, J.  Sharaku.  Munich, 1910.  New edition, 1922.

Noguchi, Yone.  Hiroshige.  New York, 1921.

Perzynski, F.  Hokusai.  Bielefeld and Leipzig, 1904.

Revon, M.  Étude sur Hok'sai.  Paris, 1896.

Smidt, H.  Harunobu : Technik und Fälschungen seiner Holzschnitte.  (Die Graphischen Künste, Vienna, 1911.)

Succo, F.  Utagawa Toyokuni und seine Zeit.  Munich, 1913–1914.

Succo, F.  Katsukawa Shunshō.  Plauen im Vogtland, 1922.

Strange, E. F.  Hokusai.  London, 1906.

Strange, E. F.  Toyokuni.  London, 1908.

Watanabe, S.  Hiroshige.  (Catalogue of Memorial Exhibition.)  Tōkyō, 1918.

## 3. EXHIBITION CATALOGUES

Fenollosa, E. F.  The Masters of Ukiyo-ye.  New York, 1896.

Gookin, F. W.  Catalogue of a loan exhibition of Japanese Colour-Prints.  Chicago, 1908.

Gookin, F. W.  Catalogue of a memorial exhibition of Japanese Colour-Prints from the Clarence Buckingham Collection.  Chicago, 1915.

Kurth, J.  Japanische Holzschnitte aus der Sammlung Straus-Negbaur in Frankfurt.  Frankfurt-am-Main, 1909.

Ledoux, Louis.  Exhibition of Japanese Figure-Prints from Moronobu to Toyokuni.  The Grolier Club, New York, 1923.

Louvre, Musée du.  Catalogue de la collection Isaac de Camondo.  (Estampes japonaises ; by G. Migeon.)

Morrison, Arthur.  Exhibitions of Japanese Prints.  Fine Art Society, London, 1909 and 1910.

Musée des Arts Décoratifs, Paris.  Catalogues by C. Vignier and H. Inada of exhibitions held 1909–1914, edited by R. Koechlin.  Vol. I, Estampes japonaises primitives; Vol. II, Harunobu, Koriūsai, Shunshō; Vol. III, Kiyonaga, Bunchō, Sharaku; Vol. IV, Utamaro; Vol. V, Yeishi, Chōki, Hokusai; Vol. VI, Toyokuni, Hiroshige.   Referred to in this work as the " Paris V.I. Catalogues."

Strange, E. F.  Victoria and Albert Museum, London.  Japanese Colour-Prints, lent by R. Leicester Harmsworth, 1913.

# INTRODUCTION

The earliest known woodcuts in the world are those discovered by Sir Aurel Stein in 1908 in the Cave of the Thousand Buddhas at Tun-huang, on the extreme western frontier of China. They are now divided between the British Museum and the Government of India.

These woodcuts are all Buddhist images, and served the same purpose in popular religion as the " Helgen," or woodcut images of saints, in the Germany of the 15th century. One of them stands apart both for its complexity of subject and its skilful cutting. It prefaces the text of the Chinese translation of a Sūtra, printed from blocks and dated 868 A.D. The other woodcuts from Tun-huang are ruder in style, though in different degrees ; two are dated 947, and another 983. We can hardly doubt that the invention of the woodcut for multiplying designs was made in China at a considerably earlier date.

Already in these Tun-huang woodcuts we find a tentative experiment in colour-printing. In the British Museum are two impressions of an image of Avalokiteśvara. One of these is coloured by hand and mounted on paper which is printed with a pattern of blue on blue. The idea of the colour-print—the printing from one block over another—is here in essentials, it only needed further application. If the invention was not carried further, it was probably due to the cost and labour involved. The same considerations would seem to have prevented the development of the colour-print in Europe. Though as many as eight blocks were used in one German print (the arms of Cardinal Lang, 1520, by Hans Weiditz), this was exceptional and extraordinary ;[1] and little was made of the invention.

The German and Italian woodcuts printed in two or three colours and in oil pigment at the beginning of the 16th century and known as " chiaroscuro " prints are earlier than any Chinese colour-print, so far as we know at present ; and Mr. Strange has advanced the interesting suggestion that specimens of these European prints may have been introduced into China by the Jesuits and given the idea to the Chinese. Since, however, we know from fragments found at Tun-huang by Sir Aurel Stein that patterns were printed on textiles in colour during the T'ang period, and we have also the evidence of the colour-printed paper mount mentioned above, it does not seem likely that the Chinese needed to get this inspiration from Europe. The earliest Chinese colour-prints known at present

---

[1] See the Catalogue of Early German and Flemish Woodcuts in the British Museum, by Campbell Dodgson, Vol. II, p. 181. Five colours were used in " The Beautiful Virgin of Ratisbon," by Altdorfer (ibid., Vol. II, p. 227).

are in a book called *Shih Chu Chai Shu hua p'u*, dated 1625. During the 17th century various other books of the same kind, intended as models for drawing, were printed in colours. The best known of these is the *Mustard Seed Garden*, *Chieh Tzŭ Yüan*, of which there are many editions.

During the last few years Chinese colour-prints, for long totally neglected, have begun to interest the curiosity of collectors. The Marées Society of Munich has issued a most sumptuous publication, reproducing with infinite care pages from the two books above-mentioned. It is even contended, here and there, that prints like these surpass the best of the Japanese prints; a symptom of the fashionable dislike of mastery in the arts.

We are here concerned with Chinese colour-prints only in their relation to the Japanese woodcuts. And there is a sharp distinction to be drawn between them. The best of the Chinese colour-prints were, so far as we know, merely reproductions of paintings already made. The Japanese prints which are the subject of this book were produced by artists, many of them artists of distinction, the best of them men of genius, who made their designs with the colour-print as their sole end in view. And, strange as it seems, the Japanese developed the colour-print by gradual stages quite independently of China, from the hand-coloured woodcut to the elaborate print from twenty or thirty blocks.

Not that Chinese prints were unknown in Japan.

In 1746 Shunboku published at Ōsaka a book of Ming drawings in colour-print, copied from a Chinese book of 1701. The only known copy of the first edition of Shunboku's book was recently presented by Mr. Arthur Morrison to the British Museum. And, as we shall see in the course of our narrative, Chinese single-sheets were imitated from time to time by Harunobu and other masters. For there is no doubt that single sheets, printed in colours, were produced in great quantities in China and in many different styles.

A distinctively Chinese form of print was the " stone-print." Usually cut on wood, this was an imitation of the rubbings from designs incised on stone, which were an ancient method of preserving and multiplying the design of pictures which were threatened with decay. Woodcuts of this type, in white on black, or white on blue, were common in China; and they were imitated by some of the Primitives in Japan. An elaborated kind of stone-print, with colour, was also devised; and this also was imitated in Japan. These prints are discussed in more detail in a later chapter (pp. 63–4). The Chinese also produced single-sheets in colour not only landscapes with sages, birds, flowers, etc.—the typical subjects of Chinese painting—but popular broadsides, in two, three, or four colours, illustrating or advertising stage plays. (A few examples of all these kinds are in the British Museum collection.) These prints are now of excessive rarity; a fate invariably attending the cheapest and commonest productions, since no one thinks them worth preserving. It is quite likely that the cheap theatrical prints were not known in Japan: since they were artisans' work, they would not be thought worth exporting, and only answered local needs. Intercourse between the two countries was extremely restricted. Some of the finer prints, of landscape and flower subjects, were known and were imitated; but they were only a side-influence, since the Japanese prints were devoted almost entirely to figure-design. And, we repeat, the Japanese, in Yedo at all events, seem to have discovered each stage of the perfected colour-print for themselves.

One great difference between the colour-prints of China and those of Japan lies in the paper employed. The Chinese printed on a thin white paper, on which the colours tell brilliantly, but without the delicacy of texture and depth of tone which the pigments took from the softer, tougher, and more bibulous Japanese paper. The finest known series of Chinese colour-prints, produced probably towards the end of the 17th century, of birds and flowers, fruit and still-life, seem to be imitating the effect of coloured porcelain; and they contrast strongly with the Japanese prints of equal refinement and elaboration, which they anticipate by more than half a century. Twenty-nine prints from this very rare series are in the British Museum, and scattered examples in other collections. Their gaiety has its charm; but they are not to be compared with the best Japanese prints, where the arts of the designer, wood-cutter, and printer are combined with a felicity unknown elsewhere in all the world.

Because of their priority in date and of their relation to Japanese work— a relation which still remains rather problematic—it is only right that some account should be given of the Chinese colour-prints, though our knowledge at present, especially in the matter of dates, is but scanty. In all essentials, however, the history of the Japanese colour-print is independent of China, and is involved in the history of a particular school of Japanese painting which grew up in Yedo in the 17th century; the school known as Ukiyo-ye, or the painting of the Transient Scene.

The early history of Ukiyo-ye has been so often told that we need only recount it in brief outline.

Just as in Europe what we call *genre* was a comparatively late development of painting, so in Japan, though scenes from daily life were introduced in an episodical or accessory fashion into scroll-paintings of the old Tosa school, it was not till the 16th century that painters ventured to make such themes the real subjects of their brush. Certain of the Kanō masters in that century painted, rather furtively, groups of people amusing themselves. Examples are reproduced in *Masterpieces of Ukiyo-ye*, Vol. I. But the first to take such motives for his chief inspiration was Iwasa Matabei, who was born in 1578 and died in 1650. He had a number of followers. But Matabei's was still an aristocratic art. Paintings were expensive, and did not reach the lower classes of the feudal system. Yet it was just in these lower classes that a demand for beautiful things was arising.

After centuries of civil war, Japan was at last at peace under the strong government of the Tokugawa Shōguns. Intercourse with the outside world was forbidden. The people were thrown on themselves. The industrial arts throve greatly. And in Yedo they began to desire a pictorial art that should reflect their own interests and amusements. The genius of Hishikawa Moronobu turned the inspirations of Matabei to popular account by utilizing the woodcut. Here was a cheap means of multiplying designs indefinitely, for all to enjoy.

The woodcut, hitherto, had been rather neglected in Japan. Originally used, as in China, for religious purposes, it began to be used about the close of the 16th century for illustrating romances. The illustrated *Ise Monogatari* of 1608 is the best known example, and one of the earliest, of these books. But in Moronobu's hands, as we shall see, the woodcut was to be transformed into something much more vigorous and alive.

This book is not concerned with the paintings, which form an important part of Ukiyo-ye, and were the most esteemed side of its production. The woodcuts were provided for a lower level of the people ; and it must for ever astonish us that a class of the population which in any other country of the world would have been satisfied with crude and gaudy productions, should have created and fostered, and kept in eager and multifarious life for nearly two centuries, an art of design as distinguished for delicate and fastidious taste as it is rich in creative power.

# CHAPTER I
# FROM 1658 TO 1695

The history of the Ukiyoye print opens at Yedo in 1658 with a book entitled *Kamo no Chōmei Hōjōki shō*, " An epitome of ' Notes from a ten-feet square hut,' by Kamo no Chōmei," a Buddhist recluse of the 12th century. The book is illustrated with woodcuts after drawings by MORONOBU, the first print-designer of the Ukiyoye school. This artist, whose real name was Hishikawa Kichibei, was the son of Hishikawa Kichizayemon Michishige Kōchiku (*d.* 1662), the most skilful embroiderer of his age, and also clever at painting and designing patterns. Kōchiku was a native of Hoda, a small village in the province of Awa, where Moronobu was born at a date not yet ascertained, but which is commonly believed to have been about 1625. At first he assisted his father in his business by painting designs for dress materials ; and, while still a youth, accompanied him to Yedo, some thirty miles from Hoda, across the present Bay of Tōkyō. Here, while continuing to assist his father, he began to study the Tosa style of painting, and later that of the Kanō school. Soon after he was attracted to the modified form of the Tosa and Kanō styles initiated by Iwasa Matabei (1578–1650), the founder of the Ukiyoye school, confining himself at first to painting and book illustration. About 1673, he began to design *ichimai-ye* or single-sheet pictures, which were printed in ink from engraved wood-blocks and were termed *sumi-ye* or ink pictures. It is recorded that visitors to Yedo took back these prints to their homes as souvenirs of their visit, and that they were popularly known as Yedo-ye. From this time until his retirement in 1694, he executed a number of *sumi-ye* as well as book illustrations. Very few of the former have survived to our time ; but the number of extant books illustrated by him reaches, according to the list given in *Hishikawa Moronobu gwafu* published in 1909, a total of one hundred and eight, of which forty-eight are unsigned.

His *sumi-ye* are all unsigned. In *Meijin-ki Shin-roku*, Moronobu's death is recorded as having occurred on the 2nd day of the 8th month of Shōtoku 4 (August 30, 1714) at the age of seventy-seven, from which he would appear to have been born in 1638. The author, the late Mr. Sekine Shisei (*d.* 1893), further states that he was buried in the grounds of a temple at Yanaka, Yedo.

The same statements are repeated in *Honchō Ukiyo gwajin-den* of 1899, written by Mr. Sekine Kinshirō. From whatever source Shisei obtained these details, they are certainly inaccurate ; for in *Sugata-ye hyakunin isshū*, published in May, 1695, Moronobu is referred to as already deceased. Santō Kyōden (1761–1816) states in his supplement of 1802 to the Ukiyo-ye Ruikō that he had been informed by Shibakawa Genryō, a physician and relative of Moronobu and a native of Hoda, that there was then in the grounds of the Buddhist temple of Rinkaizan Betsu-gan-in at Hoda, a large bell upon which was engraved : " contributed by Hishikawa Kichibei-no-jō Fujiwara Moronobu nyūdō Yūchiku on an auspicious day in the 5th month of Genroku 7, the year of Kinoe Inu." Yūchiku was the name taken by Moronobu when, after shaving his head and becoming a follower of Buddha (*nyūdō*), he had retired to his native village at some unknown date previous to that above recorded. His death must, therefore, have taken place between this date and May, 1695. In the illustrated catalogue of Japanese old fine arts displayed at the Japan-British Exhibition, London, 1910, the dates of his birth and death are given as 1618 and 1694, the former being evidently deduced from Shisei's statement that the artist was in his seventy-seventh year at the time of his death. As, however, Shisei was evidently wrong as to the date of his death, it would be unsafe to accept the age given.

Contemporary with Moronobu as print-designers were his eldest son Hishikawa Kichizayemon Morofusa ; his pupil, Furuyama Tarobei Moroshige ; Ishikawa Ryūsen ; and Torii Shōbei Kiyonobu. MOROFUSA, the dates of whose birth and death are unrecorded, worked from about 1685 till 1703, when he forsook print-designing to become a dyer. His work is to be found in about nineteen books and about half a dozen *ichimai-ye*. Among these books is the *Sugata-ye hyakunin isshū*, two large volumes already referred to ; *Kemono yehon-zukushi*, one large volume, and *Yehon Yamato-zumi*, three large volumes, both published in 1694 ; *Ka no kaori* and *Wakoku hyaku jo*, each three large volumes published in 1695 ; and *Gorei-kō*, one large volume published in the same year.

These six books bear the name of Moronobu ; but modern Japanese criticism declares them to be by Morofusa, who they believe was induced by the publishers to allow his father's name to appear as the designer in order thereby to secure a better sale.

In support of this view, the comparative weakness of brush displayed therein is insisted upon, and certainly cannot be denied. It is to be noted, too, that Moronobu was already in retirement in 1694.

MOROSHIGE, whose real name was Furuyama Tarobei, illustrated about ten books and designed about the same number of prints between 1678 and 1698. Dates of birth and death are unknown. His *Shikano maki fude*, five large volumes published in 1686, is his best-known work and was very popular at the time. It was reprinted in 1692 ; and in the following year the authorities decided to ban the book, confiscating the wood-blocks and such copies as remained unsold, whilst the author, Shikano Buzayemon, and the publisher are both said to have suffered penalties—the former being deported to a far-off island and the latter being expelled from Yedo for the time being. The book deals mainly with life behind the scenes in the theatre.

Ishikawa RYŪSEN, whose name was Toshiyuki Izayemon, was a native of the Asakusa district of Yedo. There is no record of his birth and death. Some say he was a pupil of Moronobu, perhaps on the ground that his brush name Ryūsen may be also pronounced Tomonobu ; but the style exhibited in the books illustrated by him, twelve of which have come down to us, and in one or two *ichimai-ye*, do not betray the style of that master, but rather that of Kiyonobu though only in a remote degree. His work extends from 1686 till about 1714.

Torii Shōbei KIYONOBU I was the son of an Ōsaka actor of female rôles who also painted sign-boards for the theatres of Dotombori in that city, and whose name was Torii Shōshichi Kiyomoto. In spring, 1687, Kiyomoto removed with his son to Yedo, where he was employed to paint the *kamban* (sign-boards) of the *Ichimura-za* (theatre), in which work he was assisted by his son, then about twenty-two years of age, having been born in 1664. In the same year, Kiyonobu made his debut as a print designer by illustrating Shogetsudō Fukaku's four-volume book, *Nanshoku hana no some-goromo ;* some eight years later appeared his actor-prints in *sumi-ye*, which were the first of their kind, and immediately attained an immense vogue. They were hawked about the streets ; and being cheap found ready purchasers, not only among the townfolk, but also among provincials by whom, like Moronobu's early prints, they were called *Yedo-ye*. Books illustrated by Kiyonobu prior to 1696 and still to be seen are *Tomotsu monogatari*, one volume, published in 1687, and *Kokon Shibai Hyaku-nin isshu* (alternative title, *Shibai iro-kurabe*), two volumes, published in the 5th month of Genroku 6 (1693). This latter book is unsigned ; and has, from the illustrations resembling the style of Moronobu—which was common to all work at this period—been wrongly attributed to that master. In this period, Kiyonobu designed his first *banzuke* or playbills. He died at the age of sixty-six on the 28th day of the 7th month of Kyōhō 14 (11th August, 1729).

The woodcuts in the *Isé Monogatari* of 1608 are mere journeyman's work, in which whatever delicacy the original designs may have had—and Tosa work of that period, enfeebled though the tradition had become, could be exquisite in its kind—is completely lost. The illustrations are dull and tame, repeating what had been done before a thousand times; and they show no sign of having been designed with the woodcut line in view.

What a contrast with the typical picture books of Moronobu! Here at once we see the immense difference between woodcuts which are the final expression of the artist's thought, designed in terms of the material, and woodcuts which are merely the transcription of a drawing made for the drawing's sake and with no thought of anything further.

But it is wrong to suppose that this mastery of the woodcut medium was achieved at once. Moronobu's books of the last fifteen years of his life (1680–95) are familiar to all collectors, and it is by these that he is usually judged. But when we turn to his early work, to books of 1660 and there-abouts, we find something very different. These books are rare and not well known; indeed, none of them is described in Duret's catalogue, and Duret says of Moronobu: "Les livres qu'il a illustrés sont surtout compris entre les années 1680 et 1700." In this early work, while it is evident that the artist has reduced his design to the simplest terms, it is equally evident that the wood-cutters are still struggling with the diffi-culties of their craft. There are no flowing curves; no fine detail survives the vigorous chops of the knife. The growth of the hair at the temples, to be beautifully indicated in later times with lines of incredible fineness, shows no transition between white and solid black. The formula for the mouth, usually opened in speech, is an acute angle cut down into the profile, rather like a fish's mouth. The figures are smaller and leaner than those of Tenna-Genroku periods. In fact, to pass from a book of 1660 to one of 1685 is almost like passing from some German woodcut of the mid-fifteenth century to Dürer's "Apocalypse" or "Great Passion." None the less, the technical immaturity of the wood-cutters does not smother or suppress—perhaps enhances rather—an almost fierce vitality in Moronobu's figure-drawing. A certain diminution of force may be perceptible in the designs for the later books, but the complexity and richness of the *arabesque* of black and white are immensely increased. And Moronobu's drawing of the figure is always remarkably expressive. You feel the living presence in his men and women, and in the relation of the figures to each other Moronobu often shows a keen sense of drama.

The earliest of Moronobu's surviving single-sheet prints, such as the " Target of Yasu no Yoichi," reproduced on Plate II of *Estampes Japonaises Primitives*, the first volume of the great Paris Exhibition Catalogues, by MM. Vignier and Inada, are in the style of the books of 1660–70 ; but such prints are of excessive rarity. Already the question of colour had been attacked. In some cases it is impossible for us to say whether the colouring of one of these early prints is contemporary or not. Nor can we know for certain whether it was applied by the artist, or the publisher, or even the customer. But that it was the practice to enliven prints with colour from the very first is a safe conjecture. Red lead (*tan*) and yellow, with or without a tint of olive-grey, were the pigments most favoured. And as soon as the need for colour was recognized, the invention of the colour-print was bound, sooner or later, to follow.

The history of the Japanese colour-print, therefore, may be said to begin with Moronobu, though it was not till half a century after his death that colours began to be printed from the block.

The print reproduced on Pl. 19 (2) is one of a series of twelve sheets forming a single composition and representing a procession of Korean envoys with Japanese escort. It is hand-coloured in tones of warm yellow, pale red, and pale olive. Ten prints only are known, but as these are numbered from three to twelve, there is no doubt about the complete number. These prints, in Mr. Bateson's collection, have no signature, but were attributed to Moronobu. Certainly they were designed under the prevalent influence of his style, but the types and the drawing are demonstrably not his. The reproduction on the same page of a sheet by Moronobu, dating from about 1675, illustrates the difference. And, in fact, on one of six prints of this same series, sold in the Hamilton Easter Field Collection, New York, December, 1922, there is the signature *Torii Kiyonobu fudé*. (The sheets from the Field Collection are not numbered.)

A comparison of the two sheets here reproduced brings out the difference of character in the draughtsmanship of these two masters, though the later of the two prints, probably made after Moronobu's death, is not of the kind which displays Kiyonobu's style at its most typical. Moronobu, more than Kiyonobu, creates by his supple outlines the sense of a living body. Kiyonobu's figures are flatter to the eye, and the contours less expressive of the form within, though cunningly woven together as a composition. But the Korean procession was a traditional subject, and it did not give full scope to Kiyonobu's personal powers.

Moronobu's great contribution to Ukiyo-ye was, first, his discovery of

the possibilities of the woodcut, and then, through his perfect under-
standing of the medium, the broad and firm foundation of design which he
laid for future generations to build on.  As a draughtsman he ranks high
for the peculiar animation of life which he could give to human figures,
the energy and significance he could put into the turn of a head, the
gesture of an arm, the glance of an eye.  He gives the sense of human
magnetism, of people attracted or repelled by each other.  And all is done
with the simplest means, by his instinct for the essential line.

# CHAPTER II

# FEBRUARY 3RD, 1695, TO FEBRUARY 5TH, 1730

From the death of Moronobu till the close of the Genroku period, the prospects of Ukiyo-ye were far from bright.

Morofusa, upon whom the Hishikawa mantle had fallen, was devoid of originality and did not possess the ability to be even a good imitator. His spiritless work is but the ghost of the easy yet powerful brush-work of his great ancestor.

Moroshige, though a far better artist, never quite mastered his teacher's style. Ryūsen showed some independence; but his drawings are unpleasantly stilted.

Kiyonobu was producing good work, though the Hishikawa influence was too marked to invest it with originality except as regards subject. Fortunately, he was too great an artist to remain long in this groove; and towards 1703 he evolved a robust style which, though lacking the grace of Moronobu, was almost as powerful.

His manner at this time may be studied in the books *Fūryū shihō byōbu* and *Keisei yehon*, each in two volumes, published in the 3rd and 4th months respectively of 1700.

Similar work may be seen in his *sumi-* and *tan-ye*, issued in *hoso-kakemono-*, and *yoko-ye* format, which set the fashion to nearly all the Yedo artists of the succeeding periods of Hōyei, Shōtoku, and Kyōhō.

In the beginning of Hōyei, three talented artists in the persons of Kwaigetsudō, Kiyomasu, and Masanobu made their debut. Such of the former's life-history as is known is given in Note A, where, too, the problem surrounding him and his so-called " group " has been discussed.

KIYOMASU, whose real name was Torii Shōjirō, was the eldest son of Kiyonobu, with whom he lived at Naniwa-chō, Yedo. The date of his birth has not yet been definitely ascertained. Some authorities give this as 1706; but as he was already at work in 1703, this is obviously wrong.[1] According to the *Torii Kafu* (family records) his father was married in

[1] In the chronicle of Ukiyoye Masters, dated September, 1920, forming an appendix to No. 55 of the monthly magazine *Ukiyo-ye*, the commencement of his activity is given as 1704. In the Hayashi sale catalogue, Paris, 1902, lot No. 1434, a book dated 1703 is attributed to him. Moreover, in an article entitled " Tea-talks on Ukiyo-ye " (*Ukiyo-ye chabanashi*), it is recorded that Kiyomasu was married in the summer of Kyōhō (April–May, 1724); so if we accept 1706 as the year of his birth his marriage must have taken place when he was seventeen, which appears somewhat premature. For the question of his identity with Kiyonobu II, and possibility of a 2nd Kiyomasu, see Note B.

1693, so that it is possible that he was born in 1694, in which case he would have been ten in 1703, according to Japanese reckoning. He, like his father, painted theatrical sign-boards and designed playbills. His death occurred on December 6, 1763 (Hōreki 13, 2nd day of 11th month) and not as often stated, owing to discrepancy in reading the month number on his tombstone, on January 4, 1764 (Hōreki 13, 2nd day of 12th month). His activity lasted till about 1758.

MASANOBU, whose real name was Okumura Gempachi, appears to have been born at Yedo of unknown parentage in 1691. He was self-taught, studying the styles of Moronobu, Sukenobu, and Kwaigetsudō.

His earliest work is to be seen in a theatrical booklet entitled *Kyōtaro*, published in 1703,[1] which he followed up in 1704 with a book of courtesans in which he displays so much skill that it is difficult to credit the above statement that he was born in 1691. Nevertheless, this date is undoubtedly correct; for, on a six-panel screen painting of a " theatre and performance," No. 195, reproduced on picture 124 of the illustrated catalogue of *Japanese Old Fine Arts displayed at the Japan-British Exhibition, London*, 1910, and again by the owner, Mr. Fukuba Toru, in his catalogue of *One Hundred Ukiyoye Paintings*, exhibited at Paris in 1911, the following is recorded: " Japanese painting, drawn by Okumura Masanobu in Kyōhō 16 at the age of forty-one."

On the painting the name of the play that is being performed is inscribed, namely " Fukubiki Nagoya," and the *mon* (sort of heraldic device) of the Nakamura theatre and other details concerning the actors are plainly visible. This play was, in fact, produced at this theatre in the spring of 1731; and the actors depicted by Masanobu correspond with some of those who took part in the performance. It is, therefore, unreasonable in the face of this evidence to discount Masanobu's birth in 1691 merely on the ground that a boy of thirteen could hardly have shown such talent as is exhibited in the book of courtesans referred to above.

Precocity more or less similar is found among other Ukiyoye artists. As examples, we have Kiyomasu already noted; Moronobu's granddaughter O Sawa, the daughter of his second son Moronaga, who followed her father's profession at the age of six or seven; Yamazaki Ryū, a girl pupil of Moronobu, who began to paint when six or seven and showed extraordinary talent at the age of fifteen; Shunshō's pupil Shunyei who illustrated a book when fourteen; Toyokuni's pupils, Kuninao and Kunitsugu, and Toyohiro's son Toyokiyo, who each illustrated a book at the age of twelve.

[1] Hayashi Collection sale, Paris, June, 1902, No. 1457.

Though Masanobu, Nishimura Shigenaga, and Kondō Kiyoharu are recorded in *Ukiyoye ruikō* as pupils of Kiyonobu, the writer Shikitei Samba (1775–1822) states that they were all self-taught, adding " all Ukiyo-ye at this time were done in the Torii style." Certainly an examination of Masanobu's work during Hōyei and Shōtoku leads one to the same conclusion.

Masanobu started his career as an artist, not as a bookseller as is generally believed. It was not till the Kyōhō period that he set up as a publisher in Tori Shio-chō. A picture of his in *Yedo meibutsu ganokō*, of 1733, is inscribed " Abura-chō beni-ye"; so he may have then had a branch in that street. Prior to Kyōhō, his works were issued by other publishers; and it was not till that period that he produced his own books and prints. As a publisher, he called himself Kwakujudō (his *dō-gō* or business name) Okumura-ya Genroku, and used a red gourd-shaped sign as his trade-mark or shop-sign (*iye no shirushi*), which is found on many of his prints. He had reason to complain that prints were being forged with his signature and that his own prints were being copied and sold without his sanction. At length he found it necessary to stamp his gourd seal as a guarantee, and to warn the public that only prints so sealed, and signed by him with the prefix Shōmei, or the affix *shō hitsu*, meaning respectively " genuine name " and " real brush," were his own work.

On a *hoso-urushi-ye* representing the actor Bandō Hikosaburō I upon his first appearance on the Yedo stage at the close of 1727 is the following inscription : " Genuine brush of the Japanese artist Okumura Shinmyō Masanobu, originator of a particular style of Ukiyo-ye ; Okumura-ya at the sign of the red gourd, wholesaler of illustrated books, in Tori-shio street "—(" Nippon gwakō Ukiyo-ye ichi-ryū kongen Okumura Shinmyō Masanobu shō hitsu ; Tori-shio chō yezoshi toi-ya akaki hyōtan shirushi Okumura-ya "). Probably he intended to intimate by the expression " originator of a particular style of Ukiyo-ye " that he was the inventor of the Urushi-ye or so-called lacquer picture.

Masanobu used several *gō* or " pseudonyms," the earliest of which was Shinmyō (pronounced Shimmyō). Others were Hōgetsudō, Bunkaku, Bai-ō, and Tanchōsai. The first three of these he received from his Haikai (17-syllable poem) master Shogetsudō Fukaku Sen-ō, of whom he made an excellent portrait as the frontispiece to his picture book *Tsuru no hashi*, or " The Crane's Beak," published in 1752, in which he exhibits work of the highest order. He styled himself at various times " Refined Japanese painter " (*Fūryū Yamato yeshi*) and " Yedo Japanese artist "

(*Tōbu Yamato gwakō*). He died on March 29th, 1768, his age being given by two authorities as seventy-nine, which makes the date of his birth 1690, though as already explained 1691 appears more likely. He seems to have retired from active work about fifteen years previously.

Furuyama Moromasa, a pupil of Moroshige, began work in Shōtoku. The dates of his birth and death are alike unknown. His activity extended at least to the autumn of 1772, when he designed a print of the actor Nakamura Noshio as the courtesan Takao in the play " Keisei Momiji no uchikake " then produced at the Morita theatre. He used the *gō* of Getsugetsudō. At first influenced by Kiyonobu, he later followed the middle style of Masanobu, and finally that of Kiyotsune.

Another pupil of Moroshige was Furuyama Morotane, of whom nothing is known save two paintings—one of a courtesan of the Kyōhō period in the writer's possession being exceptionally fine and somewhat in the style of Kiyomasu, and one hand-coloured *hoso-ye* in the Kunstgewerbe Museum, Berlin, of the actor Ichimura Takenojō as Kichisaburō the lover of O Shichi. A reproduction of this print is to be seen on Plate 7 of Kurth's *Die Primitiven des Japanholzschnitts*, Dresden, 1922.

During Shōtoku, Kyōto Ukiyo-ye had fallen into a languishing condition after the death of the painter and book illustrator Hinaya Rippō in 1669. Yoshida Hambei made a bid for and succeeded in gaining popular favour by illustrating books, clever in their way but certainly decadent. These books, known as *Kōshoku-bon* (lewd books), deal with degenerates called *wakashū* or *kagema*, young effeminates of attractive mien who masqueraded in women's clothes. The Bakufu or Shōgun's government issued an edict in Kyōto for their suppression. Another Kyōto artist, Ōmori Yoshikiyo, who worked from 1701 to 1716, illustrated a few books, but showed little talent. It was left to Nishikawa Sukenobu to infuse new life into the Kyōto Ukiyo-ye, which he did by a number of books chiefly depicting charming and dainty girls and women. This artist was born in 1671 at Kyōto, his personal name being first Yūsuke and then Yūkyō, and his *gō* Jitokusai and Bunkwadō. At first he studied under Kano Yeinō and then in the Tosa school, finally forming his own style and founding a school at Kyōto which was attended by numerous pupils. He died on October 19th, 1751, in the eighty-first year of his age.

The Kyōhō period stands out as one of the most important in Ukiyoye history, not only on account of a remarkable array of talented artists, but also for the advance made in technique. In *Kinsei Seji-dan*, published in 1734, we read : " Ukiyo-ye were first painted by Hishikawa Kichibei

(Moronobu) of Yedo. Afterwards, Furuyama Shinkurō (Moromasa) followed his style. The present artists are Kwaigetsudō, Okumura Masanobu, etc. Their pictures are called *yedo-ye*. Miss Ryū began painting at the age of six or seven, and became skilful. Her writing was as good as her painting. She was the best of lady painters. . . . From the beginning of Kyōhō, Izumi-ya Gonshirō of Dōbō-chō, Asakusa barrier-gate, Yedo, published Ukiyoye actor-prints coloured with *beni* (a red pigment extracted from a species of saffron), which became widely known in Kyōto, Ōsaka, and throughout several provinces. They were bought for children to play with, and were reckoned among the special products of Yedo." The famous writer Santō Kyōden (1761–1816), well known, too, as artist under the name of Kitao Masanobu, tells us in Volume I of his *Kottōshū*, published in the 12th month of Bunsei 12, that in his opinion " single-sheet prints (*ichimai-ye*) appeared some time during the Yempō-Tenna era (1673–1684), the subjects being Asahina engaged in a neck-pulling (*kubi-biki*) contest with demons, Tosa jōruri (a kind of musical drama), Rats' wedding ceremony, and such-like. The actor Bozu Kohei may have been the first theatrical print. At that time they (*sumi-ichimai-ye*) were crudely coloured in tan, green, blue, etc. Hishikawa Moronobu and Furuyama Moroshige painted them. From the beginning of Genroku, pictures coloured with tan and green pigments were termed *Tan-ye*. From about the end of this period, Torii Kiyonobu and his son Kiyomasu painted them. In Hōyei and Shōtoku periods, Kondō Kiyoharu appeared. In the beginning of Kyōhō, *beni-ye* originated. Pictures, on which a lustre was produced by spreading glue on the *sumi*, were called *Urushi-ye*. These were chiefly made by Okumura Masanobu." Illustrative of Kyōden's article is an interesting woodcut of a *beni-ye* pedlar. *Beni-ye* here refers to the hand-coloured prints.

In *Ukiyoye ruikō tsuikō*, published in 1802, we read : " In the beginning of Kyōhō, Izumi-ya Gonshirō of Dōbō-chō began to sell pictures coloured with *beni*, which were called *beni-ye*. Improvements were made by applying glue to black and by sprinkling gold-dust ; and these *Urushi-ye* were very popular."

From these extracts it would appear that *beni-ye* were invented by Gonshirō. There are prints by Torii Kiyotada, Katsukawa Terushige, and Okumura Toshinobu, and perhaps by other artists upon which is inscribed within a vase-shaped seal, " Beni-ye : original publisher Gonshirō of Dōbō-chō, Asakusa gate " (Beni-ye Kongen hammoto Gonshirō Asakusa mitsuke Dōbō-chō), which goes to prove the truth of the above statements. As to who was the first artist to design these *beni-ye* there is no direct evidence, except the names of the above artists.

There seems little doubt that Okumura Masanobu first used the glue device and perhaps the sprinkling with gold-dust, though this latter alone is found on some prints by Kiyomasu and others which may antedate Kyōhō, but this is uncertain.

KONDŌ KIYOHARU, mentioned above by Samba as having been an independent artist in Hōyei and Shōtoku, was commonly known as Sukegorō. He designed a few good *tan-* and *urushi-ye*, but was chiefly noted as an illustrator of red-covered books known as *Kompira-bon*,[1] and readers. Kondō Kiyonobu appears to have been his pupil who worked during Kyōhō in a similar manner.

An original, if somewhat erratic, artist was HANEKAWA CHINCHŌ, whose name was Manaka and who was popularly called Ōta Bungorō, Ōta being the old name of Kawaguchi village, Saitama district, in the province of Musashi, where he was born in 1679. According to Kyokutei Bakin (1767–1848), in his miscellany entitled *Yenseki Zasshi*, "he was a poor but proud *samurai*, who refused the offer of a publisher to provide him with lodging, food, and raiment on condition that he would work for him alone, saying : ' Poverty is the common lot of a *samurai*. Why should I bend my back for 5 *to* (about 2¾ bushels) of rice ? etc.'" The same author says that he would work only when in the mood, and that when it pleased him he would even paint theatrical sign-boards.

Chinchō studied under Kiyonobu, from whom he received the name of Motonobu. He afterwards, during Shōtoku, took the brush name of Hanekawa—one hand-coloured print of Daikoku standing on a bale of rice bearing the signature " Hanekawa Motonobu fude." His painting of sign-boards probably took place when he was under the Kiyonobu influence during Genroku and Hōyei.

He sometimes used the *gō* of Kwaijosai in books and prints. In 1742 he illustrated a Yoshiwara guide (*saiken*), his last known work. He died in 1754 at the age of seventy-six. His prints are very rare, consisting of 4 or 5 *tan-ye*, and 3 or 4 *urushi-ye*. He had two pupils named Hanekawa Wagen and Okinobu, each of whom designed 2 or 3 *urushi-ye* during Kyōhō.

Several new recruits joined the ranks during this period. The most important of these were the Nishimura, Shigenaga and Shigenobu ; the Torii, Kiyotada, Kiyotomo, and Kiyoshige ; and Okumura Toshinobu.

---

[1] *Kompira-bon* dealt with Jōruri chanters of Yedo.

SHIGENAGA was born in 1697 at Yedo. He was a landowner (*Ji-nushi*), not a tea-house keeper as is commonly stated, in Tōri Abura-chō. Later he removed to the Kanda quarter, where he opened a bookshop. He used the *gō* of Senkwadō and more rarely that of Yeikwadō. He was a self-taught artist, working on much the same lines as Okumura Masanobu. His death occurred in 1756.

SHIGENOBU was born in 1711. About 1728, he became a pupil of Shigenaga, and in 1731 designed his first print under the name of Nishimura Shigenobu. He also used the brush name of Magosaburō with or without that of Shigenobu. Some time after 1737 or 1738, he married the daughter of an innkeeper in Kodemma-chō, and changed his *geisei* or art surname to Ishikawa, and his *gwamyō* or art personal name to Toyonobu, using too the *gō* of Tanjōdō and Shūha. After his marriage he became the proprietor of the inn, the name of which was Nuka-ya, whence he received the popular name of Nukaya Shichibei. He died on the 25th day of 5th month of Temmei 5, corresponding to July 1st, 1785, at the age of seventy-five. His popularity may be gauged from a series of twelve *kyōka* or humorous poems each commencing with a character of his name, meaning "feeling sorrow at the death of Shūha." These poems were composed by the celebrated comic versifier Yomo no Akara, otherwise Shokusanjin (*b.* 1749, *d.* 1823).

KIYOTADA, KIYOTOMO, and KIYOSHIGE were pupils of Kiyonobu I from the beginning of Kyōhō. The first two remained at work till about 1744–1745, according to the Chronicle of Ukiyoye Masters in *Ukiyo-ye*, No. 55, appendix.[1] Kiyoshige's activity lasted till about 1758. The dates of their birth and death are unrecorded. Kiyoshige sometimes used the *gō* of Seichōken.

TOSHINOBU was the son and pupil of Okumura Masanobu. Dates of birth and death unknown ; but worked from about 1725 to 1749. He used at times the *gō* of Kwakugetsudō and Bunzen as a book illustrator, but as far as is known not as a print designer.

Several print designers of minor importance appeared during this period. Their work is scarce but in most cases of much distinction. A list of their names with approximate dates of their activity will suffice.

Okumura Kuninobu, *c.* 1733, of whom only one *urushi-ye* is so far known. He was a pupil of Masanobu.

Hirose Shigenobu, *w.c.* 1724–1735.

Tamura Yoshinobu, *w.c.* 1725–1734.

[1] See also Note B as regards Kiyotada's activity.

Tamura Sadanobu, *w.c.* 1725–1740.

Tsunegawa Shigenobu may be identical with Hirose above ; he worked about the same time.

Katsukawa Terushige, Katsumura Terunobu, Fujikawa Yoshinobu, Yamamoto Shigeharu, Kichikawa Katsumasa, Torii Kiyoharu, and Shimizu Mitsunobu were contemporaries of the above. Each did good work imitative of either the Torii or Okumura styles of this period. In Volume IX of *Kenkyō-ruitenshō* it is recorded that in the 7th month of Kyōhō 6 (1721) the authorities forbade the publication of books and picture-books concerning current events, and also for the time being the printing and peddling of *ichimai-ye* (single-sheet pictures) of the same. This may, perhaps, account for the restricted output of these artists. How long this order remained in force is not recorded. This stage closes with the death of the first Torii Kiyonobu in 1729. He appears to have retired from active work during 1727, and to have handed the succession to his eldest son Kiyomasu, who then became the second Torii, at the same time retaining his first name. It is from about this year that prints bearing either signature (i.e. Kiyonobu or Kiyomasu) are so alike in style. Many of these signed " Kiyonobu " and hitherto ascribed to the father are in reality the work of the son. For instance, out of three examples given by Kurth in the 1922 edition of his book, *Der Japanische Holzschnitt*, Plates 12 and 13 are certainly by the second Kiyonobu. So, too, is the print reproduced on Plate 14 of the same author's book, *Die primitiven des Japanholzschnitts*, Dresden, 1922. An innovation during this period was the three-sheet continuous picture called *sambukutsui*—an innovation, so far as prints only were concerned, for the term had long been in use in regard to paintings of the classical schools.

In a period like that of Genroku, an age of luxury, pageantry, and pleasure, the craving for new modes of self-expression was imperious and persistent. Ukiyo-ye was a mirror in which the Yedo public, avid of novelty and enjoyment, looked to see itself.

Moronobu, with the immense mass of his picture-books, had pictured scenes from life and legend and the history of Japan with delightful vivacity. But it was above all the passing hour, the doings and the fashions of the moment, that the public craved to see mirrored in the woodcuts to which Moronobu had given such a vogue ; its own doings, and the features and the dresses of its favourite idols.

Kiyonobu, who came to Yedo just before Genroku opened, created the actor-print; and from now till the very end—that is, for nearly two centuries—the actor-print was to be one of the two main preoccupations of the woodcut designers. The other centred in *bijin-ye*, the prints of popular beauties, especially of courtesans. Kiyonobu and Kiyomasu designed *bijin-ye*, but it is especially with the prints of actors, either singly or in a group of two—rarely more—that the Torii in the days of their glory are associated.

Till his death in 1729, Kiyonobu ranked as the leading master in Ukiyo-ye. So many of his earlier prints must have been lost, that we are not really in a position to judge of his work as a whole. One or two poster-paintings, ascribed to him, have survived; but our estimate of his art is founded upon his single-sheet prints. And in the extant prints he has his son Kiyomasu as his close rival; for few, if any, woodcuts have been preserved from days before Kiyomasu came on the scene. In gift there seems little to choose between the two, though Kiyonobu was the leader. Father and son together founded the Torii tradition which was to last so long.

With the Hōyei period (1704–1711) we come to a time when the single-sheet prints, which are our main concern, begin to appear in quantity, though doubtless only a fraction have been preserved.

From books published in 1700—the album called *Shin Yoshiwara*, for instance, a copy of which is in the Boston Museum—we can form a good idea of Kiyonobu's style at that period. The influence of Moronobu is obvious, but there is a stronger element of caligraphy in the drawing, which sweeps in the outline of a figure with a few ample curves, and the patterns on the dresses are big, bold, and simple, such as a few immensely magnified flowers, alternately black with white centres, and white with black centres, sprinkled over the form.

Kiyonobu's art was fundamentally that of the poster-designer. Such work was to tell at a distance as a stimulating pattern to the eye. There was no room for the subtle or the exquisite. Forcible black lines make an exhilarating arabesque, like the lead-lines in a stained-glass window, in which the details of form seem almost irrelevant.

During Hōyei period Kiyonobu's style in single prints becomes more personal, and at its best has an exultation and exuberance of line which reconcile us to a looseness or even a certain emptiness in the forms. He invents striking patterns; sometimes capriciously making a decoration out of Japanese characters traced in rapid caligraphy over a dress, and partly cut in gleaming white out of a field of black; the invention of the white line invading a black mass being peculiarly congenial to the wood-engraver's art, though never exploited by the Japanese as it has been in Europe. But it is above all the breadth, bigness, and impetus of Kiyonobu's sweeping outlines that give the character to his art. With all the centuries of Japanese painting behind him, all its discoveries, achievements, and sophistications, he makes a new start as with the joyous confidence of a gifted child. He exults in the force of his brush-lines for their own sake ; and they give us pleasure, even when they seem to do little but enforce and enrich the pattern of the design.

There is a considerable difference between the large prints of scenes from legend, whether direct illustrations or stage-presentments, and the small actor-prints. The former are much richer and more complex as designs, and overflow with energy. The two prints reproduced in the *Paris V.I. Catalogue*, Plate XI, are masterpieces of this kind. The violence of gesture and expression—eyes starting out of the head, contorted limbs, extravagantly sprawling action—is at times grotesque. There is a barbaric element in Kiyonobu, and the fierce orange-red and yellow filling in the strong black outlines heighten the savage effect. But this primitive effervescent energy was of great value to Ukiyo-ye at this time.

What we say of Kiyonobu applies equally to Kiyomasu. As woodcuts and as works of art there is nothing finer in their work than certain prints of hawks and eagles, of which most now extant are from the hand of Kiyomasu. Here there is less of the rapid formula which the Torii used for human form and feature. The anger-ruffled plumage of the great birds, the black and cruel stare of the eye, are given in strokes of astonishing force. Two prints by Kiyomasu, one of an eagle eyeing a monkey cowering and whimpering under a pine branch below it, the other of the eagle with the agonized monkey in its claws, are of an almost terrifying vitality.

Though 1729 is now accepted as the date of Kiyonobu's death, the majority of the prints still catalogued under his name are prints published after that date, and therefore by Kiyonobu the Second. Not only the *beni-ye* in a small, delicate style, signed Kiyonobu, which date from after 1741, must be eliminated, but also many of the hand-coloured prints which have survived—probably most of them. The records of the Yedo stage enable us to date a number of the early actor-prints, and we thus get a clue to changes of style which enable us to date others. All prints of Segawa Kikunojō, for instance, the first of that name, so famous on the stage for women's parts, date from December 1730 and after.

The residue of prints which are indubitably the work of Kiyonobu the First form a very limited series; and the genius of the first great Torii master appears, in our revised conception of him, with its exuberant vehemence heightened and enhanced. Only towards the end is this vigour a little tamed and softened.

This restless energy, and the peculiar Torii conventions—a linear style which the Japanese compare to " the wriggling of worms," must have given novelty of contrast to the style of the Kwaigetsudō prints, when they began to appear during Hōyei. These tall, stately single figures, with rather inexpressive faces, are drawn with a magnificent sweep of line, but are much more contained than the swirling forms of the Torii work. The general effect is suave and serene. If these prints were not so extremely rare, we should find them monotonous; the repertory of pose and gesture is so limited. But, few as they are, they fill a historic place in Ukiyo-ye. They have a grandeur of aspect rarely afterwards matched.

It is noticeable that in a large-sized *tan-ye* of an Oiran and Kamuro reproduced in *Masterpieces of Ukiyo-ye*, Vol. III, Plate 82, Kiyonobu is found working very much under Kwaigetsudō influence, though he gives a characteristic sway and swing to the superb figure.

But a far more fertile genius than Kwaigetsudō had already appeared in the field. Okumura Masanobu, as has been recorded, was a precocious boy. His youthful productions follow pretty closely the style of Kiyonobu and Kiyomasu (or of Moronobu in non-theatrical subjects), and he seems soon to be working on equal terms with them. In the Boston Museum is a book of Yoshiwara beauties, published in 1711, in which Masanobu repeats, almost line for line, some of the figures in Kiyonobu's *Keisei Yehon* of 1700 and similar albums.[1] Probably these books of beauties were issued every year. The full scope of Masanobu's genius was hardly revealed till after Kiyonobu's death, but he was quick to see the possibilities of a larger range of subject-matter than the Torii masters affected. The great success of Sukenobu in Kyōto and the popularity of his picture-books suggested that the woodcut need not confine itself to the Yoshiwara and the theatre. If Sukenobu had found inexhaustible material in the occupations and amusements of young women and girls, why should these not provide charming motives for single-sheets? There exist a few prints by Sukenobu, though nearly all his work is in paintings and book-illustrations; two hand-coloured woodcuts, of unusual shape, are in the British

[1] Information supplied by Mr. Kōjiro Tomita, assistant curator in the Museum of Fine Arts, Boston.

Museum collection, and another is reproduced by Ficke, Plate 2 ; but he did not exploit this favourite form of popular art as it had been exploited in Yedo. Obviously the Torii style was ill-suited to idyllic and domestic subjects. It was entirely incapable of intimacy. And if the range of the woodcut was to be enlarged in this direction, a change of style was bound to come. A more supple and delicate manner of design was required.

Throughout its history Ukiyo-ye is always under the mysterious influences of fashion. Novelty and change are a necessity to the life of this popular art. We see it alternately swayed in one direction and another. The original impulse to a new method or new motives may come from some single artist, but it is taken up so swiftly by a group or by a whole generation that it seems like a spontaneous change of outlook in the whole school. Moronobu's easy vigour was succeeded by Kiyonobu's masculine vehemence ; then under Sukenobu's influence Ukiyo-ye turns to a softer and more feminine manner. Later on we shall find similar alternations, as from Harunobu's exquisiteness to Kiyonaga's grandeur.

The point to note is, how thoroughly each manner, each field of subject-matter, was explored and exploited before it gave way to the next change of fashion.

The prints we reproduce, Plates 20 and 21, illustrate the prevailing manner of the period and the work of its chief masters. The two on Pl. 20 are typical of the work of the two chief Torii masters during the Shōtoku period. The resemblance in style between Kiyonobu and Kiyomasu is very close ; and were the subjects of these particular prints the same, the parallel would seem closer still. The exuberance of Kiyonobu's swinging lines and twirling loops and rolling curves is now just a little chastened, but the caligraphic element is still very strong. The human face and hands appear as part of the general gay pattern, on equal terms with the devices on the dresses, the subdivided areas of colour, and the black lines surrounding them.

Kiyomasu's conception of figure-drawing is essentially the same, a kind of drawing which communicates the sense of gesture and movement rather than of form ; and both gestures and movements are willingly repeated from a chosen repertory with slight variations.

The Masanobu print reproduced (Pl. 21) is later ; it belongs to mid-Kyōhō. It is a very fine example of Masanobu's middle period, after he had begun to develop a personal style and was drawing away from the Torii influence. It is one of the *urushi-ye*, or " lacquer-prints," which, as we have seen, were an invention probably of this artist. How solidly the figure is projected, how compactly designed! The silhouette is beautiful in itself. The girl's dress is soft red, deep black, and yellow. There is grey-blue on the fan, repeated on the skirt. The vivid impression of rich colouring comes from the lustrous depth of black cutting into the other colours and foiling them, while the grains of gold-dust powdered over the sash and the tea-chest slung over the girl's shoulder add a final enhancement. Masanobu has moved a long way, in reality, from the Torii models. In the Kiyonobu and Kiyomasu prints the lines twist and coil as if they had taken life on their own account and had almost parted from their function of defining the forms beneath the dress. Masanobu's brush-line sweeps firm and graceful, with ample curves, but when he had finished, the shape is there, expressed to the eyes; we feel a real, breathing body beneath the rich delightful pattern.

On an earlier *urushi-ye* by Masanobu, also in the British Museum collection—again it is the same actor, Sanjō Kantarō, as a dancing girl— is a mica ground, which has every appearance of being contemporary. It is the earliest known example of this silvery background which late in the century was to have great vogue for a time.

With the passing from favour of the crude, though forcible, *tan-ye*, and the advent of *beni-ye* with their softer colouring, at the beginning of Kyōhō, the large-sized prints, the scale of which suited the bold and telling effects of the older style, became very rare. The *hoso-ye* shape, about $12\frac{3}{4} \times 5\frac{3}{4}$ in. was the established size for actor-prints. But during Kyōhō was devised, again by Masanobu, the *hashira-ye*, or pillar-print, a form in which some of the finest of all the Japanese colour-prints were to be designed.

Whatever new technical devices or inventions were made were taken up at once by the whole school. For a number of years *urushi-ye* were popular, and were produced by the Torii, now reinforced by Kiyotada, Kiyoshige and Chinchō, as well as by Masanobu and his son Toshinobu, and by Shigenaga and Shigenobu. The colouring of the *beni-ye*, delicate and attractive in choice examples, is often rather gaudy, and the sheen of the glue applied to the blocks in the *urushi-ye* is not always happy in effect. But at its best this phase of the hand-coloured print has a glow of colouring which is peculiar to itself.

The range of Ukiyo-ye is still decidedly circumscribed. But we note the appearance of occasional landscapes, or sets of landscape prints—the " Four Seasons," or the " Eight Views of Ōmi "—usually on small upright panels. These are truly " primitive " in manner, being in a style derived from the old conventions of the Tosa school, instead of the vivid and summary synthesis of the Chinese manner. The appearance of things is registered in symbol, with little attempt at coherence and unity. Dr. Kurth, in his *Japanische Holzschnitt* (p. 37), reproduces a flower-and-bird piece by Shigenaga which is certainly in the Chinese tradition so far as the motive is concerned; but it can hardly be said to be in the "style" either of Chinese paintings or of Chinese woodcut.

The print by Shigenaga which we reproduce represents a girl carrying letters to sell. Part of the pattern on her dress is formed by the *mon* of various actors. Among these are the *mon* of Ichikawa Monnosuke I, who died in 1729, and of Ōtani Hiroji I, who came to Yedo at the end of 1727. We can therefore assign the print to about 1728. The fashion of dressing the hair has not changed greatly from that of the end of Genroku, but the "tail" at the back of the head is less full and does not lie so low. During the succeeding years it becomes still thinner, in a shape characteristic of many of the prints signed Kiyonobu, but certainly dating from after the first Kiyonobu's death. It is to be noted, however, that in their actor-prints the Torii masters clung to a certain convention of representing the hair. It may be seen in Plate 22 (1) which dates from the close of 1740, and is also found in the later two-colour prints. In these actor-prints, therefore, the style of coiffure is no guide to the date.

Shigenaga during the first Kiyonobu's lifetime rose rapidly to the front rank of Ukiyoye artists. There is something personal in his style, which we can recognize in the print reproduced, though so much in the Masanobu manner. Some of the finest *urushi-ye* are by his hand. And he designed some of the earliest *ishi-zuri*, or stone-prints, cut on wood in imitation of the rubbings from stone of which the Chinese were proud. Of these stone-prints we shall have more to say later on.

# CHAPTER III

# FEBRUARY 6TH, 1730, TO FEBRUARY 1ST, 1764

During the remainder of Kyōhō until the Kwampō period (February 5th, 1741, to February 2nd, 1743), the hand-coloured print reigned supreme. The high standard of excellence in design that had marked the earlier productions was maintained; and, except the first Torii Kiyonobu, Kwaigetsudō, and one or two minor artists, the same men were at work. The softening influence of Sukenobu became more accentuated, the virile brush-work of the sign-boards giving place to a tenderness of drawing almost bordering on effeminacy even when the subjects were of a theatrical character. From the commencement of 1739, Okumura Masanobu used for the first time the *dō-gō* of Hogetsudō, with or without the *gō* Bunkaku and Bai-ō, all of which had been bestowed upon him by his *haikai* (seventeen-syllable poem) master Shōgetsudō Fukaku Sen-ō (1662–1753). This forms a useful landmark in determining the dates of his work about this time. He also dropped the name of Shinmyō and adopted that of Tanchōsai. At the close of 1740, he originated *Uki-ye* or floating pictures —large oblong hand-coloured prints ranging in size from $17\frac{1}{4} \times 25\frac{3}{8}$ in. to $12\frac{1}{2} \times 17\frac{5}{8}$ in. The native term for these prints is *yen-kin* or " far and near." The hand-colouring comprises vermilion, tan, yellow, blue, purple, olive-green, dark red, and brown. They mostly represent interiors with the *fusuma* and *shōji* thrown open. The subjects include scenes from plays, such as " Yaoya O-Shichi," " Soga," " Taiheiki," or " Dōjōji "; the middle street of the Shin Yoshiwara (exterior view); apartments of a courtesan or of a nobleman; the Mitsui silk emporium, and such-like. These *Uki-ye* continued in favour for about four or five years, the principal artists besides Masanobu being Shigenaga, Kiyotada, Moromasa, Tanaka Masunobu, and Jōgetsudō.

TANAKA MASUNOBU appears to have been a pupil of Shigenaga about 1735. He used the *dō-gō* of Sanseidō, and continued at work till about 1771, later coming under the influence of Harunobu. There is an example from his brush of *Shiro-nuki-ye*, or " pictures picked out in white," which is reproduced in the 1902 Hayashi catalogue, Lot 291. Another, a two-colour print of his, dated 1746, is recorded in the same catalogue.

During the first year of Kwampō (1741),[1] prints coloured from two wood-

---

[1] A beni-ye actor print by Kiyomasu in the Howard Mansfield collection has been dated by Gookin the autumn of 1741, and he thinks it can hardly have been the first published.

blocks in rose and green made their first appearance, from which it would seem that the invention of printing *ichimai-ye* in colours from wood-blocks took place some time in the previous year. The writer Fujikake, in his work *Ukiyoye hangwa shi*, expresses the opinion that the Ichiwa-ichigen is correct in attributing the invention to the Yedo publisher Kamimura Kichiyemon. This book records that " in the first year of Yenkyō (1744), Yemi-ya Kamimura Kichiyemon, inventing a guide-mark (*kentō*) which is now known as the *Kamimura kentō*, produced the first colour-block pictures (*shiki-sai han-gwa*)." The guide-mark referred to was a right angle at the right bottom corner and a straight line corresponding to its lower edge at the left bottom corner of the key-block, similar marks being made on the blocks to receive the colours ; so that, by adjusting the bottom edge of the sheet to be printed on these marks, accuracy in register was secured. It may be true that Kamimura was the inventor, though the date given is later than some dated prints testify to.

It has been a matter for surprise that colour-prints from wood-blocks did not appear before this, since Chinese coloured woodcuts were made at least more than half a century previously, and were doubtless well known in Japan. According to the testimony of Mr. T. Urushiyama, as published in an article that appeared in the *Ukiyoye Magazine*, No. 13, of June 1st, 1916, the idea had occurred and been put into practice some thirteen years before. This gentleman, after reviewing and criticising Hokkyō Ōneisai's colour-book *Kyō-chū zu* of 1750–1751, Sekkōsai Tokinobu's *Saishiki gwasen* of 1767, and Tachibana Minkō's *Shokunin burui* of 1771, as not being strictly coloured woodcuts, writes as follows : " But the two-volume book, *Chichi-no-on* (compiled by Danjurō II), published in the 15th year of Kyōhō (1730), on the occasion of a requiem mass for Ichikawa Danjurō (the first), contains sixty-six uncoloured cuts by Hanabusa Ippō (1697–1760), and two pages with four coloured woodcuts that are sealed ' Kwan '—doubtless an abbreviation of Ukwansai, one of the *gō* of Ogawa Haritsu (1661–1747, a Yedo painter). I have personally inspected these latter, and declare without hesitation that they are genuine coloured woodcuts very skilfully done, and in no way resemble the gradation colouring of the above-mentioned *Saishiki gwasen*."

Not having seen the book in question, we are unable to confirm this statement, which has the appearance nevertheless of a well-considered judgment. Mr. Urushiyama does not state what colours were employed, nor does he express an opinion as to how the register was maintained. Perhaps the reason why so apparently a successful experiment was not applied to printing *ichimai-ye* of that time in colours was that the cost of extra blocks would not, in view of the paucity of purchasers, have made the process profitable. In *Baka-gatari* we are told that " at the end of Kyōhō (1735–1736), in the collection *Chichi-no-on*, by Ichikawa Hakuyen (Danjūrō II), on the occasion of the requiem of his father Saigyū (Danjūrō I), three verses by Saigyū are illustrated by means of colour-printing (*iro-zuri*) by Katsuma Ryūsui." This appears to have been a re-publication of the original book.

Colour-block printing almost, but not quite, displaced the *urushi-ye*; there are still in existence some of these, one of which, by Kiyomasu, represents Nakamura Kumetarō and Ichimura Kamezō—the former not having appeared on the Yedo stage till the close of 1748. There are at least two colour-prints which are dated 1743, and others which may be so dated from the stage records, all after designs by Kiyomasu or Shigenaga ; so that no particular artist can be said to have been the first to design for the new technique. It is unfortunate that the term *beni-ye*, which, as we have seen, was used to describe the hand-coloured prints at the beginning of Kyōhō (1716), is also applied to prints coloured from wood-blocks, a more appropriate name for which would be *beni-zuri-ye* or " beni-printed pictures " ; and this term is often used by modern native writers.

A modification of *beni-zuri-ye* is to be found in *kusa-zuri-ye* or " grass (colour) printed pictures," in which *kusa* or grass-green and yellow were used. They are rarely seen. One by Kiyomasu of Ichimura Kamezō as Inu no Hayata may be dated from the stage records December, 1747. Shigenaga and Tomikawa Fusanobu sometimes used this technique. They are referred to in some books as *rokushō-ye* or " verdigris pictures." They are less effective than the *beni* and green prints.

When Shigenobu changed his name to Toyonobu has not yet been ascertained. As a tentative date, pending further research, 1744 is suggested. He made several wide and also narrow *Hashira-ye* (of which format Okumura Masanobu was the originator), coloured by hand and dating from about this year. The dimensions of the *hashira-ye* varied from about 27 × 12 to 28 × 9 in. in height and width respectively. Later a similar format called *hashira-kakushi-no-ye* or " pillar-hiding pictures," otherwise known as *hashira-kake* or " pillar-hanging pictures," measuring about 27 in. high by 4 or 5 in. wide, came into vogue. Koryūsai especially made use of this shape.

Nishimura Magosaburō Shigenobu does not appear to have designed *beni-zuri-ye*, though there are several by him under his later name of

Tanjōdō (which some read as Meijōdō) Ishikawa Shūha Toyonobu. There are also a few by Toshinobu, who was certainly living in 1749, as a book illustrated by Kwakugetsudō Okumura Bunzen Toshinobu entitled *Protection against Small-pox* (*hōsō-jo*) was published in that year. Several new artists appeared in Gembun, Yenkyō, and Kwanyen periods (i.e. from 1736 to 1750), namely Tomikawa Fusanobu, Okumura Masafusa, Shimizu Genshirō, Yamamoto Yoshinobu, Mangetsudō, Yengetsudō, Kōgetsudō, Jōgetsudō, and other minor men.

FUSANOBU was a wholesale publisher of prints and illustrated books in Ōdemma-chō, Yedo. He became bankrupt during Gembun, and took up print-designing. His ordinary name was Yamamoto Kuzayemon. He is said to have received instruction from Shigenaga. His work extends up to about 1763. During the Hōreki period he took the name of Ginsetsu. About eight prints in all comprise his output.

MASAFUSA, also called Bunshi, was a pupil of Masanobu. He appears to have worked in the provinces. One hand-coloured print, and an illustrated book dated 1747 are all that is so far known of his work.

SHIMIZU GENSHIRŌ, by whom but one colour-print has been so far recorded, worked at Yedo. He may have been a pupil of Shimizu Mitsunobu, who was still active at this time and continued at work till about 1769.

YAMAMOTO YOSHINOBU, common name Heishichirō, chiefly illustrated theatrical play-books during Kwanyen and Hōreki. He made a few *beni-zuri-ye*. Working about the same time and much in the same style were Yamamato Fujinobu and Amano Toyonaga. Yamamoto Shigeharu[1] was still at work during Kwampō. Very few prints are known by these artists, and no details are available as to their schooling. There is at least one *urushi-ye* by Yasukawa Shigetoshi, who flourished during Gembun and Kwampō, but of whom nothing is known.

Mangetsudō, Yengetsudō, Kōgetsudō, and Jōgetsudō are all unrecorded in the old biographies. Judging from their *dō-gō*, they were pupils of Hōgetsudō (Okumura Masanobu), whose style they followed so closely that at times one could not, except from the signatures, distinguish their work from his. Prints dated 1747 by Mangetsudō and Jōgetsudō are known.

During the Gembun period, Torii KIYOHIRO, a pupil of Kiyomasu, made his début—a book illustrated by him bearing the date of 1737. He made a few *urushi-ye* and hand-coloured prints—but most of his designs were colour-block printed. He was one of the chief artists of the Hōreki period. His death occurred in 1776. His birth-date is unknown.

[1] See also p. 18.

The Hōreki period produced Torii Kiyomitsu I and Seigyū Kyōchin. KIYOMITSU was Kiyomasu's second son, born in 1735; common name, Kamejirō. He was a prolific artist, his style being a combination of that of his father and Ishikawa Toyonobu. He is said to have been the first to have used a third colour-block, but this is extremely doubtful.

The third colour-block dates from about 1754-5—black, blue, yellow, Indian red, grey in varying tints being employed.

Tints were also produced by over-printing, such as grey over yellow to produce a warm green, blue over *beni* to produce a purple, and so on.

On the retirement or death of Kiyomasu, he succeeded as the third Torii, and died on May 11, 1785; posthumous name, Kwozenin Yōdō Nittatsu (Nichidō is an erroneous reading).

Inouye (op. cit. Note B) thinks Kiyohide was Kiyomitsu's eldest son, born *c.* 1757; died Anyei 1, 12 mo., 6 day (Dec. 29, 1772) aged *c.* 16; posthumous name, Gigakuin Jōgen Nippō.

Kyōchin's work consists of but one *hashira-ye*—an excellent portrait of the celebrated professional story-teller and diviner Fukai Shidōken. This artist is recorded in the Kogwa Bikō only, as having painted courtesans as *bijin* in the Okumura manner. Possibly he was a pupil of Masanobu, who also made two *hashira-ye* of Shidōken; Mangetsudō and Ishikawa Toyonobu each drew his portrait, the former dated 1747. The following short account of Shidōken is compiled from various native sources.

*Fukai Shidōken was born at Kyōto in 1682, the son of a prosperous farmer. At the age of twelve, he entered a Buddhist monastery to study for the priesthood. Here he made such extraordinary progress in knowledge of the Scriptures that his superiors predicted a great career for him as a preacher and expounder of Buddhist doctrines. He was given charge of the novices ; but having been detected in grossly immoral relations with some of them he was expelled as an apostate. After a number of years, during which he lived from hand to mouth, he eventually reached Yedo, where he eked out an existence as a writer of tales of revenge and love-stories which he loaned out to impressionable youths and girls, spending his earnings in drink and debauchery. One day, as he was engaged in watching crowds of worshippers entering and leaving the Kwannon temple at Asakusa, it occurred to him that he might turn such fervour to his own profit by preaching popular Buddhism intermingled with pleasantries and heroic deeds. His success was immediate ; and he had but to raise his voice to draw crowds around his " pitch " under a large tree at a cross-road in Asakusa Park. Despite his ugly exterior, his powers of oratory and mimicry of the female voice so raised his fame that he rivalled Hakuyen (the 2nd*

*Ichikawa Danjūrō) in public favour ; and, on the death of the latter in 1758, he became the sole idol of the Yedo people. His jests, largely interlarded with obscenities which he emphasized with his infamous " matsudake "—an emblem of phallic significance—were received with loud guffaws accompanied by side-splitting laughter. Having amassed sufficient capital, he built and opened a booth, where he supplied his patrons with food and drink, and where they were accommodated on roomy benches. (In Toyonobu's print—a yoko beni-ye—he is shown seated therein surrounded by persons of both sexes ; hanging on the wall is one of the nostrums for the cure of ailments, especially those of women. Probably owing to their presence, he has the decency to hide his matsudake up his left sleeve.) There he also sold love-philters and horoscopes, and in fact all the usual " catch-pennies " of the mountebank. He died in 1765, at the age of eighty-five in the odour of sanctity, receiving interment at the hands of those very men at whose religion he used to deride. As a raconteur, Shidōken is said to have had no equal.*

Katsu Shunsui was at work during Kwampō. He was a pupil of Miyagawa Chōshun (1682–1752), and first called himself Katsu Miyagawa, afterwards dropping the latter. He made a few *beni-zuri-ye* during Hōreki, and was the teacher of Katsukawa Shunshō. Harunobu, Kiyonaga, and Sekiyen (the latter as a painter only) appeared towards the close of Hōreki. They will be referred to at length in the next chapter.

The period now entered, somewhat stationary in its art at first, had become brilliant before the close in its profuse and rich expansion. If it was notable above all for the invention of the two-colour print, it was hardly less important for the wealth of new talent disclosed, for the exploitation of new subject-matter and the discovery of new motives, and for the splendid series of designs by Okumura Masanobu.

For it was Masanobu who was now the indisputable leader. The Torii line was to be strengthened by two distinguished young artists, Kiyohiro and Kiyomitsu ; but it was Masanobu rather than the veteran Kiyomasu to whom they looked, and on whom they modelled their style. Kiyomasu continued to produce good work down to his retirement, changing with each change of style that came over Ukiyo-ye. But he had lost much of the fire and force of his youth. He kept in the front, but he broke no new ground. Whether the hypothesis suggested in this book, that the prints signed Kiyonobu were, after 1727, the work of Kiyomasu, be adopted or not, makes no difference to our estimate of the prints themselves. This hypothesis, though admittedly involving something entirely exceptional—the simultaneous use of two signatures by a single artist—does explain what no other solution of the difficulty explains ; and that is, the extreme closeness of style in the parallel series of prints bearing the two signatures after 1727. During the earlier part of Kyōhō, Kiyonobu and Kiyomasu were hardly distinguishable apart ; after 1727 it is not too much to say that the prints bearing the two signatures are indistinguishable. For practical purposes, therefore—whatever theory be held—it is only one master of whom we have to take account. A few years ago it was generally held that Kiyonobu II was Torii Shirō, who was assumed to have designed only two-colour prints, or a few hand-coloured prints at most. But it is now certain that many, if not most, of the hand-coloured prints signed Kiyonobu date from after 1727. The series is continuous, and it is exactly paralleled on the prints signed Kiyomasu.

It is conceivable that if the woodcut had been wholly in the hands of the conservative Torii, it might have degenerated into a fixed tradition, all repetition and no expansion, as folk-arts have so often done in other countries of the world. But Ukiyo-ye was destined to a far different fate. It was to be alive, intensely alive, alternately expanding and concentrating, perpetually sensitive to change, for many a decade to come. And this could not have happened had it not attracted to itself generation after generation of admirable designers, among whom were masters who rank with the great artists of the world. And the emulation among these was a continual spur to effort.

To Okumura Masanobu Ukiyo-ye owed enormously. The period of which we are now treating witnessed the gradual ripening of his genius, which, unlike that of many of the other great masters of the colour-print, gave no signs of flagging and exhaustion even at the end of his career. It was after his assumption of the name Hōgetsudō in 1739 that his powers seem to have come to full fruition. From 1740 to 1750 is a decade brilliant with many masterpieces.

According to Fenollosa, Masanobu, during most of Kyōhō period, devoted himself to painting and produced very few prints. In any case it is certain that, so far as prints are concerned, this last stage of his career is at once the most fertile and the most splendid.

It might have been thought that the hand-coloured woodcut would have been exhausted as a type of popular print by the time of Kiyonobu's death. But many of the finest of the hand-coloured prints were still to be produced.

Mention has been made above of some *shiro-nuki-ye*, or " white-line " prints, designed by Tanaka Masunobu. One example, at least, is known.

Another example of this type of print, one of several by Okumura Masa-nobu, is reproduced in the *Paris V.I. Catalogue*, Plate XXIV. It represents the poet Narihira riding across a bridge. The bridge, the river-banks, and the distant hills are designed in white against the black of the water and the sky. Tanaka Masunobu's print, of a poet seated in reverie looking out on Mount Ogura, is also designed in white on black.

These prints, which suggest Chinese influence in their technique, are exceptional. It may be thought rather surprising that the resources of the "white-line," which in Europe have immensely enriched the wood-engraver's art, were not more explored by the Ukiyoye artists during the long period before the adoption of colour-printing. But it must be remembered, first, that the effects of *chiaroscuro* and atmosphere, the defining of shapes by means of light instead of by a drawn contour, and the whole conception of picture-making which has become a second nature to European artists, were alien to Japanese tradition. And, secondly, the kind of subjects which would best admit the happy use of white lines and "reserves," such as the subject of Masanobu's print, just described, were out of the recognized province of Ukiyo-ye. The white line was employed in the patterns of dresses with felicitous effect; we noted in the last chapter Kiyonobu's tracing of white characters of Japanese writing on the black portions of a dress, and we find this same use in prints by Masanobu, who will also lighten solid black by a delicately incised floral motive.

In general we may say that up to the year 1741 the resources of the woodcut, within the limitations of Japanese convention, were used to the full. But now it was more in the direction of new motives that the artist's curiosity was active.

It may be that the decade 1730–1740 has not much to show of stir or change. Certainly the work of Kiyomasu seems to continue in much the same course as before.

We reproduce a print by Kiyomasu of the actor Segawa Kikujirō who came to Yedo in December 1731. It must, therefore, date from after that year. But it must be nearer 1740 than 1731, because it already shows the type of face, with the curiously swollen cheek, which is typical of Kiyomasu's early two-colour prints of about 1743. It is quieter in line than the earlier Torii work. It can in fact be dated at the close of 1740.

At the same time as this Masanobu was putting forth his full powers, and leaving the Torii master far behind. In the new large *uki-ye* he was designing spacious compositions, such as had not been essayed since

Moronobu, with European perspective more or less successfully introduced. It was the beginning of that picturing of the life of the Yedo streets and the interior of Yedo houses and the Yedo theatre, which was to yield so rich material to later artists. Shigenaga designed *uki-ye*, but in the art of composing in depth, and in the grouping of figures, he was less happy than Masanobu. A very large print of an interior by Torii Kiyotada is one of that rare artist's most important works. A copy is in the British Museum collection.

But from the æsthetic point of view these prints, though of great value in enlarging the range of Ukiyo-ye, are not to be compared with Masanobu's magnificent *hashira-ye* produced about 1740 and in the following years; overlapping, no doubt, the two-coloured prints in point of time. A number of these rare and treasured works are reproduced in the *Paris V.I. Catalogue*. One of these bears an inscription in which Masanobu calls himself the originator of the *hashira-ye*. This is one of his most splendid designs. It is the whole-length portrait of a youth holding a half-closed umbrella. The figure is superbly placed on the page. It is as imposing as a Kwaigetsudō, but how much more intimate and alive! The contours are sensitive of living shape; they are not merely related to the form, as in earlier more caligraphic work, they *are* the form, though they contain it in a design so ordered that it appeals to the senses like an air of music. Masanobu is the first great master of that supreme achievement of the Japanese colour-print, as handled later by Harunobu and Utamaro; he knows how to seize the beauty of natural attitude and movement in the human body, and to fuse that charm with the beauty of a design which simply as related lines and masses enchants our sense of rhythm. In this print, though the figure itself, in its felicity of poise and movement and placing within the frame, makes the essential and dominant interest, look with what luxury of pattern he enriches the young man's dress, with its opposition of stripes and small checks, its squares of design on which we catch glimpses of blossoming sprays and tendrils, and even horses at their gambols by a stream; such a wealth of seemingly incongruous motives as a lesser master would never have attempted, or, if he had, would have failed to subordinate to the whole form. This sort of irrepressible flowering of fancy into pattern, as if he wanted to associate his gracious human forms with memories of the beauty springing in the fields, hints of blowing wind and sunshine, is characteristic of Masanobu's work of this time, and gives an extraordinary richness of sap and life to the surface of his designs.

A gradual change from massiveness to slenderer forms is now perceptible ; and the type of face becomes both sweeter and more expressive. The influence of Sukenobu can be noted ; but Masanobu absorbs this and makes it his own, uniting the sweetness and sensitive delicacy with a larger scale and a certain grandeur of outline. In the years from 1740 to 1750 Masanobu evolves a feminine type which, in combined sweetness and dignity, is unsurpassed in all Ukiyo-ye, even by Kiyonaga in his prime. But though this is a main attraction in these prints, it is necessary to emphasize the point that where Masanobu excels all his contemporaries and predecessors, with the possible exception of Moronobu, is in the art of figure-design. It is not only that his figures are drawn with singular grace and vigour ; here he is rivalled by Kiyonobu and Kiyomasu at their best, as by Kwaigetsudō ; but the spacing of the design, even when it is only a single figure, contents and charms the eye. Look at the *hashira-ye* of a girl holding an umbrella on her shoulder and looking down ; it is reproduced in the *Paris V.I. Catalogue* (Plate XXXIV, No. 129). Everything here is *inevitable*. What is the secret which can make of the straight fall of that long fold of the dress something that enchants and thrills ? Here again the dress is subdivided into small panels of pattern, alternating dark and light tones, geometrical and natural motives of design. This is one of Masanobu's most splendid creations. But still more is Masanobu's gift revealed in the relating of two figures, as in the well-known print of a girl giving a love-letter to her little maid, where we feel the touch of the girl's hand on the child's shoulder and all the confidingness of its pressure, as the two come so close together for the whispered instructions. Harunobu will use this design later, but will not surpass it for charm of naturalness and intimate feeling.

At last in 1741 comes the two-colour print. And with that invention comes a sudden change. Perhaps it was felt that in a large and open type of design the green and rose-pink which had been adopted as the choice of opposed colours would have a garish or flat effect ; perhaps the fashion of the day, which happened to prescribe small patterns for the dresses, also contributed its influence. In any case, we find Masanobu, and all his contemporaries with him, turning to a smaller, slenderer type of figure, with delicate patterns in which small checks are a favourite feature. If there is a decided loss of boldness and vigour, as compared with the earlier hand-coloured prints, there is no question of the felicity in the decorative use of the rose and green, combined with black and white. For a time the research for elegance and delicacy above everything becomes a passion. Shigenaga especially develops in this phase an almost morbid refinement, accentuated by a love of strangely serpentining lines, which are now cut to the utmost possible thinness as if traced by a fine and even pen rather than by the brush. This phase, in which Masanobu participates, seems to culminate about 1747, to which year we can assign certain prints by Shigenaga with a calendar introduced into them, and other prints of actors.

Actor-prints of this same time, signed by Kiyomasu and by Kiyonobu, are less exquisite in delicacy of drawing, but show the same characteristics and the same small patterns on the dresses. These are so identical in style that, were it not for the different signature, no one would dream of doubting that the same hand had designed them both.

The two-colour print reproduced in colour (Pl. 1) has been chosen as a particularly happy example of the type, and also because of its exceptional state of preservation. In scarcely any surviving print has the *beni* not faded; but in this example the colour can scarcely have changed since it was printed. It is part of a triptych, cut on a single block, but the single sheet suffers nothing by separation. Though not by Masanobu himself, it shows how closely and successfully his pupil Mangetsudō modelled his work upon his master's. The impression of colour is so lively and radiant that one quite forgets that only two tints have been used. But then how cunningly the black and the white interplay with rose and green, each enhancing the other! These two-colour prints are indeed an inexhaustible study for the designer, in the infinite variations they play upon the simple themes.

Of Masanobu's masterpieces in two-colour design one might single out for special beauty the lovely print (reproduced in the Hayashi catalogue, No. 282) of the young couple walking under one umbrella, each with one hand on the handle of it. How charmingly the two forms are brought together! This print belongs to the time of the small patterns; one dress is all covered with little checks, the other has a pattern of bamboos in snow. Or, in the larger style, we might instance the well-known print of the two *geisha* going to the play, attended by a boy who carries a *samisen* in a box—a group which for sweet movement and grace of natural grouping is not surpassed in all Ukiyo-ye.

But, as the years pass, new masters arise and challenge Masanobu's supremacy, though never deposing him. In fact, these younger spirits were no doubt glad to follow where he led. Once again it is the turn of the Torii. First Kiyohiro and a little later Kiyomitsu come into the field and are soon prominent in the first rank of Ukiyo-ye. But before them comes Shigenobu, reappearing under his new name of Toyonobu, and bringing to the new colour-prints a power and distinction for which his youthful hand-coloured designs had hardly prepared us.

This is a constant phenomenon in Ukiyo-ye; the signal example being Harunobu, as we shall see in the next chapter. Toyonobu is especially famous for his nudes, so rare in Japanese art; and indeed they have an exquisiteness that reminds one of a Venus by Lucas Cranach, but with an even greater emphasis on the slimness and pliancy of youthful limbs, as they step from the bath with bending head and with hands that gather round them the folds of a flowered wrapper. Toyonobu's faces have often more animation than is usually indulged in by Ukiyoye artists, and he takes motives, such as that of two girls struggling with each other for possession of a theatre programme, which are livelier in action than most.

Kiyohiro and Kiyomitsu are also admirable artists; and the rivalry between these three is keen during Kwanyen and Hōreki. Kiyohiro's early prints in Torii style, some of which were hand-coloured, are weak and without much promise; but Masanobu's prints in two colours were an inspiration to him, and before long he was producing excellent designs in the prevailing style of that master. Perhaps Kiyomitsu was a little the more original of the two; but this is a case where one's judgment is apt to vary. We give the palm to one or the other, and then the discovery of a print by the rival artist makes one repent or hesitate. Neither Kiyohiro nor Kiyomitsu, however, is so individual a master as Toyonobu. In later chapters we shall find the same emulation in excellence; a whole group of able designers modelling themselves on a central master, and content to play variations on his themes. Now it is Masanobu, later it will be Harunobu, or Kiyonaga.

The prints by Toyonobu and by Kiyomitsu which we reproduce are in the large form, ōban, which Masanobu used for some of his finest designs. This size was not so popular as the smaller hoso-ye, but all the masters of the day, except perhaps Shigenaga, occasionally employed it. The Kiyomitsu print which we reproduce, a beautiful example of his work, can be dated 1765.

Even the veteran Kiyomasu sometimes designed actor-prints on this large scale. One of a group of three actors as Otokodate, the fraternity of men vowed to stand by each other and to help the friendless and oppressed, is in the British Museum.

It is interesting to place this print side by side with another *ōban* of about the same time in the same collection, representing a girl selling flowering plants carried on a yoke in baskets. It is by a young artist of the school of Shigenaga, scarcely known and undistinguished as yet, whose name before long will be famous and whose genius will be supreme in Ukiyo-ye, Harunobu. One would hardly guess from either of these prints the masterpieces of which the designer's hand was capable ; the one in the past, and the other in the future. Harunobu was designing actor-prints in two colours, but only a few of these have survived ; and the print above-mentioned is the best known of his rare non-theatrical designs of this period.

Kiyomasu was at the end of his career. But we have not yet taken farewell of him. Still later in date is the print reproduced on Plate 23. This is a print in three, possibly even four colours ; an excessive rarity in his work. For the artists were beginning to tire of the limitations of the rose and green. By superimposing one tint on another, an additional variation had been gained. The device is used by Masanobu in his beautiful print of the *geisha* going to the play, already mentioned (p. 37). But the result was not very happy ; it introduced a hint of muddiness into a colour-scheme, the charm of which was its luminous gaiety. Experiments were made, especially by Kiyomitsu, with a third, and sometimes a fourth colour ; yellow, olive, and a fuller red were introduced. The balance of the old, simple contrast was disturbed, but without a compensating gain. In fact, no " half-way house " such as this could really satisfy. The two-colour print was a delightful thing in itself ; but the colours were arbitrary and decorative only. Once the change was made to fuller colour, the mind unconsciously felt the claims of representation as well as decoration. The full-coloured print was inevitable. The experiments of the last years of Hōreki were no doubt serviceable as a preliminary to the achievement of Meiwa. But they are not comparable with the masterpieces of the two-colour print which preceded them, and which are for ever associated with the genius of Okumura Masanobu.

# CHAPTER IV

# MEIWA PERIOD

**FEBRUARY 2ND, 1764, TO FEBRUARY 3RD, 1772**

In the beginning of the second year of Meiwa (20th of February, 1765), there appeared a number of *surimono* into the designs of which are cleverly interwoven the long or short months of that year, either with or without the year name (*nengō*) and the E-to, Kinoto Tori. They are called *ye-goyomi* or pictorial almanacs ; *dai-shō no surimono ;* or *ryaku-reki*— abbreviated calendars. They were not for sale ; but were interchanged or distributed among friends by members of art clubs as souvenirs of periodic gatherings. These clubs or *ren* were composed of amateur art-lovers, foremost amongst whom was Kikurensha Kyosen. This man is first heard of in a book entitled *Segen Jūi*, published in the 11th month of Hōreki 8 (commenced December 1st, 1758), and comprising three volumes called Kiku, Ren, and Sha, whence his first name. He also used the *gō* of Jōsei Sanjin, and is said to have lived into the Kwansei period, though his interest in art appears to have ceased about the middle of Meiwa. *Segen Jūi* consists of seventeen-syllable poems by Kyosen, his master Saren, and his pupils ; and is illustrated by woodcuts after designs by Okumura Masanobu, Ishikawa Toyonobu, Hyakurin Sōri, and Kyosen himself. One of Toyonobu's designs was issued as a *ye-goyomi* in 1765, and is reproduced in F. W. Gookin's catalogue of a memorial exhibition of Japanese colour-prints from the collection of the late Clarence Buckingham, Chicago, 1915, No. 142. Besides the artist's signature and seal, there is that of " Kyosen renjū Rinkō," i.e. " Rinkō of the Kyosen club."

*Ye-goyomi* were also issued for the 3rd year of Meiwa (1766) ; but appear to have been discontinued after that year. It is generally believed that they were designed, engraved, and printed in the year preceding that of issue ; but this was not always the case. For instance, one for Meiwa 2 of a girl in a straw raincoat with a bundle of leaves on her shoulder and straw hat in hand, signed Sakei kō and sealed Sakei, is inscribed " first published on the 5th day of the 5th month." Many of these calendars, as in this case, are signed with otherwise unknown names to which is appended the ideograph *kō*, as to the meaning of which opinion is divided.

It has been interpreted as equivalent to engraved, or printed, or conceived in the sense of suggesting the idea of the picture. The first interpretation is certainly wrong, for alongside signatures of this nature is often found the name of the engraver.

As an example : a calendar for 1765, representing Daruma and a girl under an open umbrella which he holds over her head—*aiai-gasa* as it is called—as they walk in conversation along the bank of a stream, is signed on the right " Shisen kō," sealed " Shisen," and on the left " Suzuki Harunobu gwa " and " Sekine Kayei azusa," i.e. engraved. Here it is clear that Shisen is a different individual from Sekine Kayei. In the production of a print, three men are usually associated, namely the artist, the engraver, and the printer ; so that in the above example the ideograph *kō* appended to Shisen's name would appear to signify " printed."

A suggestion, however, that this is not the correct interpretation has been put forward by Mr. K. Tomita in No. 121, Vol. XX, of the Boston Museum of Fine Arts Bulletin, October, 1922, in an article entitled " Surimono."[1]

He thinks that one of the forms of *kō* is the first character of *ku-fū* (devised), and that another form stands for *kō-an* (conceived) ; both indicating the idea of the picture having been suggested. It is quite true that the *ku* of *ku-fū* is the same ideograph as the *kō* found appended to these signatures, and hence may be interpreted as Mr. Tomita suggests.

But the *kō* of *kō-an* is an entirely different character, which is never found on these calendars. He is further of opinion that " some of these amateur designers undoubtedly not only conceived their own designs and cut their own blocks, but printed from them as well. Most of them, however, seem to have commissioned artists like Harunobu to make drawings after their ideas, and to have engaged engravers and printers to complete the calendars."

A *ye-goyomi* for 1765, recently come to light and reproduced on Plate III, No. 57, of the collection Ch. Haviland, sold at Paris in November, 1922, goes to support the suggestion of the last sentence. The signatures are catalogued thus : " signed, on the right, Suzuki Harunobu ; engraver, Ishi-i ; on the left, Riusui Tokiofu, Rokei, ko." No special attention has been invited to the latter unique and interesting signature which trans-literated should read : Ryūsui To (Jap. Higashi) kyo (Jap. iru) fu (Jap. yome) Rokei kō ; that is, " conceived (or printed ?) by Rokei, the daughter-in-law (or perhaps wife) of Ryūsui dwelling in the East, i.e. Yedo." Ryūsui is the artist already mentioned in the preceding chapter. In 1762 he illustrated a book entitled *Umi no sachi*, two volumes, in colours (*vide* Hayashi catalogue, No. 1597). Here we find his daughter-in-law (or wife)

---

[1] The writer is indebted to F. W. Gookin for a copy of this bulletin.

Rokei taking part in the production of this calendar; and it seems more probable that she did so in the capacity of "conceiver" of the design rather than in that of "printer"—though, of course, the latter is possible. Now if this was really the case, then it is direct evidence of the correctness of Mr. Tomita's view. However that may be, he has certainly made a valuable contribution to this vexed question.

Further research is necessary before accepting or rejecting either of these views, as the following calendars for 1765 will show. No. 383 Hayashi catalogue is signed "Hakusei kō" and bears the following names: Gwakō (artist), "Suzuki Harunobu"; chōkō (engraver), "Yendō Goroku"; shōkō or printer, "Yumoto Kōshi." In the catalogue, Hakusei is stated to be another name of the engraver; another view is that he is identical with the printer. But neither view can be proved and are but conjectures based on the belief that only three men produced these prints. Mr. Tomita's opinion probably applies to this case, when Hakusei would be held to be the "conceiver" of the picture. This man's name appears alone in seal form on a calendar depicting a young couple reading a roll inscribed with the names of the year 1765 and the months, she seated on a *kotatsu* over which is spread a *futon*, and he sprawling beneath the latter. Perhaps this may appear to be a case in point of an amateur conceiving, designing, engraving, and printing the picture as suggested by Mr. Tomita. But another copy of the same print is stamped with the seal (undeciphered) of a different individual, and Mr. Gookin has expressed to the writer his opinion that from its colour qualities it does not differ greatly in date of printing, and that both impressions were issued in the same year. If this be so, it is difficult to reconcile these two men as conceivers of the same picture, and leads one to regard them rather as printers of another's design; but this conclusion militates against the interpretation of the rôle played by Hakusei in the first-quoted print. As the matter at present stands it would be premature to express a decided opinion.

*Ye-goyomi* were printed on a superior paper known as *hōsho*, so called from its having been used in writing *hōsho* or letters of instruction issued through the secretary of the Kamakura Shōgunate by order of the latter. Their size is about 11 in. high by 8 in. wide, and the printing was done with the greatest care and refinement. Some of them were issued a year or two later by regular publishers, but with the calendric symbols removed and in most cases with the colour-scheme altered. In these re-issues we frequently find the signature Harunobu substituted for the name or seal of the printer or conceiver whichever he may have been. In addition to the designers of *ye-goyomi* already named, we find the following professionals : Minkō, Komatsuken, Uyeno Shōha, Shigemasa under the name of Kage[1] (see reproduction, Von Seidlitz, London, ed. 1910, opposite p. 108), and Toyomasa. Several other signatures are found in seals, such as Hakusei, Seikō, Sōan, etc. ; but whether these were professional artists is a moot point. Some, for example Hakusei, and Seikō under the name of Sei-ichitei Nijū, sometimes appended *kō* to their signatures—which makes it difficult to decide. By far the most important and prolific, however, was HARUNOBU, whose real name was Hozumi Jihei, and who lived in Yonezawa-chō, Ryōgoku, Yedo. He died on the 15th day of 6th month of Meiwa 7, i.e. July 7th, 1770, at the age, according to *Ukiyo gwajinden*, of forty-six ; whence he was born in 1725. Shiba Kōkan (1747–1818), notorious as an avowed forger of Harunobu's signature on prints immediately after his death and which deceived even the purchasers of that time, states in his diary, *Shumbarō hikki*, published in 1811, that " the Ukiyoye painter Suzuki Harunobu, famous for his drawings of the manners and customs of women of the period, suddenly fell ill and died when over forty " ; so that the *Ukiyo gwajinden* is probably correct, though the failure so far to locate Harunobu's tomb makes verification impossible. He appears to have been the first artist to design for the polychrome prints that followed the *ye-goyomi*, and which from their resemblance to brocade were called Azuma Nichiki-ye or brocade pictures of Azuma, i.e. the eastern provinces of which Yedo was the capital city. According to the famous writer Kyokutei Bakin, in his miscellany *Yenseki-zasshi*, an engraver named Kinroku invented the process in consultation with a certain printer.

In what exactly the new process consisted is not clear. Bakin's statement is as follows : " Concerning Nishiki-ye, the block-cutter Kinroku told me that in the beginning of Meiwa he ' in consultation with a certain printer, invented a method of putting a guide-mark (*kentō*) on several blocks by means of which several colours could be applied to the one sheet of paper. Since then many printers, imitating my method, have issued these Nishiki-ye ' . . . Kinroku left this world in 7th month of Bunkwa 1 (1804). . . ." As we have seen, the guide-mark had been in use from the beginning of Kwampō (1741) and perhaps earlier, so that Kinroku's invention must have included something more than the *kentō*—unless it was an improved form.

In some of these *nishiki-ye* as many as eleven blocks were employed.

---

[1] This reading of the signature is tentative.

Harunobu also illustrated twenty books, some in colours, and extending in date from 1762 till his death.

Besides those already mentioned, the older men who continued to work during Meiwa include Furuyama Moromasa, Tamura Yoshinobu, Yamamoto Yoshinobu, Tanaka Masunobu, Tomikawa Ginsetsu Fusanobu, and the Torii—Kiyohiro and Kiyomitsu I.

New men appeared in Ishikawa Toyomasa, Torii Kiyotsune, Ippitsusai Bunchō, Katsukawa Shunshō, Kitao Shigemasa, Isoda Koryūsai, Utagawa Toyoharu, Torii Kiyohisa, and Torii Kiyonaga.

There were, besides, several followers of Harunobu, such as Fujinobu, Kishōsai Suzuki Yasunobu, Komai Yoshinobu, Harutsugu (otherwise Haruji), Muranobu, and Harushige (later called Shiba Kōkan and already referred to). With the exception of the last, it is only necessary to say that nothing is known of them except a few rare prints in which they copied their master's style with fair success.

Collaboration amongst artists forms an interesting innovation during this period. Examples of such are to be seen in the following : Harunobu, Kiyomitsu, and Kiyotsune ; Harunobu and Bunchō ; Kiyomitsu and Kiyotsune ; Bunchō and Shunshō ; and Shunshō, Shigemasa, and Toyoharu.

MINKŌ, whose real name was Tachibana Masatoshi, and who used the gō of Gyokujuken, was a native of Ōsaka or Kyōto and an embroiderer by trade. He came to Yedo about 1762, and took an active part in print-designing during Meiwa. His name, along with those of Bantō, Chiryō, Suiyō, Kisen, and Ryūshi, appears in seal form on a set of six oblong calendars for 1765 enclosed in a wrapper on which are inscribed the title, " The Fox's Wedding," their names, and those of the engraver Okamoto Shōgyo, and of the printer Harada Yoshiyuki. Another copy of Minkō's print in this set is reproduced on Plate IV, No. 60, Part I, Haviland Collection, and is inscribed : " Engraver, Yamaguchi Bokuyō (Mokuyo in catalogue)," and " Minkō made this at the request of a certain person (aruhito, not amateur as stated by cataloguer)," and followed by the seal " Tachibana Masatoshi." The two calendars are identical but for these inscriptions, which are significant in showing that two men engraved the same design. Minkō designed some nishiki-ye which are unsigned and generally attributed—as indeed are most of the unsigned prints at this time—to Harunobu. His style and colour, however, differ from those of the latter, in the one following Sukenobu closer than Harunobu does, and in the other Tsukioka Settei (1711–1787, an Ōsaka painter), one of the finest colourists of the School. Plate 27 reproduces an unsigned print undoubtedly designed by him. The colours are wonderfully pure and rich. In 1771, not 1770 as is generally stated, a book in two volumes entitled *Saigwa shokunin burui*, reproduced in colours by the stencil process, is one of the finest Japanese colour books ever produced.

The engraver was the above-mentioned Okamoto Shōgyo. The rarity of this edition is accounted for by the destruction of the plates by fire in 1772, as explained in the preface to the second edition of 1784, a very inferior production in every way. Minkō also illustrated two other books in 1769 and 1770. His activity ceased after this period. His dates of birth and death have not yet been discovered. He probably received instruction from Sukenobu and Settei before coming to Yedo.

KOMATSUKEN (may be also pronounced Shōshōken) appears to have been identical with Komatsu-ya Hyakki, who was Yedo born, and kept a drug store at Iida-machi in that city. His personal name was Sanyemon, and he died at the age of eighty, some time during Kwansei (1789–1801). Besides a few prints during Meiwa, especially calendars for 1765 and 1766, he is only known by some erotic books in which he follows the style of Sukenobu.

Of Uyeno Shōha nothing is known save that he made a few calendars for 1765.

Ishikawa TOYOMASA designed some *nishiki-ye* between 1767 and 1773. He was pupil of Ishikawa Toyonobu. Dates of birth and death are unrecorded.

Torii KIYOTSUNE was pupil of Kiyomitsu. He worked much in his master's manner between 1757 and 1779, but with less ability. His birth and death are unrecorded.

Ippitsusai BUNCHŌ was a pupil of an obscure painter Ishikawa Takamoto. His family name was Mori; personal name, not known. His life-history has been mixed up with that of Kishi Bunshō, a poet and pupil as such of Bunchō. His prints date from about 1766 to 1779, and are mostly those of actors in character. His *nishiki-ye* are rare. Birth and death are not yet known. He is said to have received the honorary title of Hokkyō.

Katsukawa SHUNSHŌ, pupil of Shunsui, was born in 1726, and had as personal name Yūsuke. As *gō* he took the names of Kyokurōsei, Yūji, Jōgwasei, Roku-roku-an, and Ririn. He worked from about 1757 till his death on January 19th, 1793.

He used at times a jar-shaped seal inscribed " Hayashi "—the name of a publisher under whose encouragement he is said to have adopted the career of artist—whence he earned the nickname of Tsubo (jar). He illustrated at least sixteen books from 1770 onwards, some in colours being of rare beauty, e.g. *Yehon butai ōgi*, three volumes, 1770, in collaboration with Bunchō ; *Nishiki hyakunin isshū*, one volume, 1775, the original issue of which, with the poems written with a fine brush, is extremely rare ; *Seirō bijin awase sugata kagami*, three volumes, 1776, in collaboration with Shigemasa, and one of the finest books of the Ukiyoye school ; *Yehon Takara no ito*, one volume, 1786, in collaboration with Shigemasa, and consisting of twelve plates—six by each artist—which had previously appeared as single prints, two on a block, about the end of Meiwa ; and *Sanjū rokkasen*, one volume, 1789.

Kitao SHIGEMASA was the son of the publisher Suwaraya Sarōbei, at whose house in Kodemmachō, Yedo, he was born in 1739. His personal name was Sasuke. In his youth, he displayed so great a talent as calligraphist that he received commissions to make the Yedo almanacs. His work extends from about 1759 till his death on March 8th, 1820. He, like his confrère Shunshō, was a prolific book illustrator, but designed comparatively few prints. He was a self-taught artist.

Isoda KORYŪSAI was of the military class. His personal name was Masakatsu. In *Zōho Ukiyo-ye-ruikō* he is said to have been a pupil of Shigenaga, but modern Japanese critics discredit this statement. He certainly studied under Harunobu, from whom he received his earliest *gwamyō* or brush-name of Haruhiro. Dates of birth and death unrecorded. His work extends from about 1765 to 1784. A book entitled *Hokuri uta*, one volume, black and white, without date, but about 1784, is signed on the last picture " Hokkyō Koryūsai," which honorary title was conferred upon him in appreciation of his paintings. His rapid drawings in ink in the three-volume book *Yamato konzatsu sōgwa* are wonderfully clever. He lived at Yagenbori close to Ryōgoku Bridge and Yonezawa-chō, where Harunobu dwelt and with whom he was on intimate terms of friendship. "Yagenbori inshi," " recluse of Yagenbori," is found sometimes prefixed to his signature from 1777. A pillar-print (see p. 77) is sealed "Yagenbori".

TOYOHARU was a native of Toyo-oka, Tajima province (some say he was a native of Bungo province), where he was born in 1735. His personal name was Tajimaya Masaki ; his common name Shōjirō, afterwards changed to Shinyemon. He first studied under Tsuruzawa Tankei (d. 1769) at Kyōto. About the close of Hōreki, he came to Yedo, and became a pupil of Toriyama Sekiyen Toyofusa, from whom he received the *gwamyō* of Toyonobu. At this time he resided in Utagawa-chō, Shiba, whence he derived his *geisei* or art surname of Utagawa. Soon after he changed from Toyonobu to Toyoharu, and took the *gō* of Ichiryūsai. He died in 1814 at the age of eighty. He is said to have painted several theatrical sign-boards.

Torii KIYOHISA was pupil of Kiyomitsu. Worked during Meiwa. Dates of birth and death not known.

Torii KIYONAGA was pupil of Kiyomitsu, upon whose death (1785) he became the fourth Torii. He was born in 1752, the son of a bookseller at Honzaimoku-chō, Yedo, named Shirokiya Ichibei. He was first called Seki Shinsuke (Sekiguchi being his surname), afterwards Ichibei; and was popularly known as Shimba no Kiyonaga. Late in life, he is said to have opened a tobacco shop. He died on June 28, 1815, at the age of sixty-four; posthumous name, Chōrin Yeiju. He, like his predecessors of the Torii line, painted theatrical sign-boards. His work extends from about 1766-7 till 1792, after which he practically gave up print-designing for painting.

Harushige is identical with the artist who became known later on as SHIBA KŌKAN. He was not a pupil of Suzuki Harunobu, whose *geisei* he assumed without authority about 1771, after having previously forged that artist's name as already mentioned. About 1782 he studied the Dutch methods at Nagasaki, and in 1784 made some interesting copper-plate engravings in European perspective, coloured by hand. These he sometimes signed Shiba Kōkan sōsei, i.e. " created by Shiba Kōkan." Some, too, are inscribed with Dutch titles, e.g. Tweelandbruk. He also tried his hand at oil painting.

Meiwa opens a new epoch in Ukiyo-ye. The art of the print-designers renews its youth and makes a fresh beginning. We may imagine the stir caused among artists and publishers by the cloud of little calendar-prints issued privately in the second year of Meiwa and circulated among groups of friends with the newly-invented choice of colours, not many yet, but delicately harmonized and no longer founded on the old contrast of rose and green with an extra colour added.

Harunobu had been working for long before 1764, but few of his *beni*-prints have survived, and these are not remarkable. Some of them were actor-prints, which he afterwards eschewed and disdained. It was only with the opening of Meiwa that he began to disclose his real genius, but then it was as if a torrent had been released. He poured out prints in rich abundance till death cut short his production in his prime; and even if we subtract from the total those prints, fairly numerous, which often pass under his name, but were really designed by other hands, the fecundity of his invention during the last five years of his life is astonishing.

All the promising young talents, and some even of the established veterans, like Toyonobu, were content to follow in Harunobu's steps. Neither Masanobu in the preceding period nor Kiyonaga in Temmei period attained quite so sovereign a position or established so complete a dominance.

Why the invention of the polychrome print should have been so long delayed is a problem to which no certain answer can be given. It can hardly have been any technical obstacles. It is more likely that it was a question of the expense of the many printings required.

The actual process of cutting and printing the wood-blocks has been described so often and is now so familiar that we need not repeat it. But though the work of the designer, the wood-cutter, and the printer, can each be imagined in detail, there are some points in the relation of the three to each other which have hitherto remained a little obscure. In what shape, for instance, was the design communicated to the engraver? Did he have a design completed in colour before him? And how much latitude or responsibility had the printer?

Major Sexton found and interviewed in Japan an old printer from whom he sought information; unfortunately the printer was so very old that he was incapable of any connected statement. Quite recently, however, a correspondent in Japan has been able to obtain a more satisfactory interview with a printer, trained in the old traditions, who had followed his profession since 1880; and the resulting notes, here reproduced, are of real interest. " The artist's original sketch was called *sumi sen on ye*, or ink-line picture. This was handed to the engraver, who cut it on a block called *ji sumi ita*, literally ' ground ink-board ' (or, as we should say, key-block); after which a printer took off the required number of correction proofs (*kyō-gō*), one for each colour. These proofs were on rough Mino paper, a tough, thick paper originally made at Mino, a village about ten miles north of the present Ōsaka. The artist painted on each proof the colour he wished to be employed; *beni, kusa* (grass-green), *shu* (vermilion), *aka* (red), *ki* (yellow), *ai* (blue), *usu-ai* (light blue), and so on; at the same time he indicated the colour by name. He then gave these correction proofs to the engraver, who proceeded to cut *iro ita* or colour-blocks for each colour, on completion of which they were examined by the printer, presumably as to their suitability for taking the colour. If satisfied, the printer applied the colour to each block as indicated by the artist on the proofs, adding here and subtracting there until he got the required *notan* or tone. This was an extremely difficult operation, as he had to rely on his own brains in interpreting the artist's intention, and it required the most careful consideration and the utmost skill, to which very few printers attained. The Ditcher, as the printer who had merely to apply *sumi* (ink) to the key-block was called, had no need to trouble about the *kentō* or guide-mark; he had but to be a quick manipulator; but the colour-printer knew that the success of the picture depended on the exact adjustment of the colours."

It is probable that this procedure followed the tradition set up in Meiwa. The division of labour made possible the extraordinary fecundity of artists like Harunobu and later of Utamaro, though we cannot cease to admire the wealth of their inventiveness in design. To Harunobu the invention of the polychrome print was a heaven-sent piece of fortune, since it set free his genius for colour; and the colouring produced by the contact of the brush-charged surface of a wood-block with the sympathetic texture of mulberry-pith paper was something different in kind from the colouring to be got on a *kakemono*.

Among the new colours now introduced were a delicate blue called *airō*, used for skies and also sometimes for water; a violet, *murasaki*; a red ochre, *beni-gara*, varying from brick-red to chocolate; and red oxide of iron. The first two, the blue and the violet, were unfortunately very liable to fade; as also were the beautiful rose-red *beni* and the fuller red *shō-yenji*, and gamboge among the yellows. Thus it often happens that we see prints in which the stable greens and yellows and especially the strong opaque chocolate have lost relation with the other faded colours, and Harunobu's harmony is destroyed.

Besides these simple colours Harunobu invented, or at least seems the first to have used, an exquisite pearly grey made by mixing ink with white lead and powdered mica. This is the opaque grey which he used for masonry, as in the print of a boy offering to sell toy-archery gear to a woman going home past the great walls of Yedo Castle. White lead was also mixed with *beni* to produce a beautiful opaque pink. With these pigments at his disposal, and with all the range of pale grey to deep black to be obtained from Chinese ink, Harunobu was, of course, able to create modulations of colour altogether outside the scope of what his predecessors had achieved with their simple schemes, and never surpassed by his successors. Of all the Ukiyo-ye masters Harunobu is the subtlest and most magical colourist. In all his best work—and the level of his work is very high—the colour is fused with the design to create an emotional effect.

The influence of Sukenobu on the Yedo artists during the preceding period has been already noted. That influence was all in the direction of grace and suavity, softening the violent exuberance of Kiyonobu's style, and infusing an atmosphere of intimacy. It was congenial to something in Okumura Masanobu's nature, though it did not weaken his art. Harunobu was a pupil of Shigenaga, but it was to Sukenobu that his art owed most. Sukenobu had a fertile gift for animated and graceful compositions. Harunobu was not more inventive, but his inventions were more exquisite, more " final " in their form. He was more imaginative. He took up the same subject-matter as Sukenobu, but showed his genius in discovering motives that concentrated the sentiment of a scene in an expressive design, to which every line and every tone of colour contributed. None of the Ukiyoye masters before his time approached him in the keenness of his sensibility. His prints have about them the same sort of exquisite poignancy that the scent of the narcissus has, breathing out the very essence of spring. It is the springtime of life that preoccupies him ; the bloom, the shyness, the sensitiveness, the trouble, the passions, the thrilling joys of adolescence. There are prints of his which are night-pieces, though, according to Japanese convention, all is visible as in daylight, but relieved against a black sky ; and against this black sky he loves to set the white blossoms of the cherry, perhaps illuminated from below by a lantern carried by one of a pair of lovers, the blossoms appearing so in isolation as a miracle of fugitive but motionless beauty, each perfect in its white shape. The enchantment of the spring flowers appearing out of the darkness, and their very fragrance, is communicated to our senses even through the wood-cutter's translation of the scene ; but we should not feel this as we do, were not those young human forms intimately related to that apparition of beauty in the design, so that we seem to share their heightened senses in the intoxication of a spring night.

In preceding phases of Ukiyo-ye the finest prints had aimed at a certain largeness, both in the forms and the design. But now it was the exquisiteness of small things that Harunobu set out to reveal. The chosen size for the print was now smaller and approaching the square ; and the human types portrayed were delicate flower-like forms, with small faces and with arms and hands of an infantine grace and an incredible slimness. It is an art that might be reproached with effeminacy but for the intensity of its perception of the real charm of youth.

Gainsborough's little picture in the National Gallery of his two daughters as children chasing a butterfly is a true Harunobu subject ; and if we imagine our English master following up that vein and inventing a hundred of such motives for pictures, we might have had a parallel to Harunobu's little world of beauty. But the 18th century in Europe was in general all too prone to a prettiness dependent on the reminiscence of a smiling face, a blooming complexion, a happy attitude ; it ran to the vignette. When we turn to Harunobu we see what a difference is made by an art which, underneath the feminine charm, the favour and prettiness, has a strong basis of design, knows how to relate the forms to one another with felicity and variety, and keeps always a certain squareness in the main plan. Harunobu's sweetness is never sugary. See with how sure a composer's instinct he loves to relieve the living curves of his young figures, warm with life, against straight lines and angles. The rare and beautiful print reproduced (Pl. 2) is a good example. Compare also the famous and often-illustrated print of a girl going up the stone stair of a temple, where the hard parallels enhance the slender form as she turns upon her steps.

Between 1765 and 1770, though the fashion of dress and coiffure scarcely alter, there is a perceptible change in Harunobu's work. At first there is a kind of diffidence and timidity in design and colouring, though associated with an unusual grace. But this soon passes into the assured enjoyment of mastery and the delighted exploration of a chosen range of themes. The earlier prints show a rounded type of face, which little by little becomes longer, and with that comes a slightly taller and slimmer type of figure. The colouring again assumes stronger harmonies. And with the employment of more colours we find Harunobu completing his outdoor scenes with a blue sky. But the blue, a vegetable colour, was a fugitive one, sensitive especially to damp, and it is rarely found in its pristine state, having usually faded to a pleasant sort of buff tint, on which traces of soft blue remain. This completeness of representation and fullness of colour might have led to literalism and loss of style ; it would assuredly have done so in Europe, where a step nearer illusion has almost always been hailed as " progress." But in Japan the public supported the artist ; and the artist was not led astray by a dull desire for naturalism, but pursued his own instinct for choosing and emphasizing what in a given scene stirred his emotion and offered him his design. Moreover, the tradition, inveterate in Asia, which eliminated shadows from a picture, gave a certain ideality to the colour-print, even in the hands of its poorest practitioners; it made a remove from the actual, a certain formal grace, which might be compared to the use of verse in drama.

We find, too, that this blue sky, which with Harunobu, Bunchō, and Koryūsai was never more than a flat tint, suggesting the ambience of sunlit air rather than imitating weather, appears only occasionally, and in the next period was generally abandoned in favour of a blank sky. It was only when Prussian blue was introduced in the 19th century, and Hokusai began to design his great landscape prints, that a strong but graded tint became of universal usage in the skies of landscape subjects.

We have spoken of the special beauty of Harunobu's night-scenes. Something must also be said of the beauty of his snow-scenes. Here he makes much use of the device of embossing (*gauffrage*), which was a refinement of printing introduced by him to vary and enrich the surface of prints, and in this case to give to banks or lumps of snow a suggestion of mass and also of luminous edge. One of his most famous and sought-after prints is the one of two lovers walking under one umbrella on a morning after snow. The youth is in black, the girl in white, but there are reds and purples, where the under-dresses show. The blue of the sky has generally faded. The uneven surface of the snow is indicated solely by embossing. Of this print there is more than one version. Undoubtedly the finest is that in which the snow on the umbrella has no black outline. It is reproduced in colour as frontispiece to Gookin's *Japanese Colour-Prints and their Designers*. The key-blocks in the two versions are different; it is not a question of a different state, since in the one just mentioned there is a willow-bough at the left reaching down almost to touch the umbrella, and this is not in the other version. Is this a case of a contemporary forgery, an unauthorized print issued by a block-cutter?

Four beautiful girls were favourite models for Harunobu's brush: their names are O Sen, O Fuji, O Nami, and O Natsu. O Sen was a waitress in the Kagiya tea-house at Kasamori; O Fuji was the daughter of a seller of cosmetics and perfumes; the other two were attendants in the Temple of Yushima Tenjin. All were famed for their beauty and charm. O Sen and O Fuji especially inspired Harunobu. As we see these girlish figures in the prints, there is little to individualize their features; and one wonders how much they were reshaped in his imagination, and how much the actual form and face contributed to mould that chosen type, which we see again and again in so many different surroundings. Such motives as Masanobu had discovered—the girl walking on a windy day, for example,

bent towards the wind and holding her skirts round her slender legs—
were found anew and in infinite variety by Harunobu and enriched by the
completeness of his new method. The sweet, slim girl crosses a bridge in
the snow ; or blows soap-bubbles in an April garden for her little brother ;
or listens to the vanishing cuckoo, or to the evening bell from the near
temple ; or she dances demurely in a ceremonious temple dance ; or buys
from a fan-seller stopping, with his pile of black fan-boxes on his shoulder,
at her door ; or sends a love-message by a little maid ; or is parting from
her lover. Harunobu rarely takes his subjects from the Yoshiwara ; but
even when the girl is a courtesan, how innocent in her delicate aloofness
she appears !

In one of these rare night-scenes, in which Harunobu seems to excel
himself, we see a girl with a lantern so entranced with the beauty of the
blossom against the dark sky that she stands as in a dream, oblivious of
her lover who holds her hand and seeks to draw her within the opened
shutters of the room. It is reproduced in the *Paris V.I. Catalogue*, Plate
XVII. The gesture of the youth, so gentle in its entreaty, is typical of
Harunobu's art. The faces allow themselves so little of expression, they
appear so serene ; but in the shy touch of two hands, what a world of
feeling !

Harunobu's disdain for the theatre, and his ambition to raise the whole
level of Ukiyo-ye, makes it interesting to consider his relation to classic
art and the subject-matter of the classic schools.

Ukiyo-ye from the first had been fond of parodying the stock subjects of
the Kanō, Chinese, and Tosa painters. But when we say " parody," we
are using the word with a different shade of meaning from that to which
we are accustomed. Parody with us is usually the parody of manner. But
with these artists it is the matter which is translated into another sphere.
Some historic or legendary episode is taken for theme, and a parallel to it
found in the everyday life of the people. And though often a humorous
colour is thus given to the subject, this is by no means always the case.
The allusion, the association, is in itself sufficient. What is to be observed
in this extraordinary Yedo public is its obvious familiarity (through the
public story-tellers and through stage-plays) with all the legendary lore,
the heroic histories of Japan, as well as with the personages of popular
religion and famous figures from the past of China and of India. It is as
if they loved to link together all that world with every passing incident of
their own existence. And Harunobu adds to this allusiveness the world
of classic poetry.

We look at these colour-prints and are charmed by their design and colour. For æsthetic satisfaction we demand no more. But we shall not understand their full significance in relation to those for whom and by whom they were produced, unless we realize how steeped they are in allusion and association, and perceive how many a delightful motive has thereby been given to the artist.

The older art of Japan, as of China, is of course far more traditional in choice of subject than European art. Only in religious art has Western painting been traditional to a comparable degree. Ukiyo-ye continues this love of tradition, only it gives each of the old motives a new setting.

Among subjects derived from China are such sets of themes as the Twenty-Four Paragons of Filial Virtue, and The Seven Sages of the Bamboo Grove. To these, and even to the subject of the Three Wine-tasters—Confucius, Lao-tzŭ, and Buddha tasting wine from a jar and each finding a different savour in it—homely counterparts are invented. The most famous of Chinese love-stories, the passion of the Emperor Ming Huang for his fascinating concubine Yang-Kuei-fei, affords a favourite motive. There is a lovely print by Harunobu—it is reproduced in the *Paris V.I. Catalogue*, No. 153—of two lovers seated by a stream, the youth showing the girl how to play the *samisen*. No inscription indicates the allusion; it was unnecessary, for every one would recognize the parallel to the emperor seated by his mistress and teaching her how to place her fingers on the flute.

Even the classic Chinese landscape themes are—we would not say travestied, for the intention, though playful, is not to turn to ridicule—paralleled rather, in domestic life. Every one who has studied Chinese art knows the Eight Famous Views, motives taken originally from two lakes in China, and found again by the Japanese in the Omi Hak'kei of their own Lake Biwa. Nothing is commoner in the colour-prints than to find one of " Eight Views of the Day " (or some such title), imitating the " Vesper Bell from an Evening Temple," or some other of the classic eight motives. If Koryūsai draws two girls sailing toy-boats in a basin, it makes a pretty perversion of the " Boats returning to Yabase."

Then of allusion to Japanese historic subjects there is no end. Harunobu is especially fond of the story of Komachi, most famous of the old poetesses of Japan, famous for her wit, her beauty, her lovers, in her youth, and for the desolate wanderings of her old age. Once he portrays her, a full-length standing figure, in the fine brocades of Fujiwara times, against a background of blue. In that print there is no hint of a connection with the Ukiyoye world. But for the chosen "seven moments" in her life, consecrated by traditional art, he finds some situation in the life of courtesan or maidservant, yet treats it quite seriously, with no hint of burlesque. Such allusiveness is common to most of the masters of Ukiyo-ye, but it pervades Harunobu's work more than that of any of the others. And how many of his prints have inscribed above them a poem from the classic anthology of the Hundred Poets, the *Hyaku-nin Isshū*, with which he links his idyll of the day! Sometimes the allusion is an occasion for fun, at other times it is just an allusion for its own sake.

To all this we have hardly a counterpart in European art. The attitude of mind of an Ukiyoye painter like Harunobu is not like that of, say, a Rowlandson, whose sense of grace in line and colour finds inexhaustible material in the passing scene, but whose frank enjoyment of human nature is contented by anything that life presents to his eye just for its own sake; still less has it the bitterness, irony, satire, of masters like Goya or Daumier. There is a singular absence of comment or criticism in the Ukiyoye attitude. Even when the intention is playful, the drawing itself will often give no hint of it. If we seek a parallel, we might find it perhaps in a picture like Manet's "Olimpia," where the intention is obviously to challenge the Venuses of Titian with a counterpart from real and contemporary life, or in his "Déjeuner sur l'Herbe," where the composition is taken "word for word" from an old Italian print, but a river-god leaning on his trident has become a Parisian gentleman sitting on the grass and leaning on his cane.

Truly it was an amazing public, this public of artisans and small shop-keepers,[1] for whom these colour-prints, to the *samurai* class of Japan so vulgar, to us so exquisite, were made. One of the most beautiful of all Harunobu's pillar-prints is a print of the famous highway-robber Shirai Gompachi, disguised as a *Komusō*, with the big basket-hat, meant to cover the face, and used by persons wishing to conceal their identity, in one hand, and a flute in the other. In contemporary England Jack Sheppard was likewise a hero of the populace; but how strange an apparition, like a creature from fairyland, would this slim feminine youth, refined and serious, make in Hogarth's world of thieves and vagabonds!

Towards the end of his life Harunobu turned more frequently to the pillar-print, and in this shape some of his finest designs are to be found.

---

[1] And their women-folk. In book-illustrations of publishers' shops women are seen examining prints and books. And in several texts there are references to women's taste for actor-prints.

He had made some experiments in two-sheet composition, but does not seem to have been happy in the diptych form, though we note his experiments as a stage on the way to the diptychs and three-sheet designs of Kiyonaga. The two-colour " triptychs " were printed from a single block, and in a fair number of examples are found as a still undivided sheet; they form a set of three, rather than a design thought out in three compartments. But Harunobu's diptychs are, like some rare two-colour prints in oblong shape, composed as a single complete design. They are very rare, but possibly more exist than have hitherto been suspected, since each sheet, though only half of a whole, might often be mistaken for an independent design. This is the case also with many of the triptychs of the later masters. Examples are the " Girl at a garden-gate to which her lover approaches," reproduced in the *Paris V.I. Catalogue*, Plate XVII; the parallel to the story of Kosekiko and Chōryō—a girl picking up a fan dropped in a stream by her lover (*ibid.*, Plate XIV); " Osen in Kagiya Temple grounds " (*ibid.*, Plate XXII), and the charming print of girls shooting darts through blow-pipes at a target, which is in the British Museum.

But this horizontal expansion of space suited Harunobu's genius less well than the vertical expansion of the *hashira-ye*. The tall, narrow sheet was a challenge to invention; and just as European artists have found a stimulus to invention in such difficult forms as the spandrel, Harunobu rejoiced in triumphing over the contracted limits of the pillar-prints, so that if we place a blank sheet of the same size beside one of these compositions we are amazed at the ingenuity which has filled the space so naturally without any sense of cramping, and are beguiled into the illusion that there is room to spare in a form that it would have seemed almost impossible to fit a figure in with any ease. The grandeur and amplitude of Masanobu's big *hashira-ye* Harunobu does not attain or aim at; but he knows how to unite dignity of form with exquisite feeling.

The most beautiful print of Gompachi has been already mentioned, and it is considered by some to be Harunobu's masterpiece. There we note how the repetition of two or three diagonal lines suffices to disguise the extreme narrowness of proportion. In another hardly less beautiful sheet a girl in white descends some steps to fetch oil for the lamp, and the red diagonals and horizontals of the steps perform the same function. In another print it is the lines of a *samisen* held by the girl who is tuning it. A fine set of *hashira-kake* is the set of Six Tamagawa, with old poems written above in a square, and on a smaller panel a little portrait of the poet. To this set belongs another and a later " Gompachi disguised as a *komusō*," in which that fascinating young robber and lover is coming from right to left instead of from left to right. It is not equal to the earlier version, missing something of its subtle simplicity and supreme distinction.

In this form of the pillar-print Koryūsai rivalled and even surpassed his friend.

Koryūsai was an artist of rare gift who was unfortunate in being over-shadowed during his most productive years by the genius of Harunobu. He was content during Meiwa to have Harunobu for his master, and to follow him so closely that occasionally, in the absence of a signature, one might be deceived. But he is never wholly dependent on Harunobu ; he has his own individuality, felt especially in his colour-schemes. Less delicate, less sensitive as a draughtsman than Harunobu, he is of robuster fibre. A personal note in his colouring is the vivid rust-red which he is so fond of introducing into his schemes, sometimes as the dominant tint, as if he craved an astringent to the suave harmonies of his master. He worked the same vein of youthful idyll that Harunobu had made so popular, and designed in the same squarish sheet. But in the *hashira-kake* he seems to have found a form especially congenial ; and whereas Haru-nobu rarely ventured to bring two figures into the narrow design, Koryūsai often did this with complete felicity.

During Meiwa period Harunobu was, as we have said, the supreme master. Even so great an artist as Koryūsai had to take a second place. All his contemporaries, old and young alike, fell under the enchantment of his new style. The Torii line, after its half-century and more of sustained and prominent effort, was in temporary eclipse. Kiyomitsu and Kiyohiro made no serious attempt to compete in the new manner ; and the young Kiyotsune, though he produced a certain number of agreeable prints under Harunobu's influence, made no special mark. Another veteran, Toyonobu, designed a few prints early in Meiwa quite in the new style—a calendar-print for 1765 is in the British Museum—as did also Tanaka Masunobu. But the race was now to the young. The new-comer Minkō has already been mentioned. " The Fox's Wedding " set, to which he contributed, is contemporary with Harunobu's first prints in the new manner, being published as a calendar for 1765. Two of the set are reproduced in the Danckwerts sale catalogue (Sotheby, July, 1914).

Toyonobu's pupil, Toyomasa, designed some attractive prints, his favourite theme being the games of children. A set of the Twelve Months, all children subjects, is his best known work.

But next to Koryūsai, the most important of the younger generation who made a name during Meiwa are Shunshō, Toyoharu, Shigemasa, and Bunchō. We find the first three of these collaborating in a set of twelve prints, four of which are reproduced in the sale catalogue of the Blow Collection (Sotheby, July 2nd, 1912), and others in the Danckwerts sale catalogue (Sotheby, July, 1914). One by Toyoharu is also given in Von Seidlitz's book (English edition, p. 114). Each artist contributed four designs. These prints are curiously composed, being divided diagonally into two compartments, the upper one being on a more distant plane, with smaller figures.

Toyoharu, founder of the Utagawa school, later to play a prominent part in Ukiyo-ye, was less under the influence of Harunobu than the others. He was drawn to historic subjects and to topography rather than to idyllic and domestic scenes. We shall have more to say of him in the next chapter.

Shunshō and Shigemasa were also both drawn to the heroic legends of their country; to such famous episodes as the fight in the sea-shallows between the beautiful youth Atsumori and the old warrior Kumagaya, who was afterwards to repent so sorely of the life he took that day; or again the feat of the archer Nasu-no-Yoichi, who shot away the fan from the mast of the Taira ship; or the rivalry of Kagesuye and Takatsuna at the fording of the Uji river. But both Shunshō and Shigemasa designed idyllic scenes in the Harunobu manner, sometimes with wonderful success. There is a beautiful print of Gompachi and Komurasaki reproduced in Gookin's catalogue of the Chicago Exhibition in 1908 (No. 261), in which Shunshō rivals Harunobu. We reproduce Pl. 26 (2) an early Shigemasa of about 1766. The two collaborated in the well-known " Silk-worm Set." This set of twelve prints, closely imitative of Harunobu, is in the style of about 1767–1768, though it was published as a picture-book so late as 1786. This friendly rivalry and collaboration was continued after Harunobu's death in a famous book, which will be mentioned in its place in the next chapter.

Meanwhile, Shunshō's special line was already being developed. The eclipse of the Torii had left an open field in the theatrical print. And Shunshō seized the opportunity. As early as 1765 he was producing actor-prints, though he did not mature his style or show the full vigour of his gift till Meiwa was ended. But by 1770 his position as a designer of actor-prints was well established. In that year he collaborated with Bunchō in publishing one of the most important picture-books yet produced, the *Yehon Butai Ōgi*, in which the actors' bust portraits are given in fan-shaped panels.

Though Shunshō was to be the most eminent and prolific actor-print designer of his time, during Meiwa it was Bunchō who was the more interesting and distinguished of the two.

Kurth, in his book on Harunobu, reproduces a print of an actor and an *oiran* in which Harunobu and Bunchō collaborated, the girl being drawn by the former and the actor by the latter. This is an early instance of a practice which later became more common.

Bunchō is, of course, best known by his actor-prints in *hoso-ye* size, though he published also a certain number of non-theatrical prints, in the vein of Harunobu.

Even his actor-prints are comparatively rare. All his work has a peculiar fascination. The very rare print which we reproduce is perhaps Bunchō's masterpiece, unless a preference be given to that other portrait of Kikunojō, the actor famous as a player of feminine parts on the stage, walking all in white on the bank of a stream under snow-laden willow-boughs. This other print is reproduced in colour in the Paris catalogues.

Bunchō's figures are taller than Harunobu's and supremely elegant in their pliant attitudes and fluid lines. He was a wonderful colourist, being fond of unusual combinations in which a vivid grass-green, foiled with white, often played part. The Kikunojō here reproduced (Pl. 4) is superb in poise and swing, and in the contrast of the red and yellow asters with the deep black of the background.

Bunchō worked on for some years after Harunobu's death—a print by him of Onoye Matsusuke as Munetō in disguise can be dated 1778–1779—but his main activity seems to have been in the latter years of Meiwa.

Some essays in the theatrical field were now being made by the youthful Kiyonaga, Kiyomitsu's adopted son ; but these efforts to uphold the Torii tradition look weak and timid beside Shunshō's and Bunchō's work. Kiyonaga also followed Harunobu in domestic scenes, though no one could have divined as yet his future power.

If Shiba Kōkan was the author of all the prints signed Harushige, as presumably is the case, he was a singularly skilful imitator of Harunobu's manner. Some of the Harushige prints are beautiful and, so far as we can tell, show independent invention. Certain characteristics found in these prints—a long nose, and an exaggerated slenderness of figure—seem to mark some of the prints signed Harunobu as forgeries by Kōkan. But this is a problem on which there will probably always be difference of opinion. What we can be reasonably sure of is that the internal evidence of Shiba Kōkan's hand is not to be found (as some have thought) in semi-European conventions of foliage, for it was not till Temmei period that he began to study from the Dutch.

Towards the end of Meiwa we find a new influence coming into Ukiyo-ye, and, though not affecting its general character, enlarging its range with new motives and a new manner.

Harunobu definitely aimed at lifting Ukiyoye art to a rivalry with classic painting; and in Japan there is no reference to the classics without a reference to China. Beside all the multitude of his idyllic scenes we find a certain number of prints which are not strictly Ukiyoye subjects at all, but are designs of flowers and birds with a suggestion of landscape. In these Koryūsai competed with him. Some are unsigned, and it is doubtful in some cases to which master they should be attributed. These designs follow the Chinese tradition, revived among a group of Kyōto painters who were stimulated by the settlement of a Chinese artist at Nagasaki in 1731. It is noteworthy that Shiba Kōkan in his Confessions tells us that he expressly imitated the famous and popular Chinese *genre* painters of the 16th century, Chou Ying and Chou Ch'ēn. Already in the time of the hand-coloured print we find occasional experiments by Okumura Masanobu and Shigenaga in flower-and-bird motives, but these were tentative and crude, and not be to compared with the prints we are now considering. And it is not merely an imitation of Chinese painting that we find in Harunobu and Koryūsai, it is an imitation of Chinese colour-prints. The well-known and exquisite print of a " Vase of Flowers with a rising Moon," by Harunobu (unsigned), is certainly of Chinese inspiration, though the idiom is Japanese. We are reminded of the brilliant set of Chinese colour-prints, printed in many colours on a white paper and with richly embossed effects, best known from the examples which have been in the British Museum since its foundation, and were bought by Sir Hans Sloane with the collections made by Kaempfer, the historian of Japan.

But in certain *naga-ye* we get even closer to Chinese prototypes. A *hashira-kake*, by Harunobu, reproduced in the *Paris V.I. Catalogue*, Plate X, No. 110, is a Chinese landscape and imitates a Chinese woodcut. But the most beautiful of these pillar-prints are *kakemono-ye* by Koryūsai. As these were probably produced in Anyei period, after Harunobu's death, we will return to them in the next chapter.

On the other hand, two pillar-prints of falcons attributed to Koryūsai in the Hamilton Easter Field collection, sold in 1922 in New York, are in all probability not Japanese at all, but Chinese. Two very similar prints are in Mr. Bateson's collection in London ; they were bought at a sale of Chinese prints, and have been pronounced quite definitely to be Chinese work by Japanese connoisseurs. When placed side by side with Koryūsai's work, the difference is quite perceptible, though difficult to describe in words.

The technique of these prints is peculiar, being based on the *ishi-zuri* or stone-print. This does not necessarily mean printed from stone. The Chinese, from remote times, have been accustomed, when a picture was falling into decay, to preserve the design by incising it on stone. Rubbings were taken from the stone and served the purpose of reproductions made by engraving. Some *ishi-zuri* may have been printed from engraved stones ; but wood was obviously a much more convenient medium ; and *ishi-zuri* generally means a woodcut made in imitation of a rubbing from incised stone. The rubbing made on thin paper had certain peculiarities which were imitated in this kind of woodcut, for which a technique of its own was developed.

In its simplest form the " stone-print " is a print in which the design is in white on a black ground. Examples of such are found among the Primitives, as we have seen already (pp. 24 and 34), in the work of Masanobu and Shigenaga.

But the later coloured *ishi-zuri* become much more elaborate. The process has been described in an article by the late Mr. Wilson Crewdson, Chairman of the London Japan Society, in an article in the *Studio*, May, 1914. After the wood had been incised, so that the design would show white on black if printed, a very thin sheet of paper was damped, laid on the block and pressed into the hollows made by the engraver. But instead of the wood-block receiving the colour, as in the ordinary process, it was the surface of the paper to which the colour or ink was applied, with a pad, not with a brush. The design itself did not take the colour, because it was pressed below the surface of the block into the engraved hollows and escaped the application of the pad ; it remained white. When the thin paper was taken up, it showed the design standing out in white with a raised and crinkled edge to the white lines where the paper had been pressed into the block. It was then laid down on thicker paper.

Before we take leave of Meiwa, and of Harunobu's exquisite April world, let us mention a noteworthy print which must be assigned to about 1770.

This is a triptych by Shunshō of a scene from the Civil Wars; warriors fighting outside the walls of Kurosaki Castle. An example is in the British Museum collection. It is remarkable because it is not one of the small *hoso-ye* triptychs, but a composition on three full-sized sheets. It has hitherto been assumed that Kiyonaga was the first to design these full-sized triptychs in the 1780's. But this print by Shunshō bears the form of signature which he used about 1770; it also bears the inscription *Ukiye sammai tsuzuki* (three-sheet perspective picture) on the first sheet, and on each of the others the words *One of three;* which points to its being an innovation. We shall see that with the next period, Anyei, the larger size of single sheet comes into fashion; but that triptychs of this size were designed so early has not been suspected. Naturally for heroic subjects the large sheets were more fitted than the small sheets preferred by Haru-nobu; and it seems probable that Shunshō's triptych was the precursor of other compositions of similar subjects, anticipating Kiyonaga, though perhaps only known at present in their divided state as single sheets.

# CHAPTER V

# ANYEI PERIOD

## FEBRUARY 4TH, 1772, TO JANUARY 23RD, 1781

The prints of Anyei, as compared with those of Meiwa, present some
striking differences. There is a great increase in the number of pillar-
prints, chiefly due to the partiality of Koryūsai for this format. The square,
medium-size print (*shikaku-ye*) gives place to the large, upright print
(*Ōban tate-ye*) ; and the superfine *hōsho* paper is no longer in use. The
human figure assumes a robust type, far removed from the fragile models
affected by Harunobu and his contemporaries. A radical change takes
place in the women's coiffure, brought about by the use of a contrivance
called *binsashi*, a flexible piece of metal, tortoise-shell, or bamboo inserted
into the hair so as to expand the *bin* or side-locks on either side of the
head. This method of hair-dressing was known as *Tōrōbin* or lantern side-
locks, from its supposed resemblance to the *tōrō* or lantern made of paper
stretched on a bamboo frame. It formed an admirable setting to the
face ; and much of the charm of the Shunshō, Shigemasa, and Koryūsai
drawings of women at this period is due to this. In the print by Shikō
(II ʃ) reproduced on Plate 41, the *binsashi* is held by the girl seated on the
left between the thumb and forefinger of her right hand. The charming
effect of the *Tōrōbin* coiffure may be conveniently studied in the famous
and delightful coloured picture-book by Shigemasa and Shunshō, jointly
published in the 1st month of 1776 under the title *Seirō bijin awase sugata
kagami*, by Yamazaki Kimbei and Tsutaya Jusaburō, who under his *dō-gō*
of Kōshodō contributed the preface, from which the following excerpt is
taken. " There is an obscure Chinese saying to the effect that in painting
the background is everything. Now though this may be true regarding
Chinese pictures, yet the tastes of artists vary as the ages roll by. Thus
is it that in Japanese pictures the great masters of the three principal cities
have ever painted the fashions of costume and hair-dressing prevalent at
each age, which pass as rapidly as does an infant growing to manhood.
Here in these three volumes of Snow, Moon, and Flowers, which I have
entitled *A Mirror of Rival Beauties*, the two flourishing artists of the day
—Kitao and Katsukawa—labouring with brush and palette, have with
indefatigable zeal depicted the graceful forms of the courtesans of the
Enclosure (i.e. the Yoshiwara) as they appear when on promenade or within
the precincts of their elegant chambers. I have ordered their pictures to
be engraved, not only as a permanent record of their art, but also in the

hope that the book will cause my house to flourish even as flourished the flowering cherry tree from which the blocks were made." It is noteworthy that both in the preface and at the end of the book precedence was accorded to Shigemasa, though he was thirteen years junior to Shunshō. The reason was that the younger man was considered by his contemporaries to be the greater artist, except in the realm of stage portraiture, in which Shunshō was acknowledged as pre-eminent. A contemporary engraver named Yegawa Hachizayemon has left on record that " though Shunshō was pre-eminent in his own special sphere of portraiture of actors in character, yet he was less versed in the laws of general painting than Shigemasa, from whom he was ever ready to seek advice and receive instruction." The *Mirror of Rival Beauties of the Green Houses* was published when Tsuta-jū, as Tsutaya Jūsaburō was popularly called, was a small bookseller near the great entrance gate of the New Yoshiwara. As this remarkable man was destined to play a leading part in the fortunes of both Ukiyo-ye and Literature till death overtook him in 1797 at the early age of forty-eight, it is fitting that a brief account of his career should find place here. His birth took place at Yedo in 1750. His real name was Maruyama Kari (may be also pronounced Karamaru), the first of which he changed to Ki-ta-gawa. He was a man of great enterprise and no mean scholar ; and possessed in a marked degree the gift of recognizing genius. Thus it came about that he gathered around his humble abode young men of talent, who for one reason or another had fallen on evil days, and who were willing to work for him alone in return for food, raiment, and lodging. Chief amongst these were Bakin, Shokusanjin, Kyōden, and Toyoaki— afterwards Utamaro ; all of whom but for his insight and encouragement would probably have been lost to Literature and Art.

He it was, too, who first published the works of Chōki, and who was the sole publisher of Sharaku's designs.

As a writer and humorous versifier he called himself Tsuta no Karamaru, which latter is occasionally found, modified to Karamaro, imprinted in seal form on some of his publications ; as is also his *dō-gō* of Kōshodō. In the 9th month of Temmei 3, he removed to Tōri Abura-chō, where he had purchased the commodious premises and godowns of the old firm of Maruya Kohei ; and from that time forward he imprinted on his publications his trade-mark of an ivy leaf surmounted by a triple peak. After his death, the firm was carried on by his head clerk during the minority of his heir ; but, though it lasted till the middle of the 19th century at a new address, it gradually sank into a comparatively insignificant position.

Two other publishers, who by their refined taste and business acumen, did much to foster Ukiyo-ye during this and subsequent periods, were Senkwakudō Tsuruya Kiyemon and Yeijudō Nishimuraya Yohachi. The former was the scion of a very old Kyōtō family of *jōruri* (kind of musical drama) booksellers, who established a branch in Yedo during the Yempō period (1673–1681) in the Ōdemma-chō. One of the earliest known prints issued by this firm was a twelve-sheet composition showing the arrival of the Korean Embassy in Yedo, the 7th sheet of which is reproduced (Pl. 19).

It was not, however, till the present proprietor took over the business that Ukiyoye prints were issued by him in large numbers. Yeijudō was born about 1720, and started as a wholesale publisher at an early age; one of his first prints being a *hoso-urushi-ye* by Kiyomasu of the actor Segawa Kikujirō as the courtesan Katsuragi, issued at the close of 1740 (see Pl. 22).

About 1790, an excellent portrait of the old man at the age of seventy-one was designed by Toyokuni I and published by himself. Date of his death and that of Senkwakudō are unrecorded.

Prints issued by these three publishers are remarkable for the high standard of engraving and printing.

During Anyei, Bunchō, Shunshō, Shigemasa, and Koryūsai were at the height of their powers. Kiyotsune continued to design a few actors in character; but his pupils Kiyosato and Kiyohisa appear to have ceased work.

Katsukawa SHUNKŌ, Shunshō's first pupil, was born in 1743. His family name was Kiyokawa; his personal name is unrecorded. He worked from 1771 till the autumn of 1791, when palsy deprived him of the use of his right arm, and compelled him to give up. Shaving his head, he became a lay *bonze* in the Zenshōji monastery at Asakusa. He used a jar-shaped seal enclosing the character *Hayashi* after the example of his master; sometimes, instead of *Hayashi* we find the ideograph *Ki* which is really one half of the former character. He died on December 1st, 1812, aged seventy years. There is a painting on a *fusuma* (paper sliding-screen) by him in the above monastery, inscribed " Drawn by Shunkō with his left hand at the age of fifty-seven."

In the beginning of Anyei, Toriyama Sekiyen devised a method of gradation colour-printing called *Fuki-bokashi no saishiki-zuri*, which he first applied in practice to a two-volume folio book entitled *Sekiyen gwafu* (alternative title, *Toriyama Hiko*), which appeared in 1773. This method was but rarely resorted to during the remainder of the 18th century; but it was largely employed, by Hokusai and Hiroshige especially, during the next century. The grading was effected by a judicious wiping of the block upon which the colour had been spread. Sekiyen also illustrated a series of books, each of three volumes (in which he applied the *fuki-bokashi* method to monochrome), under the generic title of *Hyakki-yagiyō*, dealing with the night wanderings of demons. These appeared in 1776, 1779, 1781, and 1784; and in all, as well as in the *Sekiyen gwafu*, Shikō is described as his pupil. This is the artist who about 1788 changed his name to Chōki. The problem surrounding the name of Shikō is discussed in a separate essay (Note C).

SEKIYEN was born at Yedo in 1713, his real name being Sano Toyofusa. He was taught painting by a Kanō artist named Gyokuyen Chikanobu, from whom he received the brush-name of Sekiyen. About the beginning of the Hōreki era (1751) he turned his attention to Ukiyo-ye, and created a stir by offering as an ex-voto to a temple a painting of the actor Nakamura Kiyosaburō, famous for his impersonations of women. This he signed Toriyama Sekiyen, the former being the art surname (*geisei*) which he had adopted. About 1700 he established a school in which he taught Ukiyo-ye and Haikai (seventeen-syllable poetry). Amongst his pupils were Shikō, above-mentioned, and Toyoaki. He died on September 2nd, 1788, at the age of seventy-six, and was buried in the cemetery of Shinkōmyō-ji, Asakusa. On his tombstone was engraved his art surname, Toriyama, his art personal name Sekiyen, and his real family or surname Sano. He designed no *ichimai-ye*.

TOYOAKI (UTAMARO), whose real name was Kita-gawa Yūsuke, was born according to some authorities in 1753, according to others in 1754; but as the age at which he died is not recorded in the register of deceased parishioners (*kwakochō*) kept at the temple at which he used to worship, it is uncertain which of these dates is correct. Most authorities, however, incline to the former. His birthplace is also uncertain; some say that it was Kawagoye in the province of Musashi. Whether this is true or not, it is certain that, as some biographers state, he was not born at Yedo, whither he was brought at a tender age by his mother, then a widow. His father's name is not known; but the fact that it is not recorded in the *kwakochō* alongside that of his mother and himself shows that he was not residing at Yedo at the time of his death. It has been said that his mother, unable to support the boy, entrusted him to the care of Sekiyen, with a view to his being eventually trained as an artist. Certainly Sekiyen's postscript to Utamaro's *Yehon Mushi erabi*, written in the winter of 1788, makes it probable that this statement is correct.

" To form pictures," writes Sekiyen, " of living things in the mind and then to transfer them to paper with the brush is the true art of Painting. My pupil Utamaro, in depicting these insects, has produced ' pictures from his heart.' I remember how Uta-shi in his childhood acquired the habit of observing the most minute details of living creatures ; and I used to notice how absorbed he would become when playing with a dragon-fly tied to a string or with a cricket held in the palm of his hand. Oftentimes had I to caution him, fearful lest he might take their lives. In presenting us with these tokens of his mature talent, his brush has become famous. . . ."

It will be seen that Sekiyen distinctly states that Utamaro was his pupil, whom he had known as a child and whom he calls Uta-shi—a term of respect rather than one of endearment.

Neither claimed any blood-relationship, and there seems to have been none ; certainly not that of father and son as has been put forward. The facts that their family names were different and that they were buried in different cemeteries negative any such theory. Even supposing there had been a quarrel, as some have asserted, resulting in the expulsion of Toyoaki from the paternal roof, the eulogistic manner in which Sekiyen speaks of his pupil proves that the quarrel had been long forgotten and that the pair were then—some nine months previous to Sekiyen's death—on the best of terms ; and hence there could have been no obstacle to their interment in the same burial-ground. About the middle of Anyei, Toyoaki was received into his house near the Ōmonguchi, Shin Yoshiwara, by Tsutajū as a *kakari-bito* or dependent ; and some time during 1779, he adopted as his art surname the family name of his protector, namely Ki-ta-gawa, and as his art personal name Uta-maro, doubtless derived from Tsutajū's *gō* of Kara-maro. One of his last prints under the name of Kita-gawa Toyoaki represents the fifth Ichikawa Danjūrō in the rôle of Arakawatarō Makezu in the play " Date nishiki-tsui no yumitori," produced at the Morita theatre in the winter of Anyei 7. Utamaro has been described as a debauchee ; partly perhaps from the fact that he selected his models of women frequently from the licensed quarters, and partly on account of his alleged portrait in the British Museum painted by Yeishi, in which he is depicted as an old worn-out roué. There is little doubt that this is in reality a portrait of his undistinguished follower Baigadō Utamaro II ; for not only was it painted nine years after the death of the first Utamaro, but a second painting by Yeishi representing him as he doubtless was has come to light. His face and figure show none of the repellent and bloated appearance of the British Museum painting. He is, on the contrary, represented as an intelligent, middle-aged man, seated with his hands on his lap, his left grasping a rosary. It is evidently a memorial portrait ; and, though it bears no date, was assuredly executed soon after his death on the 31st of October, 1806. It is common knowledge that the licensed quarters were visited by writers and artists for the purpose of obtaining material for their work unobtainable elsewhere.

The novelettes and Ukiyoye prints were written and designed for the middle and lower classes ; and courtesans, actors, *geisha*, wrestlers, and tea-house beauties naturally provided the material necessary for such works. Turn to the last plate of the artist's famous two-volume book, *Seirō nenjū gyō-ji*, or " Transactions in the Green Houses all the Year Around," where he depicts himself painting the *Hō-ō* (Chinese phœnix), palette in one hand, brush in the other, on his knees and surrounded by the materials of his art—a man intent on his work, earnest and painstaking. The great artist was laid to rest in the burial-ground of the Buddhist temple Senkwō-ji, Kita-matsuyama-chō, Asakusa, under the posthumous name (*hō-myō*) of Shūyen Ryōkyō shin-ji.

In the register of deceased parishioners, his name follows soon after that of his mother, whose *hō-myō* was Risei shin-nyō, and who was buried on the 2nd of November, 1790.

Harunobu's death in 1770 left an immense gap in Ukiyo-ye. Who was left to take his place ? There were three outstanding masters at the beginning of Anyei who were each of them brilliantly gifted ; Koryūsai, Shigemasa, and Shunshō. At any moment it seemed as if one of these might forge ahead, create a new type of print and open a new chapter in Ukiyo-ye.

But for a few years nothing novel appeared. Harunobu's idyllic vein was almost exhausted. What was wanted was a new direction such as Harunobu himself had given to Meiwa ; and this was lacking. There was a sort of lull.

By 1776 a new type of face and figure had come into fashion, as we see from the famous book by Shigemasa and Shunshō, published in that year, which is the chief landmark of the period. This shows a great change from the types of the end of Meiwa. When did this change come about ?

In his recently published book on Shunshō, Herr Succo has reproduced two actor-prints, dated, as sometimes happens, in contemporary handwriting. One is dated Anyei 2 or 1773, the other Anyei 3 or 1774. The latter represents an actor playing a woman, and we see from this that the hair is dressed much as in Meiwa, though fuller at the sides. The new style with the *bin-sashi*, described above, has not yet come in. We may presume that it was introduced in 1775.

To these first four or five years of Anyei belong most of Koryūsai's finest pillar-prints, as well as the set of small prints called *Fūryū Jorō Hakkei*, and such prints of medium size as the sets *Meichō Zashiki Hakkei*, Eight Views of interiors, each with a bird ; and the set *Fūryū Goji Hajime*.

In each of these sets there are charming compositions, in which one sees occasional symptoms already of a feeling for an ampler sweep of line.

But Koryūsai's pillar-prints and *kakemono-ye* are the special glories of this time. The " Parting of Atsumori from his Mistress " is one of the earliest prints of Anyei period. Here Koryūsai's expression of emotion is unusually eloquent. The young warrior in his armour and with a quiver full of arrows at his back, but bare-headed, stands looking sorrow-fully down on the girl Tama-ori, who has sunk on one knee at his feet. She turns away her head, but with one small hand she takes hold of the great horned helmet which her lover was about to put on, detaining it in spite of his protest. Within the narrow space of the *hashira-ye*, the two figures are beautifully and tenderly related, each having a hand on the helmet in the middle of it, and form a natural group, while the design is a rich interplay of lines and colours.

Of about the same time is a design of noble simplicity, " The Young Poet by the Sea," a youthful figure in blue and slaty purple seated on a red balcony above the sea. A pine tree thrusts up from below the balcony ; distant sails are on the water ; the broad sun is rising red out of mist. The youth with raised writing-brush looks out in reverie.

Even more beautiful, perhaps, and exquisite in sentiment, is the print of two young lovers praying with raised hands at sunrise as they stand on the seashore. It is a sort of parallel to the " Ancient Couple of Takasago," the theme of a famous *Nō* play. Here it seems as if no other shape than this tall narrow one could have been possible for the subject, so happily does it conspire with the mood evoked. The long lines of dresses and figures seem to flow upwards, like smoke in still air.

Others of these *hashira-ye* might be mentioned, to illustrate Koryūsai's singular felicity in inventing motives for this form.

Probably to this time also belong some magnificent *kakemono-ye* in

Chinese style. In the last chapter we mentioned some experiments in landscape in this style by Harunobu. In the *ishi-zuri* technique is a striking *kakemono-ye*, signed by Koryūsai, of the " Fight between the Dragon and the Tiger." The dragon sweeps down out of great swirls of inky cloud, and the tiger leaps up to attack him from the shore of a sea, the blue waves of which are shrouded by the shadowy cloud from which the dragon emerges. But in the finest of these large prints Koryūsai uses a mixed method. For example, in the " Hawk on a Rock," reproduced in colours (Pl. 5), the bird is designed in the ordinary way in black on white, while the rock and the water are designed in white on black. This splendid print, like the " Dragon and the Tiger," is extremely rare. Both are in the British Museum collection. Still more impressive, and superb as a decorative design, is the " White Falcon," which is famous and was perhaps the greatest treasure in the Alexis Rouart Collection, sold in New York in February, 1922. The great bird stands proudly with head reverted on a rock, relieved against a black night-sky. Behind the rock shoot up tall banana leaves, and at the foot of it is a chrysanthemum. This, unlike the " Hawk on a Rock," is signed. It is Koryūsai's masterpiece in its kind.

We have mentioned in the last chapter certain prints of birds and flowers by Koryūsai and by Harunobu. It seems probable that Koryūsai continued this class of print into Anyei, when he was taking more to painting than before. The most famous of these pieces is the " Crow and Heron," which has been often reproduced, the black and white of the two birds as they stand on a branch of snow-laden willow against a clear blue sky making a most effective design. Harunobu had made a similar contrast in a print of a white and black buffalo near a blossoming peach tree.

Toyoharu also designed a certain number of pillar-prints in these years, the motives being usually figures from legend, or analogues of classic themes. At the same time Shunshō published *hashira-ye* of heroic subjects. 1775 is the date of his book, *Nishiki hyaku-nin isshū azumi ori*, " the Hundred Famous Poets."

But Shunshō's main sphere of production was, as always, the actor-print. And in his actor-prints he was steadily growing in strength and decision of line and in the power of seizing and rendering character. But though acknowledged to be supreme in theatrical prints, Shunshō had no such dominant position as Harunobu had enjoyed. Probably it was no longer possible to win such a position as a master of actor-prints alone, and Shunshō's excursions into other fields were only occasional. He also developed slowly. It was from his brilliant young friend Shigemasa rather that the public expected the great things to come. Shigemasa was never very abundant in his production of *nishiki-ye*, but he, more than any of the others, seems to have created the type which we associate with Anyei period. The tendency of the day was, naturally enough, in reaction from the feminine delicacy and exquisiteness of Harunobu. Larger sheets and broader design were coming into vogue. By 1775 Harunobu's style, which at the beginning of Anyei was still being followed with little modification, had become a thing of the past.

Koryūsai's famous series, " New Patterns for Young Leaves," *Hinagata Wakana no Hatsumoyō*, was being published. The medium-sized squarish print of Meiwa was superseded, and in its place we have the large upright sheet which from now onwards was to be the regular size for all prints except the actor-prints. The more conservative Shunshō kept to the smaller *hoso-ye* size in these designs, with comparatively few exceptions, till his death in 1793.

Koryūsai's new series shows a complete change from his Meiwa manner. There is no background. The types are taller and more massive. Each group of three, the beauty with her two little maids, is combined in a system of ample, sweeping curves. The colouring is more vigorous than delicate, Koryūsai's favourite rust-red appearing in force, foiled with black, yellow, and olive tones, though pinks and purples are also used. We note a novelty of realism in the print of " Nanakoshi of the House of the Fan," who wears black velvet over pink and white, and the texture of the velvet is reproduced in the woodcut. It is a striking series, but not wholly successful. Of about the same time is the fine print which we reproduce in colours (Pl. 6) ; also one of the finest of all Koryūsai's pillar-prints, notable for its splendid drawing of the nude, the print of a girl in bed under a net from which she tries to drive the mosquitoes, while a young man pulls the net aside.

If Koryūsai's set of fashion-plates, for such they virtually were, was a bid for leadership by Koryūsai, it was soon answered. Shigemasa and Shunshō's *Seirō Bijin Awase Sugatami*, or " Beauties of the Green Houses," appeared in 1776, and is generally thought to be the most beautiful of all the coloured picture-books of Ukiyo-ye. It certainly has few rivals. Many of the motives are charming, such as that in the double-page design where a group of girls come out on a winter morning, and one of them lifting the dipper from the round cistern finds it frozen into the ice and brings up a crystal round of ice with it.

The feminine types in this book have been enthusiastically praised, but cannot wholly escape the charge of being a little " dumpy." Reaction from Harunobu's fairy grace has brought about a sort of squareness and solidity which seem to demand taller stature for really felicitous proportions.

This slightly taller stature is seen in Shigemasa's series of single prints, probably dating about 1777, called *Tōbō Bijin no zu*, or " Pictures of Beauties of the East," which is unsigned. Other prints, without title or signature, seem as if they belonged to this set, and at any rate were published at the same time. We reproduce one in colours (Pl. 7). Here is the new style triumphant ; and we cannot help wondering why it was not followed up and imposed by Shigemasa on the whole of Ukiyo-ye for some years to come. We note in one of these prints the rendering of the texture of black velvet, as in Koryūsai's series, also the use of a red and yellow stripe in a dress, afterwards to be a favourite colour-device of the Temmei period. But what strikes one chiefly is the use of broad masses of opaque colour, and the avoidance of delicate small patterns breaking into the design. Breadth, dignity, and a certain massiveness are the qualities aimed at and achieved.

Shigemasa, however, having matured this fine type of design, did not, like Harunobu before him, and Kiyonaga after him, pour out an abundance of prints developing and expanding his achievement. He produced a few very fine pillar-prints in this manner, one of which, notable for its suggestion of depth and atmosphere, is illustrated in Mr. Ficke's book (Plate XVIII). But he seems to have cared more about designing picture-books than single-sheets, which from this time onwards become extremely rare.

Shunshō meanwhile continued to pour out his *hoso-ye* of actors. The types show the change of fashion, they become more massive, less gracefully pliant. But some of Shunshō's finest designs date from these years. His line grows more nervous, the face and the whole body of the actor represented becomes more intensely expressive of the part in which he is absorbed. Like Shigemasa, Shunshō employs opaque colour more freely ; he is fond of a deep brick-red, used sometimes in a strong mass ; and his use of black can be quite magnificent. His pupil Shunkō follows him with marvellous closeness. At times the two are hardly, if at all, distinguishable. There are unsigned actor-prints of Anyei period which it is impossible to attribute more definitely than to " Shunshō or school." These *hoso-ye* seem to have been issued in threes, printed from one block, but are usually found divided as single prints. As time goes on Shunshō gradually tends to make the three figures more of a single design, but in his earlier work the three are designed independently and are only related to each other by look and gesture, the poses being stationary or in arrested movement.

The British Museum possesses sixteen triptychs by Shunshō, and sixty-three diptychs (as well as thirty-eight by Shunyei) which doubtless lack the third completing sheet. In only a few of these can it be truly said that the design gains by completion, though there are cases where the gain is striking. This is especially true of those prints where the background is more elaborated. Often there is merely a suggestion of undulating ground, coloured a tawny yellow or green. Many prints have a decorative frieze of floral design across the back ; others have a river or seashore conventionally pictured. In no case are the surroundings emphasized. It is on the actor's presence that Shunshō concentrates. The enormous amount of Shunshō's production, in which naturally there is much uninspired work, and also the repetition of standing figures, each set within its narrow frame, make a superficial impression of monotony. Yet the average is astonishingly high ; and the more one studies Shunshō's work, the more one is compelled to admire the contained force of his draughtsmanship and the richness, within the narrow limits chosen, of his gift as a designer and a colourist. He has not the exquisite sensibility, the haunting charm and emotional quality of Bunchō, but he has greater reserves of power. What has been recorded above of his relations with Shigemasa seems to indicate that he was slow in developing, diffident rather than bold, but of a nature that knew how to enrich and strengthen itself by experience. Always virile, he is at his best in depicting concentrated passion, and as a rule is better in masculine than in feminine portrayal. His designs of actors in women's parts are often rather stolid, though now and then he depicts a woman in some desolate attitude with an extraordinary dignity of beauty, using restrained colours and a full depth of black. All through the Anyei period he continues to design these actor-prints with unfailing vigour, and though sometimes there are symptoms of fatigue, he seems always ready to respond to the challenge of a fresh inspiration.

And what of the younger men ? Ukiyo-ye, so far, had never failed in supplying a new generation of varied gift. Nor was it wanting now. There were, in fact, three young men now at the opening or in the first phase of their careers who were destined to become three of the very greatest of Ukiyoye masters, although it was to be many years before two of the three, the men afterwards known as Utamaro and Hokusai, shone forth in the full splendour of their powers. The third was Torii Kiyonaga.

As we have seen already, Kiyonaga had begun his career during Meiwa, but had shown no precocity of talent. Still less was this the case with Utamaro, whose earliest known work, the illustrations to a novelette, *Kembutsu Tayema*, published about 1773, when the artist was about twenty, give little hint of the mastery to come.

Reproduced on Plate 28 is the earliest known *ichimai-ye* by Utamaro, signed Kita-gawa Toyoaki, and dating from the year 1777, when Yoshizawa Iroha, the actor represented, played the part of O Sato. The example in the British Museum—it is otherwise unknown—is exceptionally well preserved, the delicate colouring unfaded. Gracefully designed as it is, the print is not otherwise remarkable. From the three remaining years of Anyei only a few prints by Utamaro survive.

Kiyonaga, on the other hand, was active all through Anyei, though he had not yet matured a really distinctive style. There is a certain strength in his drawing, verging on the heavy ; but the designs are seldom interesting. Even as late as 1779, which is the date of a set of prints of the Kanda Festival, Kiyonaga's manner seems rather cramped, his types are rather stolid ; there is no hint of the amplitude so soon to come.

# CHAPTER VI

# TEMMEI PERIOD

## JANUARY 24TH, 1781, TO JANUARY 25TH, 1789

The average high quality of the work produced during the eight years of the Temmei period causes it to stand out as perhaps the most brilliant in the annals of the Ukiyoye school. At its commencement, Shunshō was a veteran of fifty-six and still retained his vigour unimpaired; his senior pupil Shunkō, aged thirty-nine, had earned a reputation for strength of brush almost equal to that of his master, of whom he was regarded as the *alter ego*; Toyoharu was in his forty-eighth year and had acquired a working knowledge of European perspective which he applied with no mean skill to a series of *Uki-ye* which were a great advance on the efforts in that direction of Okumura Masanobu and his contemporaries some forty years previously. The words *shim-pan*, meaning new publication, often found prefixed to the titles of Toyoharu's *Uki-ye*, convey the sense of a " new style " differing, as they indeed did, from the old *Uki-ye*. The versatile Shiba Kōkan was prepared by a study of Dutch copper-plate engravings for similar work, to which he gave expression in 1784 by a series of views both native and foreign, printed from copper plates and coloured by hand. Kiyonaga and Utamaro were developing their extraordinary talent at the comparatively early ages of thirty and twenty-nine respectively.

Moreover, a number of capable men made their début about this time; and, what they lacked in originality, they amply compensated for by a uniform excellence of draughtsmanship and harmonious colour-schemes. The women's coiffure changed from the *Tōrō-bin* of Anyei to a fan-shaped style known as *Sensu-bin* or folding fan side-locks, from the ends of which the *binsashi* are often seen to project. The *mage* or queue also underwent some modifications, which may be studied from the various styles shown in a book entitled *Onna Imagawa*, a large volume illustrated by Kitao Shigemasa in 1786, and published in the beginning of 1787. Among the new-comers were Shunshō's pupils Shunrō, Shunchō, Shunzan, Shunjō, Shundō, Shunkyoku, Shunrin, Shunkwaku, Shunsen, and Shunyei; Shigemasa's pupils Masanobu, Masayoshi, and Shunman; Sekiyen's pupil Sekiga; Yeishi and his pupil Gokyō; Bunkyō; Yenshi; Sanchō; Rekisentei Yeiri; Toyokuni I; Toyohiro; and Toyomaru.

SHUNRŌ, known in later years as HOKUSAI, the founder of the Katsushika sub-school, was born in the autumn of 1760 at Honjō, Yedo. His father,

Nakajima Isé, was a mirror-maker. As an infant, he was given the name of Tokitarō, which was changed to Tetsuzō after he had grown into boyhood. At the age of thirteen, he found employment with a bookseller; but the work proving uncongenial and the youngster failing to satisfy the requirements of his employer, he was soon dismissed. In the following year, 1773, he was apprenticed to a wood-block engraver under the name of Nakajima Tetsuzō, and studied the art till 1777, when he was received by Shunshō into his studio as a pupil. On completion of his training, his master bestowed upon him the brush-name of Katsukawa Shunrō. It has been said that in 1785 Shunshō forbade him to use the school appellation of Katsukawa on account of his having studied the methods of the Kanō school. This, however, is open to doubt for the following reason. Out of thirty-six novelettes known as *Kibyōshi* or yellow covers, published from 1780 till 1796 inclusive, we find the signature Shunrō in thirty, the last dated 1796; that of Gumbatei in four, published in 1785 and 1786; that of Kakō in one; and that of Katsu Shunrō in one, published in 1786. If Shunrō had been forbidden the use of Katsukawa as a *geisei* or art surname, in 1785, how is it that in the following year he signed Katsu Shunrō? Further, it is improbable that he would have continued to use the name of Shunrō under the circumstances, and to revert to it after having assumed the *gwamyō* of Gumbatei and Kakō. Shunrō's earliest print that has so far come to light is one of the actor Ichikawa Monnosuke II as the toilet vendor Rokusaburō in the play " Kataki-uchi adana kashiku," produced at the Nakamura theatre in September, 1779. Nearly all of Shunrō's prints, with the exception of a few *Uki-ye* and *Bijin-ye*, one rare example of which is reproduced on Plate 30, are of actors in character. This artist died at the advanced age of ninety in 1849, after an eventful life replete with interest as showing his character and method of work. These matters will be mentioned in their proper sequence later on.

Katsukawa SHUNCHŌ appears to have left Shunshō's studio about the end of Anyei, as his earliest prints date from about 1780. They are usually signed Shunchō gwa, but this signature is occasionally prefixed by the *dō-gō* of Yūshidō and followed by that of a seal reading Chūrin, an abbreviation of his *gō* Chūrinsha. The dates of his birth and death have not yet been discovered; but his work extends to about 1795.

Katsukawa SHUNZAN is recorded in several native biographies as a pupil of Shunyei, which is evidently an error; for he designed prints in 1785 and perhaps earlier. One of these represents the actor Nakamura Nakazō I as Kudo Suketsune in the drama " Yae hitoe koto-no-ha Soga," produced at the Kiri theatre from February, 1785. In this year Shunyei was but eighteen, and could hardly have set up as teacher at so early an age. It is certain, therefore, that Shunshō was his master. Most of his prints are signed " Shunzan " or " Katsukawa—sometimes abbreviated to Katsu— Shunzan " ; but occasionally we find a print signed " Shōyū " or " Izumi Shōyū," a brush-name which he used about 1787. It is highly probable that Izumi was his real family name. His personal name is so far undiscovered, nor are the dates of his birth and death known. He worked from about 1782 till 1798. As far as is known, he designed no *surimono*.

Katsukawa SHUNJŌ, whose real name was Yasuda Ganzō, is likewise stated in some biographies to have been a pupil of Shunyei. He was, however, undoubtedly a pupil of Shunshō, for at the date of his death— August 13th, 1787—Shunyei was only twenty. After quitting Shunshō's studio about 1781, he illustrated *kibyōshi*, and does not appear to have designed prints—all of actors in character—till about 1784–1785. He and Shunyei were relations, but in what degree is not exactly known. The date of Shunjō's birth remains undiscovered.

Katsukawa SHUNDŌ was a pupil of Shunshō, not of Shunyei, who had a pupil of the same name, but with the last character *dō* written differently, with whom he has been confounded. Nothing is recorded of his life. He used the prefix of Rantokusai, and on some of his prints which are scarce and of good quality he used the jar-shaped seal containing the ideograph Hayashi, after the examples of Shunshō and Shunkō. Nearly all his prints are of actors in character in *hoso-ye* format. He worked between 1780 and 1792.

Katsukawa SHUNKYOKU started his career about 1779 as an illustrator of *kibyōshi*, in which he proved himself to have been a clever artist. In these he follows the style of Shigemasa rather than that of Shunshō. He does not appear to have worked beyond 1785–1786 ; and so far only one print —a *hashirakake* signed Katsukawa Shunkyoku and reproduced in the Happer sale catalogue, London, 29th April, 1909, on Plate XX, No. 532— has been recorded. Dates of birth and death are unknown.

Of Katsukawa Shunrin and Shunkwaku we only know that they were Shunshō's pupils and designed a few *hoso-ye* of actors in character during Temmei. These show little power and are unimportant.

Katsukawa SHUNSEN was at work about the middle to the end of Temmei. His prints, all *hoso-ye* of actors in character, are powerfully drawn and beautifully coloured. Unfortunately they are rare. No biographical details are available of these last three artists ; the first two appear, however, on Shikitei Samba's chart of Ukiyoye painters in his *Okusetsu nendaiki*, published in 1802.

Katsukawa SHUNYEI was born in 1768. His real name was Isoda Kyūjirō. While still a boy, he became a pupil of Shunshō, his first work being to illustrate a book entitled *Ōsaka miyage Yamato nishiki*, which appeared in 1782, when he was but fifteen. During Kwansei he established a school of painting. His death took place on December 13th, 1819, in the fifty-second year of his age.

KITAO MASANOBU was both artist and writer, in which latter capacity he usually signed himself Santō Kyōden, though we sometimes find that his designs are similarly signed, especially those for books and albums; as, for instance, the scene in the kitchen of a Yoshiwara house which forms part of a book of poems illustrated in colours and published in the 5th month of Kwansei 7 (June, 1795) under the title *Yomo no haru*. He was born in 1761, his personal name being Iwase (some say Haida) Denzō. His father is said to have been Iwase Nobuaki (or Nobuyoshi, according to another account), who left the service of a certain *Daimyō* in the province of Ise on account of ill-health and settled at Yedo where he married a Miss Ōmori, by whom he had two sons, Kyōden and Kyōzan. At the age of twelve or thirteen, Denzō became a pupil of Shigemasa, who bestowed upon him the brush-name of Kitao Masanobu. His first work is to be found in a *kibyōshi* published in the beginning of 1778, and two years later he assumed as a writer the pseudonym of Santō Kyōden. His prints and illustrated books were published by Tsutajū, with whom he is said to have been employed in return for board and lodging. His famous album of Yoshiwara courtesans (*Yoshiwara Keisei shin bijin awase jihitsu kagami*), published without date, but certainly in February, 1784, and consisting of seven diptychs (undivided), is signed Kitao Rissai (not Shinsai as is sometimes stated) Masanobu. Two fine books in colours of portraits of popular comic poets of the day, under the generic title of " A sackful of humorous poems," appeared in February, 1786 and 1787 (this latter undated), and were both signed Kitao Denzō Masanobu. About 1789, he abandoned the name of Kitao Masanobu, forsaking art for trade and literature, and died on October 27th, 1816.

Kuwagata Keisei was a native of Yedo, born in 1761. As a boy, under the name of Sanjirō, he was trained in painting by Shigemasa, from whom he received the brush-name of KITAO MASAYOSHI. In later years he also used the *gō* of Keisai and Shōshin. His work during Temmei consists of illustrations to *kibyoshi* and of designs for prints, chiefly *Uki-ye*, in all of which he closely followed his master's style. His most original work belongs to Kwansei and Kyōwa periods. He died in 1824.

Kubota SHUNMAN was born at Yedo in 1757. His personal name was Yasubei. He first studied Shikunshi (a collective name for the four plants, the orchid, bamboo, plum, and chrysanthemum), under Kajitori Uwohiko (d. 1782), who gave him the brush-name of Shunman; but the character Shun being the same as that of Shunshō and his pupils, he found it convenient to alter it to another with the same pronunciation. He studied Ukiyo-ye under Shigemasa. He sometimes used the dō-gō of Shōsadō, and wrote novels under the name of Nandaka Shiran. His death occurred on October 30th, 1820. He designed many surimono.

Kinchōdō Sekiga received his training and name from Toriyama Sekiyen, and not from Ippitsusai Bunchō as has sometimes been surmised. His few prints are of actors in character of mediocre quality. No biographical details are known.

YEISHI was of gentle birth, being the eldest son of Hosoda Tokiyuki, a descendant in the third generation of a Minister of Finance in the Tokugawa Government. He was born in 1756 and called Hosoda Jibukyō Tokitomi. He was taught painting by Kano Yeisen and a certain Bunryūsai; and, as an admirer of the nishiki-ye of Torii Kiyonaga, he assumed the gō of Chōbunsai, derived from the first character of Tori-i which is pronounced Chō in Sinico-Japanese and that of Bun-ryū-sai. His work extends from about 1788 till 1800, when he abandoned print-designing for painting. He died August 1st, 1829.

Of his pupil Gokyō nothing is known save that he designed a few prints in his master's style at the end of Temmei and beginning of Kwansei. These are signed Yeishi monjin (pupil) Gokyō. Yeishi had several other pupils during Kwansei.

Sakuragawa Bunkyō is identical with the novelist Sakuragawa Jihinari, a native of Yedo (b. 1767, d. 1830) and variously stated to have been a potter, a scabbard maker, or metal carver. He designed but few prints—only three have so far been seen—at end of Temmei and beginning of Kwansei somewhat after Yeishi's style, but with a distinct personal touch, of whom, however, he does not appear to have been a pupil, though he may have been his fellow-student under Bunryūsai, whence his brush-name. On one print, he appended to his signature the words gi-gwa, the literal meaning of which is "drawn for amusement." Yeishi and his pupils Yeiri and Yeishō, as well as in later years Hiroshige and Kuniyoshi, sometimes used the same expression, which was probably intended to convey in a humilific sense the idea that the picture was of little consequence and not to be taken as serious work. It will be remembered that Kwaigetsudō sometimes used a prefix with much the same intent. Neither this artist nor ANGYŪSAI YENSHI are mentioned in the old biographies or on Samba's chart. Judging from the few *bijin-ye* of the latter, he worked from about 1787 till 1793 inclusive, somewhat in the manner of Yeishi, especially as expressed in that artist's series of Genji triptychs. His colour, however, approximates rather to that of Shunchō. He designed at least one actor-print of Segawa Kikunojō III, dating about 1794, and signed Angyūsai gwa. He was probably identical with Angyūsai Shūdō, this being his earlier name, who illustrated *kibyōshi* in 1779 and 1780 much in the style of Kiyonaga. The *Ukiyo yeshi benran* records a " Mongyūsai Shūdō, who illustrated *kibyōshi* during Anyei," who is doubtless the same artist, *Mon* being a misprint for *An*. Under the name of Shūdō, he designed one or two prints of actors and wrestlers.

Furukawa Sanchō appears on Samba's chart and in *Ukiyoye Bikō*, but with no details. In the middle of Temmei, he illustrated *kibyōshi* and designed a few *nishiki-ye*, in both of which he follows Kiyonaga's style, but with a certain pleasing individuality. He was writer as well as artist, and appears to have been self-taught.

REKISENTEI YEIRI's earliest illustrations are in a *kibyōshi* published in 1788, and shortly after he began to design *nishiki-ye*, which are somewhat in the manner of Yeishi, of whom, however, he was not a pupil. In No. 1 of the Tōkyō edition of *Kono Hana*, he is said to have probably been identical with Busentei Yeiri, who illustrated books in 1802 and 1805. The *Ukiyo yeshi benran* gives him, as a pupil of Yeishun, a pseudonym of the Kyōto artist Hasegawa Mitsunobu ; but as his style has nothing in common with that painter, this statement cannot be relied upon. According to another book, he was a pupil of a Yedo artist whose *gō* were Shosekidō and Rekisentei in affiliation with the Hosoda sub-school. He designed but few prints, and these during the Kwansei period. His one pupil, Rekisentei Sorin, designed two or three prints towards the close of the same period.

TOYOKUNI I was born at Yedo in 1769, the son of a carver of wooden images named Kurahashi Gorobei. His personal name was Kurahashi Kumakichi—changed later to Kichiyemon, and on leaving Toyoharu's studio was given the brush-name of Utagawa Toyokuni. As *gō* he assumed that of Ichiyōsai. He illustrated a *kibyōshi*, his first work, in 1786, and continued such work during the rest of his lifetime. He established a school in the latter half of Kwansei, and died on February 24th, 1825.

Utagawa TOYOHIRO was born at Yedo in 1763 (some say 1773; but former date is certainly correct). His personal name was Okajima Tōjirō, and he became a pupil of Toyoharu about 1782, receiving the brush-name of Utagawa Toyohiro. As gō he used the name of Ichiryūsai. One of his earliest prints is a hoso-ye of the actors Sawamura Sōjūrō III and Osagawa Tsuneyo II as Mohei and O San respectively in the second act of the play " Imagawa honryō mitsuki no iri-bune," produced at the Nakamura theatre from August, 1787. His death occurred in 1828. He established a school during Kwansei, training Hiroshige.

TOYOMARU, whose dates of birth and death are unrecorded but whose work extends from about 1785 to 1796, under the brush-name of Kusamura Toyomaru or Toyomaru alone, was a pupil of Utagawa Toyoharu. According to Ukiyo-ye bikō, he was afterwards called, as a pupil of Shunshō, Katsukawa Shunrō, and though no date is given for this change of name, yet it probably occurred in 1796–1797, when Hokusai had given up that brush-name. How long his career continued after this date is uncertain. As Shunrō, he appears to have mostly designed Uki-ye, somewhat after the style of Toyoharu. One of his earliest prints is that of the actor Osagawa Tsuneyo II as the maid (koshimoto) Magaki in the play " Ō-ichō kongen Soga," produced at the Nakamura theatre from February, 1787. A print signed " Toyomaru gwa " is illustrated in the Hayashi sale catalogue, No. 1057 (Paris, 1902), and is dated 1790, from which his style may be studied.

It is opportune to remark that nearly every artist of the Ukiyoye school, especially during the Anyei, Temmei, and in a lesser degree the Kwansei periods, made their début as illustrators of kibyōshi.

This was due to the number of talented writers of fiction during this time, the demand for whose works with suitable illustrations was insatiable. Edition after edition were published until the blocks were worn out; and yet, in spite of the enormous numbers printed, comparatively few have survived to our day, and generally these are late issues which give but a feeble idea of the artist's ability. When well printed these little volumes afford valuable data in this respect, more especially as most bear dates of publication. A list of books, illustrated by Kiyonaga and prepared by Mr. K. Shibui, is given in Volume II, No. 1, of the illustrated quarterly journal, Ukiyo-ye no kenkyū, published at Tōkyō in November, 1922, and comprises no less than 169 items, 157 of which are kibyōshi mostly issued in Anyei and Temmei. The practice of admixing text and illustration on the same page distinguishes the novelette from the picture-book proper (*Yehon*).

Kiyonaga is the glory of Temmei. He dominates the period, and all the many fine talents beginning to be active during these years were content to be under his influence. And yet when Anyei closed, the immediate future of Ukiyo-ye might well have seemed quite uncertain ; there was little to indicate the advent of any one artist to such supremacy as Kiyonaga within three or four years was to attain.

Koryūsai had given up designing prints, preferring to illustrate books and to paint pictures. But the veteran of the school, Shunshō, was as productive as ever and much of his finest work was still to come. Shunkō, and the younger pupil Shunjō, supported him with great ability. The most famous of all Shunshō's pupils was not to show his real greatness till the 18th century was well over ; Hokusai, at this stage a youth in his early twenties, was still Shunrō and working in Shunshō's studio.

Of the other masters who had worked through Meiwa and Anyei, Toyoharu was now devoted to topography and perspective. The study of linear perspective fascinated him as it had fascinated Piéro della Francesca in Italy centuries before. He delighted in long vistas and the recession of long buildings. But these studies, learnt from Europe, did not prevent him from remaining Japanese. He pictures the sea-coast under a night of stars, yet shows us clearly defined in the distance, and larger than life, all the incidents of the battle of Ichi-no-tani. One of his prints, copied from some European source, depicts the ruins of Rome.

Shigemasa, as we have seen, after doing brilliant things and seeming to have the leadership of Ukiyo-ye within his grasp, had not cared seriously to pursue his successes in the domain of the *nishiki-ye*. None the less he was the most influential master in Anyei. Kiyonaga certainly appeared the likeliest to succeed to his place, but much of his activity was given to book-illustration, and in the designing of single-sheets, though he had shown vigour and energy, he had given as yet, in 1781, no proofs of overwhelming power. And suddenly in the first years of Temmei there was to appear a brilliant youth, who, ten years Kiyonaga's junior, challenged all Ukiyo-ye by his gifts. This was Shigemasa's pupil Masanobu. It may be worth while to mention in passing that some of Shigemasa's unsigned prints, of the type described above, p. 78, have often been attributed to Masanobu. This is manifestly impossible, since the fashions are those of a time when Masanobu was a boy and had not begun to publish. Masanobu, when he entered the field, lost little time in tentative experiments. He was only twenty-three when the now famous picture-book of *Autographs of Yoshiwara Beauties* dazzled the Yedo public. We will return to this in a moment. But let us first see what other possible rivals were in the field. Only one year younger than Kiyonaga, Utamaro was so gradual in developing his personal style that one is apt to conceive of him as belonging to the next generation. We know no print of his earlier than 1777, and during the remaining years of Anyei he does not seem to have produced much. But early in Temmei, in the years 1781–1783, he published some diptychs which, though still superficially under the influence of Shigemasa, are of extraordinary beauty and originality. The finest of these is the diptych reproduced (Pl. 8). It is not quite the Utamaro with which we are familiar ; but in essential qualities it owes nothing to preceding masters ; it reveals already his genius for figure-design, and considered simply in itself is an enchanting masterpiece. The variation in repetition of the swinging lines make a beautiful rhythm running through it ; and the strong upright of the post near the centre, repeating the less definite upright lines of the figures, enhances the delicacy of the girlish form sitting on the boat's prow and clinches the whole composition. Note the value, too, of the outline of the wide sun-hat worn by the girl who stands foremost on the landing-stage. And how charming is the invention of the girl's face peeping through the young man's diaphanous dress which she has caught in her hand for a veil ; how beautifully drawn the movement of the foot of the girl in the centre ! Here there is a subtlety, a complexity, made to look simple, natural and spontaneous, such as no other artist of Ukiyo-ye could rival. Beside such work as this, all that Kiyonaga had done in Anyei seems almost crude and clumsy. This surely, one might have said, was the coming man of Temmei. And yet Utamaro, with all this marvellous gift, was content to bide his time, and made no effort during Temmei to dispute the paramount place with Kiyonaga. He had not caught the public taste ; and when Kiyonaga triumphed, Utamaro adopted something from his style.

But in 1783 it was a question whether Kiyonaga or Masanobu was to win the leadership. The great masters of Ukiyo-ye were few of them precocious. Masanobu is exceptional in attaining independence at so early an age. He was two years younger than Hokusai, but Hokusai, under his name of Shunrō, was quite inconspicuous now and for many years to come. At this time he was designing actor-prints in the style of

Shunshō, showing occasionally a vigour equal to his master's, as in the *hoso-ye* diptych of Danjūrō with his foot upon a great axe and Hangōrō with a skull in his hands.

He also designed small idylls, of no special note, and a few *uki-ye* in the manner of Toyoharu.[1] One print of a group of beauties is reproduced on Plate 30, and is noteworthy because it has hitherto always passed as Shunshō's work. It is usually found, indeed, with a signature of Shunshō on it ; but this is a forged addition. The earlier state which we reproduce has no signature, but is sealed *Shunrō*. Its date is about 1781, and it is one of Hokusai's earliest colour-prints.

Masayoshi, another pupil of Shigemasa, was the same age as Masanobu, but he again is one of those whom we associate with a later generation, since though he designed some attractive prints in Temmei, his most characteristic work is in the books that he published in Kwansei and later.

We return then to Masanobu. Nothing quite like the seven large double-page designs of the *Yoshiwara Keisei Shin Bijin Awase Jihitsu Kagami* had been seen before. The prints are not like the usual diptychs, each sheet of which can stand as a separate design, though completing each other. The compositions are indivisible. From the point of view of subject, the prints are interesting. Each depicts a rival pair of beauties, with their younger attendants ; and the set of prints takes its title from the autograph poems engraved on each in the handwriting of the girls portrayed, mostly poems from the classic anthologies. Nothing could more vividly illustrate the atmosphere of culture and refined accomplishment in which these prisoners of the Flowery Quarter lived. In design and colour also the prints are remarkable. It was as if Masanobu had intended to show the world the utmost resources of the colour-printer. Never before had so many colour blocks been used. Every available tint seems to be used, if only for some small detail of pattern here and there. The figures are related to another in a system of curving lines, into which the mosaic of colour is fitted, with a rather bewildering effect, since the over-complicated pattern seems almost as if it had been separately designed, and distracts from the drawing of the human forms. The feminine types derive from Shigemasa, but the faces are longer and heavier.

Imposing and novel as these prints must have seemed on their first appearance, they cannot rank as masterpieces. The intricate colour-

---

[1] Shunshō, Hokusai's master, also designed *Ukiye*. One example in the British Museum, a view of Enoshima, is remarkable for having cast shadows. The date of the print is uncertain, but it was probably made in Anyei.

schemes are not really mastered and harmonized. The synthesis is imperfect. But though altogether inferior to Utamaro's diptychs of the time, they were more striking to the ordinary eye. They were more of a novelty also; and in Ukiyo-ye novelty counted immensely.

One thing impresses at once, and that is the majestically tall proportions of the principal figures. This was something new; for during Anyei the fashionable type of figure had been rather short than tall.

Was it Masanobu or Kiyonaga who set the fashion for these types of women of grand build and stature? It is certain that by 1783 Kiyonaga had matured the special type for which he is famous and which was to be the model for all Temmei. But his finding of this splendid type seems to have been strangely sudden. The profusion of prints in this stately style which now broke forth came with a rapidity that reminds one of Harunobu's swift expansion of genius at the beginning of Meiwa. Kiyonaga's work in Anyei, often vigorous but often dull, does not prepare us for this explosion. The print of the "Child Caligraphist" which we reproduce is fortunately dated "the year of the Hare," that is, 1783, the same date which is found on one of the prints of Masanobu's famous picture-book. This print is in Kiyonaga's fully formed and masterly style in its earliest phase. It is possible that other prints in the style preceded this, but if so, hardly by more than a year. Was it Masanobu who challenged Kiyonaga's sudden putting forth of his full powers? Or was it Masanobu who stimulated Kiyonaga's genius to its rich outburst? Or was it coincidence merely? In any case the two must have seemed for the moment, in these early years of Temmei, as close rivals.

But the rivalry was not to last. Masanobu, like Shigemasa, did not follow up his success. He produced at least one masterpiece, again a double-page composition rather than a diptych, the group of holiday-makers in an iris garden listening to a cuckoo. This rare piece would be one of the prints most sought by collectors, if the chance of acquiring it were not so remote. It is reproduced by Ficke, Plate XXXIV, and in the *Paris V.I. Catalogue*, Plate XLIX, from the only two copies known at present. But after this time Masanobu practically disappears, to become more famous as a writer under the name of Kyōden.

Certainly Kiyonaga altogether surpassed Masanobu in the creation of a beautiful feminine type. In Masanobu's type the face is larger, the nose longer, the chin squarer, and the whole countenance heavier than in Kiyonaga's type, which, as we see in the print of the "Child Caligraphist," was developed originally from Koryūsai's later type, but has become sweeter and more expressive, with rounded cheek and a small chin.

The prints of the series *Tōsei Yūri Bijin Awase*, three of which are illustrated in the *V.I. Catalogue*, Plates XIX and XX, are possibly very slightly earlier in date. But the transition from Kiyonaga's Anyei style seems in any case to have been abrupt. From a print of Shunshō's which can be dated 1780, we see that the coiffure of that year shows no sign of the coming change to the mode we associate with Temmei. It is the same as in Kiyonaga's series of the Kanda Festival (p. 80) which dates from 1779. The change must have come, therefore, in 1781 or 1782.

To the first years of Temmei we may refer some pillar-prints, the most famous of which, and the most beautiful, is the girl walking against the wind under wistaria blossom, with a black hood pulled over her head. There is a walking figure in the *Tōsei Yūri Bijin Awase* which is very close to this. In these pillar-prints Kiyonaga seems to rejoice in a new-found power of line, using his brush with a confident force, such as Ukiyo-ye had not known since the days of the Primitives. Just as Harunobu at the opening of Meiwa found his genius as a colourist released, so with the first years of Temmei Kiyonaga realizes for the first time, and exults in, his splendid draughtsmanship.

This air of joyous and serene confidence in power marks the great array of prints which were now to come. All through Temmei the type of face changes little, though in the later prints the line of the cheek is a little less rounded than in the prints of 1783, and the chin is a little fuller. The fashion of hair-dressing also does not change in essentials. At the beginning of the period the side-wings are widely extended, the bow of the *bin-sashi* being flattened, and the ends of it showing beyond the hair. Then the *bin-sashi* becomes more curved, and by 1789, the end of the period, the side hair is dressed in smaller, blunter, and compacter shape, the ends of the *bin-sashi* being hidden. The only decided change is in the varying proportions of the figures. These are supremely tall and stately in the earlier years, about 1784, but gradually decline to normal proportions.

As if he had shed all hampering influences and begun life anew, Kiyonaga now created one masterpiece after another. Two famous sets of prints stand out above the others; the set called *Fūzoku Azuma no Nishiki*, " Brocade of the East in Fashion," and the set of twelve diptychs called *Minami Jūnikō*, " Twelve Months of the South." Some of the former set are known to be diptychs; perhaps all were; but most are now known only as single sheets.

The most famous of these prints have been reproduced many times and are familiar to students. In the first set is the " Murasame and Matsukaze," the sisters of the *Nō* play who turn to each other as they walk by the seashore carrying salt-pans slung from yokes over their shoulders, and with long hair unbound. The British Museum collection has Kiyonaga's original sketch for this print, differing in details from the final design. Such studies are extremely rare, not having been thought worth preservation, as is shown by the fact that this sketch was found inside the binding of an album when it was taken to pieces. It had been used merely as stuffing. The print is typical of Kiyonaga's new style of simple grandeur. No trivial accessories, no variegation of colour, no intricacy of pattern, interfere with the serene dignity of these two figures, so admirably placed within the frame. In others of the series we find a group of three or four figures placed in processional order, and relying on the majestic effect of vertical lines. In one print a family is taking a young child to visit a temple, and the little girl lifted high in her stiff ceremonial dress on the shoulders of a man-servant varies the vertical composition only by an added emphasis. This processional arrangement is typical of Kiyonaga. He gets monumental effects out of it, though it was soon to become monotonous. Two of the finest prints of this set are less stiffly arranged. In one, perhaps the grandest of all, three women have just come from the bath, with loose wraps about them. Two stand together, one with her firm bust showing bare under the dress cast negligently over her shoulders ; the third squats on the ground and is trimming her toe-nails. In the other, less imposing but more charming, two girls are buying from a seller of miniature trees, and in the foremost girl's face there is a vivacity, a lift of the eyebrows, and smiling playfulness (found also in some of the *Tōsei Yūri Bijin Awase* series) which surprise us. Kiyonaga rarely invents motives beyond the simplest to relate his figures to one another ; and his most characteristic women are proudly impassive. He is content with the solid pose of his majestic forms, as if to bend or sway them toward or away from each other would mar their dignity. But out of these so simple harmonies what a magnificent whole he creates, consummate in its equilibrium and authority ! If his resources as a designer are strangely limited and easily exhausted, within those limits he is perfect, and he is a splendid draughtsman. His superb feminine forms, calmly sweet in a stable world and breathing the unconscious air of perfect health, are drawn with no parade of power, but impress as by the sensation of actual presence, so wonderfully does the contour evoke the shape of the rounded limbs that it encloses. This discovery of a type at once winning and stately, a type founded on reality but imaginatively enhanced so as to be in truth an ideal creation, is one of Kiyonaga's great achievements.

It is an impersonal art, this; no violence of expression or of restless line disturbs the poise of these harmoniously moving or statue-like goddesses, or the adjusted folds of their garments. Only at times in the extreme emphasis of stature does the artist seem to yield to some inner emotional pressure, as in that print from the *Minami Jūnikō* series (the second sheet of the diptych has not been traced) where two girls crouch on the floor deciphering a letter by the light of the paper-screened lantern, while above them towers against the window a woman majestically tall and pensive, looking out on grey night over the sea, and the half-moon in the sky, and the flares of fishing-boats like sparks on the remote water. This wonderful print anticipates by its sense of mystery in simple things and by the beauty of its strange proportions some of the later creations of Utamaro. But it is exceptional.

The most famous and familiar of the series of twelve diptychs *Minami Jūnikō*, one of the classic masterpieces of Ukiyoyé, is the holiday group on a balcony overlooking Shinagawa Bay. It is a composition simple in its symmetry. At the left is one standing woman immensely tall; at the right two girls standing close together. In the centre are four seated or kneeling figures, a youth and three girls, arranged in groups of two. It is an hour of peace and idleness; one of the seated girls touches her *samisen*, and the imagined notes of music seem to hold the group in happy stillness; only the gesture of the girl, crouching beside the youth and holding up a lacquer wine-cup as she turns her face to the woman behind her, lends a touch of animation. But of what value to the composition is that central space of air and prospect of seashore! What largeness and infinitude seem drawn in among those idle figures! Here is Kiyonaga's new gift to Ukiyo-ye; completeness, "envelope." The landscape is no mere adjunct, it is an integral part of the conception. There is no effort at realism, no colour in the sky; the evocation is made by the simplest means; but one smells the seaweed on the sands and the salt moist air of evening at low tide, one seems to hear faint voices from the distant groups of people near the little cluster of stranded fishing-boats.

Of Kiyonaga's "processional" composition the happiest example is the night-piece in this series, where a youth and six girls are strolling out with lanterns in the dusk. He repeated this kind of design indefinitely, but was never inspired to so absolute a felicity as here.

Of the same date as this series, but apparently not belonging to it, is a diptych of " Evening on the banks of the Sumida " which rivals and perhaps surpasses the " Shinagawa " we have described. Again the motive is of the simplest. In one sheet are two girls standing by a low bench on which a third is seated. In the other sheet three other girls are taking leave of them to walk along the river bank, the breeze blowing their skirts into long curves. The contrast of gentle action with stillness is just enough to animate as with a musical slow movement this enchanting design. The tall figures with their beautiful calm carriage are breathing creatures ; hands and feet are drawn with sensitive sureness and exquisite truth to natural movement. It is as if one felt the actual touch of the two clasping hands of the girls who move away. And the river, the quiet even ing, the little houses opposite ; it is magical how it is all brought to our senses with such simple means.

Look, again, at the print we reproduce in colours (it is the left-hand sheet of a diptych, or possibly a triptych), and note the little procession of people moving along the ridge of the high green bank above the temple gate. The clear wash of light and air is round them. In this sense of out-of-doors atmosphere, and the relation of human figures to their natural surroundings, Kiyonaga is without a rival. But the figures remain always the dominating interest.

Temmei is the period of great triptychs. It has generally been assumed that these triptychs on the large scale were Kiyonaga's invention. We have already noted at least one triptych on this scale by Shunshō which dates from about 1770 ; so it was not a new thing. But certainly the form had never been exploited before as it was by Kiyonaga, and it was par-ticularly congenial to his spacious compositions of outdoor scenes. Boating parties on the Sumida gave him motives for a number of splendid triptychs, notably the landing from a pleasure boat, in which the great black prow tells so finely. And the groups of figures are beautifully harmonized with their landscape setting. An extraordinary air of happiness seems to pervade these serene and poised designs. There are other triptychs of the close of Temmei which we shall mention later. Splendid as they are, none of these triptychs quite reaches the absolute felicity and concentration of the masterpieces in diptych form, some of which have been described above.

Small wonder that Kiyonaga's triumphant works of early Temmei took the public captive ; and small wonder that all the rising generation of artists modelled their style as closely as they could on his. Even Utamaro assimilated his types to those of his victorious contemporary, though his design remained entirely his own. During Temmei perhaps the finest, certainly the most distinctive, work of Utamaro's is to be found in the wonderful *Book of Insects and Flowers*, published in 1788. The originality and felicity of the designs are matched by the exquisite truth of the drawing, the inconceivable delicacy of the printing. The book surpasses everything of the kind ever done.

Only one master remained in his old paths : the veteran Shunshō. He followed the fashion indeed when the extravagantly tall figures were in vogue ; but he continued to design his actor-prints in the old *hoso-ye* shape, and his small triptychs were still of single figures, each on one of the three sheets and only occasionally so connected that the composition suffers by the division. It is true that we find prints in the larger form (*ōban*) done by Shunshō. These are sometimes of heroic subjects, and in that case one may suspect them to be usually parts of triptychs published probably during Anyei, like the early one already mentioned (p. 65). There is also a series of large prints of actors in the green-room ; and a few large prints of groups of actors on the stage.

The example by Shunshō's able pupil Shunkō, which we reproduce, dates from 1785. But the fine example of Shunshō's late work which we illustrate dates from about 1791, after Temmei was ended, and proves that even at this late date a little before his death and when Kiyonaga's career as a print-designer was virtually over, Shunshō kept to the old traditions of his school. The point may be emphasized, since it is often assumed that during Temmei Shunshō had given up prints for painting.

Kiyonaga became head of the Torii line when Kiyomitsu died in 1785, and did not neglect the traditions of his house, which had always been connected with the theatre.

During Meiwa he had, as we saw, designed actor-prints in the Kiyomitsu style, rather feebly ; but during Anyei he seems to have left this field almost entirely to Shunshō. In Temmei, however, he resumed the designing of actor-prints, usually triptychs, with a row of musicians or reciters at their desks behind the players. They are massive and imposing, but one returns with more satisfaction to Shunshō's quiet dignity and fine colour. We reproduce (Pl. 32) one of a rare set of actors in private life, which show Kiyonaga's emphatic power to advantage.

Those of Shunshō's pupils who kept to theatrical prints were but slightly affected by Kiyonaga. The one who showed most original talent was the young Shunyei. In 1787, when he was twenty, he published a large head of Ichikawa Yaozō III as Sukeroku in the play " Ō-ichō Kongen Sōga," produced in Yedo in the February of that year. This is in the Shunshō style, on a large scale, and is very forcibly drawn. It is remarkable as the earliest known example of this type of print, the large heads of actors, which have generally been assumed to have originated with Sharaku. But it is not the only example, as we shall see in the next chapter, which can be dated before 1794, when Sharaku first appeared.

But apart from Shunshō and certain of his school, the whole of Ukiyo-ye fell under Kiyonaga's spell. Even some of Shunshō's most gifted pupils altogether forsook their allegiance, and their work is entirely associated with the Kiyonaga manner. This was especially the case with Shunchō, who follows Kiyonaga's footsteps like a shadow. We reproduce (Pl. 28) a most charming example of Shunchō's little-known early work, when he was emerging from Shunshō's influence. It dates from about 1785.

During the latter part of Temmei Shunchō designed a great number of single sheets, diptychs, triptychs, and pillar-prints all so close to Kiyonaga in style that at times one might attribute a print of his to the greater master were it not for the signature. He was not so forcible a draughtsman, though by no means lacking in vigour, especially in some of his *hashira-ye*. But he was eminently graceful and sensitive; and he was a delicate and distinguished colourist, as can be seen from the very rare and unusually shaped oblong print reproduced (Pl. 10). This could never be mistaken for a Kiyonaga, and not merely on negative grounds. What Shunchō would have achieved had he worked on independent lines we can only conjecture.

Shunzan was another of Shunshō's deserting pupils. For some years he produced actor-prints in the Katsukawa style, and scenes from history; then, going over to Kiyonaga's group he surrendered entirely to that master, and in his manner designed many a delightful print. The triptych of the "Pilgrimage to Ise" and the "Niwaka Procession" are well-known examples. But his dependence on Kiyonaga was complete.

Shunman, who came over from the Kitao school, was more original. His prints are comparatively few, but have a peculiar charm. He occupies in Temmei something of a similar position to that of Bunchō in Meiwa; and his relation to Kiyonaga resembled that of Bunchō to Harunobu.

Working in the style of the dominant master, each of these artists had a very personal quality; and in both there is more of emotional atmosphere than is usual in Ukiyo-ye. Shunman is especially noted for prints designed in a harmony of silvery grey and black, with a few delicate notes of colour. His most important work, a six-sheet composition of "The Six Tamagawa," is in this manner ; only a sober green and sparse touches of pink relieving here and there the prevailing black and grey. His figures and draperies prolong themselves in sinuous subtleties of line ; there is a touch of the fantastic in his designs. A rare but well-known triptych of his represents a party going home in groups at night from a poetry-class. As is usual in Japanese art, the darkness is not allowed to prevent our seeing everything clearly ; but here everything is in the black or grey of night except just where the lantern-light is cast and shows up what it illuminates in colour. This, of course, was no tentative naturalism, but a playful caprice that amused the artist. Shunman's frequent avoidance of colour was perhaps wise, for in his rare full-coloured designs he was not altogether happy in his control of vivid tints, finely composed though they are.

The prints of Temmei, apart from actor-prints, can rarely be dated precisely. But one diptych of Utamaro's can be referred to the year 1788. This is a print depicting a party at Mio-no-Matsubara, the legendary scene of the angel's dance in the famous Nō play, the " Robe of Feathers," and celebrating the admission of a saké merchant Shurakusai (himself portrayed in the print) to a club of poets called " The Yoshiwara Circle." It has all the delicacy of Utamaro's draughtsmanship at this period—it was in 1788 that the *Insect Book* was published—and is exquisitely composed.

Of about the same date are two fine triptychs of Kiyonaga's ; and we find that by now Kiyonaga's proportions have become normal. These triptychs are the " Visit to Enoshima " and the " Cherry Blossom at Asuka-yama." The first is reproduced in the *V.I. Catalogue*, Plate XXV, the second in Gookin's *Japanese Prints and their Designers*, page 36. Kiyonaga's drawing of simple action and gesture, as in the maid tying her mistress's sandals in the " Enoshima," is as masterly as ever ; and in both the out-of-door atmosphere is wonderfully realized. The " Asuka-yama " is notable for its daring colour ; the pinks and blacks of the dresses stand out against broad masses of vivid green grass. No modern impressionist of Europe has, with all the contrast of shadow, more successfully evoked the splendour of spring sunshine among the blossoming trees.

Utamaro's diptych, and other prints by him of the same date, like the " Women drying clothes on a roof," are more learned and subtle in design ; but the Kiyonaga triptychs with their greater amplitude and simpler harmony were no doubt likelier to capture the public. Kiyonaga's prestige was by now enormous. Besides Shunchō, Shunzan, and Shunman, the latest recruits to Ukiyo-ye joined in imitation of his style. These were

Yeishi, Toyohiro, and Toyokuni; the last hardly out of his teens. Kiyonaga, indeed, might have complained that

> *Most can raise the flowers now*
> *For all have got the seed.*

So easily, it seemed, this whole generation stepped into possession of his
felicities. The reflection may occur that something was lacking to these
felicities if they were so delightfully imitable. In fact, what these younger
artists were able to imitate, with more or less of personal variation, so
successfully, was, chiefly, the feminine type which Kiyonaga had created.
Nor was it difficult for an able draughtsman, even if with little original
gift for composition, to group these tall and gracious figures with much of
Kiyonaga's dignity. For the master's resources in relating figures to each
other and to the framing space seem to have been exhausted with the
splendid masterpieces of the earlier years of Temmei. His motives
repeat themselves again and again, and are further repeated by his followers.
The absence of mannerism in Kiyonaga's work of the Temmei time, its
love of normal beauty, preserved these followers from carrying any one
feature to excess or copying the master's weaknesses merely. They were
besides men of real talent and sensitive hand, and the youngest of them
were soon to develop styles of their own.

# CHAPTER VII

# KWANSEI PERIOD

## JANUARY 26TH, 1789, TO FEBRUARY 12TH, 1801

Owing to physical incapacity, death, or some other cause, many of the foremost artists of Temmei gradually disappeared during the Kwansei period. Shunkō, paralysed in his right side, had perforce to quit his calling during 1791; and, after shaving his head in token of retirement from the world, he entered the monastery of Zenshōji at Asakusa (Zena-pukuji is believed to be a biographical error).

Shunshō died on January 22nd, 1793. Kiyonaga, for some unknown reason, practically gave up print-designing soon after 1790 when about forty years of age. Kitao Masanobu, too, almost entirely abandoned art for literature at the early age of twenty-nine. Shunman, when about thirty-four, devoted his talents to composing *kyōka* and to designing *surimono* and book illustrations, especially *orihon* or folding albums. Masayoshi, at about the same time as Masanobu, turned his attention to illustrating books mostly with rapid drawings of considerable ingenuity known as *ryaku-gwa-shiki*. Shigemasa, Toyoharu, Shunchō, and Shunzan designed very few prints after Temmei. Thus the depletion was serious; and, had it not been for the two great geniuses, Utamaro and Sharaku, coupled with men like Yeishi and his pupils, Chōki, Toyokuni, Shunyei, Kiyomasa, and other talented but less known artists, the Kwansei period would have anticipated the decadence that overtook Ukiyo-ye in the beginning of the 19th century. As it was, the combination of talent enumerated above, and especially that of Utamaro, Chōki, and Sharaku, resulted in work no whit inferior to, and certainly as important as, that of Temmei. Moreover, a number of *orihon* or folding albums containing coloured woodcuts that rank as high as the colour books of Anyei and Temmei, already mentioned, were issued by Tsutajū at the commencement of this period. Utamaro contributed the *Waka Yebisu*, 1 vol. with 5 colour-plates, undated, c. 1789; *Kyōgetsubō*, 1 vol. with 5 colour-plates, 8th month of 1789; *Ginsekai*, 1 vol. with 5 colour-plates, 1790; *Fugenzō*, 1 vol. with 5 colour-plates, 1790; *Shiohi-no-tsuto*, 1 vol. with 8 colour-plates, undated, c. 1790; and *Momo chidori kyōka awase*, 2 vols. with 15 colour-plates, undated, c. 1791. In the Hayashi sale catalogue (Paris, 1902), and elsewhere, 1786 is given as the date of *Waka Yebisu*, but the album bears no date nor does the style warrant the ascription of so early a date. Kurth (*Utamaro*, Leipzig, 1907, page 303) gives c. 1780 for the date of *Shiohi-no-Tsuto*, though the style of the figure subjects of the first and last plates is clearly that of early Kwansei. Kitao Masayoshi contributed the *Yehon Kwachō kagami*, alternative title *Kai-haku raikin zu-i*, 1 vol. with 12 coloured plates (10 of birds and flowers, and 2 of Chinamen), published by Gungyokudō Matsumoto Zembei in 1789, which has been sometimes wrongly attributed to Utamaro. Though this book is of great artistic beauty and a triumph of skilful engraving and printing, the designs are not original, but were copied by Masayoshi from paintings made by Bakushin Seki Yeibun in 1788.

Another book, published by Yamazaki Kimbei in 1 vol. dated 1789, entitled *Sanjū Bok'kasen* (alternative title *Kasen Kumo-ino Hana*) and illustrated in colours by Shunshō, is certainly the finest presentation of the celebrated thirty-six poets in existence. Each of these volumes in the original issue with the colours fresh and untarnished forms a precious heritage of the Kwansei period.

Such biographical details as are at present available of the new-comers are recorded below.

Chōkōsai YEISHŌ, Ichirakutei YEISUI, Choyensai YEISHIN, YEIRI I, YEIJU, YEIRYŪ, YEICHŌ, and YEIRI II were pupils of Yeishi, and worked at various dates during Kwansei from about 1793 much in the style of their master with more or less pronounced individuality, especially noticeable in the work of the first-named four. Dates of birth and death of these artists are unknown. It is remarkable that, though Yeishi had, as we have seen, pupils, yet neither he nor they used a school appellation such as Katsukawa, Utagawa, Katsushika, and so on. It is, therefore, not strictly correct to speak of the Hosoda school in referring to this group. Their prints, many of which are signed " So-and-so gi-gwa " (drawn for amusement), lead one to conjecture that they considered themselves rather as amateurs than professionals. They eschewed the stage and Uki-ye, though Yeishi himself frequently added as backgrounds to his pictures little vistas of natural scenery—a practice common to his contemporaries Kiyonaga, Shunchō, Shunzan, and Utamaro, and that admirably served to break the monotony of figure-subjects.

Torii KIYOMASA was the son and pupil of Kiyonaga. He was born 1777; the date of his death is unknown. He worked from 1793 to 1795 inclusive; but very few of his prints have survived. His two best are bust portraits on white mica ground, signed " Torii Kiyomasa gwa," of Takashima O Hisa and Naniwaya O Kita, which were published by Tsuruki (Tsuruya Kiyemon) about 1793, and in which the influence of

Kiyonaga is striking. These two girls were tea-house waitresses famed, from about 1789 to 1793 inclusive, as Yedo's most popular beauties.

Utamaro and Shunchō also drew their portraits which were printed in the same technique. The tea-houses (*Mizu cha-ya*) in which Hisa and Kita served were situated at Ryōgoku and Asakusa respectively, whence they were called after the parlance of the wrestling-ring " Champions of the East and West," Ryōgoku being east of Asakusa. On one of Utamaro's prints, published about 1790 by Marubun (Maruya Bunyemon), in which a young girl presents O Kita with a cup of tea, whilst a matron seated on a bench, fan in hand, looks on, are inscribed three poems, from one of which we may gather her immense popularity. Its meaning is as follows : " Rival guests come in crowds to Naniwaya, where through white plum blossoms is wafted the fragrant scent of infused tea."

Kiyomasa sometimes signed as the "humble son" (*segare*) of Kiyonaga.

Tōshūsai SHARAKU was the brush-name of a *Nō* actor named Saito Jūrōbei, formerly in the service of the Daimyō of Awa. Without apparently any instruction in drawing or painting and relying on his natural talent he suddenly appeared in 1794 under the ægis of Tsutajū (Tsutaya Jūsaburō), and bewildered the Yedo public with a succession of portraits of actors in character which were looked at askance and regarded as exaggerations almost amounting to caricatures of their favourites.

Happily connoisseurs were not wanting who recognized their merit, and it is to the discrimination of these men that we owe the prints that have come down to us. Despite this cold reception, Tsutajū, with his innate perception of genius, continued to publish Sharaku's work until he was compelled by continued losses to discontinue after 1795, when Sharaku disappeared. His death occurred in Kyōwa 1 (1801) when he was known as Yūrin, under which brush-name he is said to have executed some oil paintings, though none have so far come to light.

Dr. Julius Kurth, in his work on Sharaku published in 1910 (second edition in 1922), attempts to prove that he was at work as early as 1787, and reproduces a print signed Sharaku gwa of the actor Onoye Matsusuke in the rôle of Otoha Obā which he attributes to that year. As a matter of fact, this actor took this part in the play " Oyama Beni-tsui no Hademono," produced at the Kawarasaki theatre from the 5th month of Bunkwa I (June–July, 1804). Moreover, a glance at the print will convince one that it is not the work of Sharaku at all. Probably a dishonest tradesman imprinted Sharaku's signature upon the unsigned work of another artist, and fraudulently passed it as a genuine Sharaku.

Kurth also reproduces a genuine Sharaku portraying a wrestler-boy named Daidōzan Bungorō, which he attributes to the year 1790. On the face of this print is an inscription giving details of the young prodigy, and the words *U no hassai*, which he interprets as meaning that Daidōzan was born in the year of the Hare (*U*) and that the portrait was drawn when the boy was eight years old (*hassai*); further, that as the year of the Hare referred to was 1783 the print must have been drawn in 1790—that is, eight years later, according to Japanese reckoning. But this interpretation is incorrect; for the words merely mean that the portrait was drawn in the year of the Hare when the boy was eight years of age, not that he was born in the year of the Hare. Chōki and others also drew portraits of Daidōzan, inscribed " Year of the Tiger, seven years "; so that, if we follow Kurth's interpretation, the unfortunate prodigy was also born in the year of the Tiger (1782), an obvious absurdity. But, apart from this, Daidōzan's birth took place on the 15th day of the 2nd month of Temmei 8 (22nd of March, 1788), and he was eight years old (according to native reckoning) in 1795, which is the date of the print by Sharaku; that of Chōki's being 1794, when also Utamaro drew his portrait.

In the *Ukiyoye Ruikō* the following account is given of Sharaku's period of activity : " Sharaku, pseudonym Tōshūsai, drew portraits of stage actors from life ; but, because he exaggerated the truth, they were shapeless and hence were unpopular ; he ceased work in a year or two." Though the years are not given, a comparison of Sharaku's work with stage records proves, when identification has been possible (for owing to the incompleteness of these records many rôles are still untraced), that 1794 and 1795 are meant. Unless therefore definite proof is obtained that Sharaku's designs for the wood-block were made in any years but these, it would be unwise to ignore the direct statement of the *Ruikō*.

Attempts have been made by Kurth and others to place a chronological order on Sharaku's prints according to their size, or to their being bust portraits, or full-length figures, etc.; but the identification of many of the rôles proves this to be abortive, as the following selection will show :

A. *Ōban tate-ye*. Two full-length figures, signed " Tōshūsai Sharaku gwa," in which powdered mica has been applied to a background coloured either with pale pink or with white lead mixed with purple.

1. Ōtani Oniji II as Ukiyo Kohei and Ichikawa Omezō I as Tomita Hyōtarō in play " Nihon matsu Michinoku sodachi," at Kawarazaki-za from July 27th, 1794. Kurth, No. 17c (Plate 30).

2. Sawamura Sōjūrō III as Nagoya Sanza and Segawa Kikunojō III as the Keisei Katsuragi in play as above. Kurth, No. 17A (Plate 28).

3. Sakata Hangorō III as Fuwa Banzayemon and Ichikawa Yaozō III as Kosodate no Kwanon-bō in play " Keisei sambon karakasa " at Miyako-za from autumn of 1794. Kurth, No. 17B (Plate 29).

4. Nakayama Tomisaburō as the Shinmachi keisei Umegawa and Ichi-kawa Komazō II as Kamiya Chūbei in play " Yomo no nishiki kokyō no tabiji " at Kiri-za from September 13th, 1794. Vignier, No. 331 (Plate 99).

B. *Ōban tate-ye.* Large head and bust portraits, signed " Tōshūsai Sharaku gwa," on dark mica ground.

1. Matsumoto Kōshirō IV as Banzui-in Chōbei in play " Shimekazari kichi-rei Soga " at Kawarazaki-za from March 21st, 1795. Kurth, No. 201 (Plate 44).

2. Ichikawa Monnosuke II as Katanaya Hanshichi in second act of play " Go-hiiki no hana aikyō Soga " at Kawarazaki-za from January 31st, 1794. Kurth, No. 20G (Plate 40).

3. Onoye Matsusuke as Hakuhatsu (grey-haired) Sasaki Ganryū in play " Kataki-uchi nori-ai banashi " at Miyako-za from September 28th, 1794. Kurth, No. 20N (Plate 46).

4. Morita Kanya IX as Uguisu no Jirosa, a sedan-chair bearer, in same play as the last (3). Kurth, No. 20M (Plate 45).

5. Ichikawa Omezō as Teraoka Heiyemon, about to slay his sister O Karu on her confessing that she had read Lady Kaoyo's letter to Yuranosuke, in play " Chūshingura " at Kawarazaki-za from June 21st, 1795. Kurth, No. 20H (Plate 41).

6. Segawa Kikunojō III as Tsukubane, the wife of Ashiya Dōman in play " Ō-uchi kagami " at Miyako-za from October 13th, 1795. Kurth, No. 20X (Plate 56).

C. *Hoso-ye.* Full-length figure on yellow ground, signed " Sharaku gwa."

1. Sakata Hangorō III as Yawazu no Yadahei.

2. Ichikawa Danjūrō VI as Mimana Yukinori. Kurth, No. 7B, C (Plate 18).

3. Nakayama Tomisaburō as the cowherd O Fude.

4. Ichikawa Yaozō III as the spirit of Chūjō Sanekata.

5. Sakakiyama Sangorō (described by Kurth as Fujikawa Murajirō) as Odai-hime, the daughter of Michinaga. Kurth, No. 7A and No. 8B, C (Plate 19).

6. Nakayama Tomisaburō as Kiri Kamuro, and Ichikawa Yaozō III as Sendai-za Tōhagi-no-Ichi in a *shosa* (mimetic dance). Kurth, No. 6 A, B (Plate 17). All the above from play " Otokoyama O Yedo banjaku " at *Kiri-za kaomise* (opening performance of a play) from December, 1794.

D. *Ōban tate-ye.* Bust portrait on yellow ground with actor's *ya-gō*, *haimyō*, *Jō-mon*, and *Kae-mon*, signed " Sharaku gwa."

1. Yamashita Kinsaku II as Satsuki, the wife of Takeda Mitsuhide, in play " Tokiwa ima kuruwa no hanamichi " at *Kiri-za* from April 29th, 1795. Kurth, No. 15C (Plate 26).

It has sometimes been stated, probably in the belief that Sharaku was at work at an earlier date than 1794, that he was the first to use mica for silvering the background ; also that his profession as a *Nō*-actor influenced his art, since he would have before his eyes the masks worn in performances of the *Nō*; and that he was the first to design prints of large head and bust portraits. As regards the first point, Utamaro used the white mica grounds from 1790, four years before Sharaku's debut. There is, moreover, a *hoso-urushi-ye* by Okumuru Masanobu in the British Museum collection (No. 6, p. 20 of the catalogue by Laurence Binyon, 1916), in which mica is used for the background and was apparently contemporary with the print. We also find touches of mica in three books of the Anyei and Temmei periods.

In respect to the second point the facial expression and the gestures of the actors portrayed by Sharaku, full as they are of intense human emotions, are far removed from the impassive mien of the *Nō*-masks and the studied gestures of the *Nō*-actors. As for the third point, we have recorded (p. 98) a large head by Shunyei dated 1787, and reproduce another of 1790. There is also a large head by Shunkō of Ichikawa Monnosuke II as Soga no Gorō Tokimune in the play " Shunshoku Yedo-ye Soga," produced at the Ichimura-za from February, 1791.

KABUKIDŌ YENKYŌ worked during 1796, for about six months only, in feeble imitation of Sharaku, but the public considered his prints so unskilful that he was forced to give up. No publisher's name, seal, nor trade-mark are as far as is known to be found on his prints. Possibly he was an amateur admirer of Sharaku's genius and strove under this name to emulate him.

Utagawa KUNIMASA was a pupil of Toyokuni. According to *Zōho Ukiyoye ruikō* he worked from the end of Kwansei and during Kyōwa and Bunkwa; and, according to *Ukiyoye Meika Shōden*, he died in the 11th month of Bunkwa 7 (began November 27th, 1810) at the age of thirty-eight. If this was so, he was born in 1773, and was but four years junior to Toyokuni. But these statistics are wholly unreliable for the following reasons. His name appears amongst the contributors to the monument erected by his pupils and others to Toyokuni's memory in mid-autumn, 1828, at which date, therefore, he was still living. There exist, moreover, a print and a *surimono* by him of Danjūrō VII as Sada-mitsu in a *shibaraku* act in the play "Yama-mata-yama," produced at the Ichimura-za in December *kaomise* of 1823, which cannot be by Kunimasa II, who was only born in that year. Judging from his work, he entered Toyokuni's studio about 1794–1795, and began designing prints in the latter year. He continued up to and including 1823, after which he painted actor's masks for sale. His personal name was Jinsuke; but the actual dates of his birth and death remain to be discovered.

Just prior to Sekiyen's death (September 2nd, 1788), Utamaro established the Ki-ta-gawa sub-school, his first pupil being YUKIMARO, a book-illustrator only whose first work (a *kibyōshi* suppressed by the authorities) was published during 1788. A second and a third pupil were TOYOMARO and KIKUMARO. The former designed a few prints signed "Utamaro's pupil Toyomaro" about the first half of Kwansei. Kikumaro worked about 1795 to 1805 inclusive under that studio-name, and then under that of Tsukimaro. He gave up print-designing about 1820. His personal name was Rokusaburō. Dates of birth and death of these three and the following ten artists are unknown. TAMAGAWA SHŪCHŌ was at work in the latter half of Kwansei, as were also his pupils Senchō and Bunrō and Yenjutei Banki, a pupil of Sekiyen. Shūchō designed *Ukiye*, *Surimono*, and *Kwachō*, in addition to figures, the other three confining themselves to the latter.

Sawa SEKKYŌ was a pupil of Tsutsumi Tōrin, and made a few prints of birds, *uki-ye*, and small landscapes about the close of the period and the beginning of the 19th century.

Katsukawa Hōshō and Katsukawa Shunyen, Shunri, and Shunrin were pupils of Shunshō. Hōshō designed a few actor-prints during the first half of the period, the remainder during the latter half. Shunyen, who designed but three actor-prints as up till now recorded, showed uncommon strength, and one regrets that his output was so limited.

Rekisentei Sorin, a pupil of Rekisentei Yeiri, designed a few prints about 1799 to 1802.

Katsukawa SHUNTEI, common name Yamaguchi Chōjūrō, was born in 1770, entered Shunyei's studio about 1795, and during the latter half of Kwansei designed actor-prints in his master's style. Most of his work belongs to the Kyōwa and Bunkwa periods, and consists of battle scenes, warriors, and landscapes, these latter much in the manner of those of Hokujū in which European influence is very striking. He died in 1820.

At the close of 1796, Shunrō changed his name to Hyakurin Hishikawa Sōri, having succeeded to the title as the fourth of the name, the third being the illustrator to the "Segen Jūi" of Kyosen already mentioned, published in 1758. The first two Sōri were painters only. In 1797 he added the name of Hokusai to that of Sōri, and in 1799 assumed that of Kakō without, however, discarding that of Hokusai. During this year he bestowed the name of SŌRI on his pupil Sōji, who thus became the fifth Sōri, and who also used the art surname of Hishikawa. This artist was a designer of *surimono* and book-illustrations. A *surimono* of three ladies playing a game of *Ken*, and dated Spring of the Monkey year 1800, is signed Tawara Sōri, Tawaraya being the name of the two first Sōri. A book entitled *Yehon Shokunin Kagami*, 1 vol., in colours, published by the firm of Tsutajū in the beginning of 1803, is signed "Hishikawa Sōri." The illustrations to this book had already appeared as *surimono* signed Sōri and dated beginning of 1802. This artist was Hokusai's first pupil, when about the close of 1796 the former established a sub-school of his own. Though Hokusai is said to have studied under various masters such as Sumiyoshi Hiroyuki, Shiba Kokan, Tsutsumi Tōrin, and the third Sōri, it is more likely that he studied their styles only, taking a wrinkle from one and a hint from another, and finally forming his own style. An interesting and rare set entitled "Yedo hakkei," eight views of Yedo in the semi-European style, each measuring a little less than $3\frac{1}{2} \times 4\frac{1}{2}$ in., appeared about 1799. On the envelope in which they were issued, besides the above title, are the words "Oranda gwakyō Hokusai sensei no zu," that is, "A pictorial mirror in Dutch style, drawn by the Master Hokusai." They were printed on glazed paper, the colours being indigo, yellow, dark green, and brown, being very similar to those used later by Shuntei, Hokujū, and Shinsai in their semi-European landscapes.

Hokusai himself always maintained that he was "self-made." About 1797, Sōri IV (i.e. Hokusai) began to design *surimono*, the literal meaning of which is "printed thing," but which is in practice the term applied to a style of colour-print quite distinct from the *Nishiki-ye*. At this time he was in very straitened circumstances, but managed to support life by illustrating *kibyōshi*, designing *surimono*, and hawking red pepper and calendars. *Surimono* had, on rare occasions, been printed long before this, one in the British Museum collection being by Moronobu; but the Sōri *surimono* with their delicate tints and exquisite refinement were an innovation. Several of these from the beginning of 1800 are signed " Hokusai, the man who is painting mad " (Gwakyōjin Hokusai). In this connection, it is to be noted that Mr. F. W. Gookin, in his catalogue of the sale of the late Alexis Rouart (New York, February 6th and 7th, 1922), under item 350 : " The apparition of Yamauba," a rôle played by Yebizō (Danjūrō V) on or about November 29th, 1796—is of opinion that as this print is signed Gwa-kyō-jin Hokusai he must have used this signature some years earlier than has hitherto been supposed.

Teisai HOKUBA was a pupil of Hokusai about 1799. His real name was Arisaka Gorohachi, and he was born at Yedo in 1771. His work almost entirely consists of book-illustrations and *surimono*, one of the latter bearing the date of Spring 1800. A very rare and interesting book of poems, privately printed and issued in the 1st month of Kyōwa 2 (1802), and consisting of two volumes entitled *Kyōka maku-no-uchi*, contains several of his illustrations in black and white, typical of his style.

By the close of Temmei period it seemed as if Ukiyo-ye must have exhausted its themes. What new field could be found, when all the daily life of the Yedo populace had been so richly illustrated ? In depicting the outdoor amusements and festivals of the people, with their landscape setting, Kiyonaga and his followers had completed the work of his predecessors. In fact, so far as subject-matter was concerned, Kwansei period was to add little to what had been done before, though Utamaro did bring in new motives, as we shall see. Beautiful women of the day, the reigning beauties of the tea-house and the Yoshiwara, and the famous actors, continued to provide—the former even more than before—endless material for the artists' brushes. But the change now to come was less in the choice of subject-matter than in the method of handling it. The new intensity of Sharaku in theatrical prints, and the new intensity in figure-design by Utamaro, were the two great contributions of Kwansei period to Ukiyoye history. A period of concentration succeeded to a period of expansion. And yet there was expansion, too ; not indeed in the conquest of fresh material, but in the field of design and composition. Here, where

Kiyonaga's range was narrow, Utamaro was inexhaustible. His work is full of surprises, which are not only surprises but felicities. There is no end to his invention in the arrangement of figures. But "arrangement" suggests a cold deliberation, whereas Utamaro's ways of relating one figure to another have the quality of inspiration.

Round about 1790 is a sort of halcyon period. No new force seems to be stirring; an atmosphere of serene harmony reigns. Kiyonaga no longer astonishes by the energy of his creations; that energy is a little waning. He still produces beautiful prints, but is content to let his followers exploit to the full what his earlier efforts had won. Proportions have become normal; the feminine types are sweet and gracious with a lovely natural-ness of mien and gesture. This is a time of numerous noble triptychs. Let us instance a few of special note. As typical of Kiyonaga's latest work at its best we may take the well-known print of girls taking refuge from a shower in a temple porch. It is a happy motive, to be repeated by Utamaro, and again by Toyokuni in the triptych where all the famous actors of the day, each represented in character, take shelter under a great tree. In Kiyonaga's design the charm of natural movement and gesture—note the man wringing out the wet from his sleeve in the left-hand sheet, which is the most fortunate part of the composition—is a delightful element; but how changed are these rather small figures, drawn with a staid line, from the magnificent creatures and the confidently sweeping brush-strokes of ten years before! It is undeniably a tamer phase into which the master passes at the close; almost as if he were harking back to Harunobu. And now, in his ripe manhood, at a time of life when some of the other masters of Ukiyo-ye were only beginning to put forth their greatest powers, Kiyonaga retires.

These Japanese artists disconcert all our Western preconceptions. We should have expected, and would have confidently conjectured, that the works of Kiyonaga's last phase preceded instead of following the triumphant masterpieces which are the glory of Temmei period. They seem like the work of one who is still a little cramped, who has not quite found himself, rather than the work of one whose gift has "gone to seed" from over-production. However it be, we observe no sign of a fresh start or new inspiration in Kiyonaga's last phase. He seems content to close the book, and leave others to continue.

The spirit of this particular time, its mellow and serene charm, finds no more perfect expression than in the series of Genji triptychs by Yeishi. Nowhere is Ukiyo-ye more aristocratic, without ceasing to be itself. The famous amatorious romance of Prince Genji, written by the poetess Mura-saki Shikibu in the 10th century, was the favourite theme for illustration of the painters of the Tosa school. Yeishi, unlike most of the Ukiyoye painters, was trained as a painter in the classic tradition, though it was not to the Tosa but the great rival school of Kanō that he originally belonged. In drawing scenes from a classic romance he came to his theme as one to the manner born. It is true that he translated it into Ukiyoye terms. It is not a direct illustration of the romance that he attempts. Before the title is put, as so often by the print-designers when parodying traditional subjects, the word *Fūryū*, which means "in the mode of the day," "up-to-date," or "popular." But it is not a travesty in the sense which that word has come to connote. There is no satiric, nor even playful intention. It is simply as if the painter said, "Why should the Tosa academicians monopolize our national romance? Ukiyo-ye shall have its Genji, too." And so he draws his illustrations to various chapters, but instead of ladies in the familiar costume of the court ladies in the old *makimono*, with long hair trailing down their backs over stiff brocaded robes, posed in immobile attitudes, we see gracious figures clothed and coiffed in the fashions of the hour. Yeishi's instinct for elegance serves him admirably in these beautiful compositions. The colour is choice and reserved. Reds and pinks are excluded; and a harmony of blacks and greys, foiled by yellow, purple, and green, makes a felicitous scheme. The most beautiful of all these Genji triptychs is the "Concert." It is one of the less rare and best known of the set.

But it is obvious that work like this, belonging to the culmination of a certain style, and characterized by balance and a sort of golden serenity, cannot be repeated indefinitely. Kiyonaga's vein is worked out. A certain glorious phase of Ukiyo-ye is over. What is to follow? Who is to make the fresh start? Just as after Harunobu's reign there is a natural reaction from his almost feminine delicacy and his small forms, so now there is a reaction from the balanced serenity of Kiyonaga—a reaction towards something more poignant and intense.

As we have seen, Kiyonaga's brilliant followers are nearly all, from one cause or another, dropping out. The chief men left are Yeishi, Utamaro, Shunyei, and Toyokuni.

It is true that Shunshō was still alive and still working at the opening of Kwansei. The print reproduced on Plate 32 proves that his powers were as vigorous as ever. It bears the *kiwame* seal and cannot therefore be earlier than 1790, and it represents Ichikawa Monnosuke II, probably as Sagami

Jirō, disguised as a rustic in the play " Iwa-no-hana mine-no Kusunoki," performed in December of that very year.

But in 1793 the master who had worked with such consistent power and distinction all through Meiwa, Anyei, and Temmei, died. We have seen already that the assumption generally made that Kiyonaga had driven Shunshō from the field is unfounded. Not only did Shunshō maintain his own style of actor-print to the end, but that style was continued into Kwansei by his pupils Shunkō and Shunyei. We noticed in the last chapter a large head of Ichikawa Yaozō III by Shunyei, published in 1787. In 1791 appeared a large head of Monnosuke II by Shunkō, a striking portrait drawn with energetic strokes of a full brush. More than a decade before, during Anyei period, Shunkō had designed portrait heads of actors, two on a sheet, either side by side or one above the other ; and probably he was also the first to design the single portrait heads on a large scale. But, so far as we know at present, the print of Yaozō III published by Shunyei in 1787 is the first of these. We reproduce (Pl. 34) a characteristic head by Shunyei of Ichikawa Kōmazō II as Sadakurō, in the play " Chūtō Ryōgoku ori," produced at the Nakamura theatre in the autumn of 1790.

But Shunyei had not abandoned the *hoso-ye* print ; there are designs of his in this form of a later date than this.

Vigorous and dashing, with a fluent brush, Shunyei, still quite young, now took a prominent place ; but he had not sufficient originality to become a real leader. In non-theatrical prints he followed the prevalent style of Temmei. He collaborated at times in single sheets with Shunchō and also with Utamaro.

At some time early in Kwansei, perhaps about 1792, Shunyei designed a series of whole-length figures of actors which are his most distinguished work.

One of these, an actor as Yuranosuke, the chief of the Forty-seven Rōnin, is specially notable for its dignity and the simple beauty of its colour-scheme of dull salmon relieved by green. And much about the same time he published a series of prints of whole-length figures of wrestlers which are immensely forcible and effective. The huge burly figures fill the page, and the contrast of a few chosen colours tells to admiration. Nevertheless, Shunyei, even at his strongest, is always just a little empty.

Yeishi had followed Kiyonaga very closely. Was he strong enough to advance on lines of his own ? As the Kiyonaga influence fades out of his work he appears for a brief time uncertain, then responds to the stimulus of Utamaro's swiftly expanding genius and takes his cue from him, as we shall shortly see.

Toyokuni, in his fine five-sheet print of the " Main Street of the Yoshiwara " and in some contemporary triptychs, shows how cleverly he has assimilated the Temmei style and is obviously a master to be reckoned with, one of the coming men. Yet we feel that the nobility of Kiyonaga's manner is only superficially imitated in his prints. A certain stiffness of composition is a fault that experience can overcome; but in his types, if we compare them with Shunchō's or Yeishi's, not to mention Kiyonaga's, there is a certain callousness of drawing, a lack of delicacy, which betray a latent coarseness of fibre. Toyokuni craves for the emphatic; his art has a need of sharp condiments.

And what of Utamaro? During Temmei his most distinctive work had been the exquisite book of Insects, which we have described, and which he followed up with the Shell book and the Birds and Flowers, published probably in 1790 and 1791. As far as *nishiki-ye* were concerned, he had produced comparatively little. He had not challenged Kiyonaga's supremacy, and had taken something from his style. Kiyonaga's influence over him has been generally exaggerated, however, for his methods of composition were always his own; but it is certainly true that his full range and capacity did not appear till Kiyonaga had retired from the field. It is plain enough that of all the masters now left Utamaro is by far the most original force. He seems in no haste to assert himself, but we have only to compare his prints of this time with those of his compeers to perceive, under the general similarity of style, a very real difference. The triptych in Chinese style, a translation into Ukiyoye terms of a Chinese or Kanō subject, with its groups of figures on a terrace with pavilions on the shores of a lake, makes a sort of parallel to Yeishi's Genji series produced at the same time, and seems to be inspired by a similar intention of asserting the claims of Ukiyo-ye as serious art. But this is but a passing experiment. Two other triptychs of the same time depict scenes on the seashore; one is of girls and children watching Awabi fishers, and the other is a companion piece of holiday-makers fishing with rod and line. In these prints there is a freshness and sweetness that is quite delicious. They are in the style of Temmei, but with a difference. Compared with the work of the other masters of the close of Temmei and the beginning of Kwansei, they have the spirit of spring rather than autumn. One would say they belonged to the youth of a period rather than to its culmination. The Kiyonaga types are here, and the outdoor scene, the sense of fresh air, the landscape setting, are what Kiyonaga had brought into Ukiyo-ye. But again, as before, there is very perceptible that genius for design, for relating figures and groups to one another with natural felicity and freshness, in which Utamaro was to excel all his compeers, his predecessors, and successors; and with that a buoyancy, a playfulness, a sweetness, such as had hardly appeared in Ukiyo-ye since Harunobu. At the same time it must be said that Utamaro has not yet shown the true measure of his gift. Put this early triptych of Awabi fishers beside the famous masterpiece of the same subject which he was to produce some eight or nine years later, and it appears small and petty in comparison.

To this time (1790) belong the beautiful bust-portraits of beauties of the tea-houses, O Kita of Naniwa-ya, O Hisa of Takashima, or of the Green Houses, like Hana-ōgi of Ōgi-ya, or chanters of *jōruri* like Toyohina, which were printed on mica ground. These portraits with their novel beauty of printing no doubt made a stir in Yedo, and they were imitated by other artists. Then came the set called *Seirō Niwaka onna geisha no bu*, not to be confused with an earlier set of the same title, of half-length figures of girls dressed for the Niwaka festival, this time not portrayed singly, but in a group of three, pyramidally arranged.

As something of a freak, we must mention the rare three-quarter length portrait of O Kita printed on both sides of the paper. It is well reproduced in colours in Kurth's *Utamaro*, opposite page 208. Such playful ingenuities served to draw attention to the artist, who was now entering on a period of confident productiveness, casting off the lingering traces of Kiyonaga's dominant influence and emerging with a formed style of his own.

This style is triumphantly asserted in the prints of about 1793. Utamaro still continues the half-length figures of women which had found such favour. In the series *Kasen Koi no bu*, a set devoted to " types of love," some of the prints, grandly designed, have an individuality of portraiture and an intensity of delineation such as Ukiyo-ye had never known before; for example, the bust portrait of the young married woman " anxious in love," leaning her cheek on her hand in a listening attitude (*Paris Catalogue*, Plate XXXIV). This series has a pink mica background, another novelty. Masterpieces are also to be found in two other sets of this time, the one called *Fujo Ninsō Jippin*, " Ten Types of Women's Physiognomies," and *Fujin Sōgaku Jittai*.

Both these sets have a white mica ground, the title being on a tablet with three vertical divisions. These prints are of singular beauty, and among them are things which, in their own kind, the half-length figure,

Utamaro never surpassed; especially we may mention the girl looking at her lacquered teeth in a hand-mirror (reproduced in colour in the *V.I. Catalogue*, Plate XIV), which in spacing and design is incomparable.

Utamaro's interest in character as expressed in the features is constant throughout his career. His nature was fastidious and critical, and he was inclined to moralize.

A few years have made an extraordinary difference in Ukiyo-ye. The mellow calm of the last years of Temmei is exchanged for an atmosphere of excitement and enterprise, recalling earlier days when new experiments in printing spurred the rival masters to surpass each other in exploiting them, the days of Okumura Masanobu when the first *beni*-prints were produced, the first years of Meiwa, and the days when Kiyonaga's first big sheets took Yedo by storm. Utamaro is now the centre, the inspiring spirit. About this time Tsutaya published a print in which Utamaro has portrayed himself at work on an ink-painting, a landscape, with O Kita and O Hisa looking on. This is less well known than the much later portrait of the artist painting a huge *Hō-ō* bird in the Yoshiwara, which forms a double-page design in the book called *Seirō yehon nenjū gyōji* of 1804, but is of great interest as showing Utamaro in his prime. He had an aquiline nose and finely featured face.

As a change from the mica background, white or mixed with colour, a yellow ground also appeared about 1790, and for a time had a great vogue. To 1793 or 1794 we may assign Utamaro's superb triptych of women cutting and measuring stuff for dresses. The left-hand sheet of this, depicting a woman holding up and examining a piece of diaphanous grey material while a small child sprawls across her knee and plays with a fan, is the best known part of the composition; but the whole triptych is designed with complete mastery, and the other two sheets add a rosy red to the colour-scheme, which with the wonderful blacks and greys and the ground of full yellow is light and strong at once. The design gives a sense of something significant to what is ostensibly a most ordinary household scene. Selection and emphasis are everywhere at work, but so subtly that there is no hint of anything adventitious, of means forced to produce an effect; on the contrary, it is the sheer beauty of natural movements in people who are absorbed in what they are doing which takes us captive.

To the same time belongs a single sheet which is one of Utamaro's master works. This is the toilet scene, reproduced in colours in the *Paris V.I. Catalogue*, Plate XLII. A woman sits on the ground bending forward and looking with intent scrutiny into her mirror with her hair half done, while a companion with her back turned sits close beside her and looks into her own mirror as she also knots a ribbon in her hair. This print has the yellow ground. The two mirrors with their round form and their positive lustrous black form integral parts of this most original design; the intent attitude of the two girls is accentuated by the opposed directions in which their figures bend, and the effect is such that the forms of the design seem to have an energy altogether transcending the limits of the space within which they are set. We note above all the singular intensity of the woman's gaze. Utamaro has often drawn women consulting a mirror; it is with him a favourite subject. But nowhere has he put more pregnant power into this simple motive. With his imagination for the elemental fact, he sees woman resorting to that truth-telling oracle, and knows that never priestess interrogated the mysteries of her shrine with more passionate absorption. The beautiful body, the young lineaments, the treasure committed by abounding Nature to her charge; in the little lucid world of the mirror how precious these seem, how anxiously to be scrutinized, how jealously watched and cherished! It is this seizure of the aboriginal, the essential, the instinctive, in feminine humanity that distinguishes Utamaro among all the artists of the world.

The novelty of the yellow-ground prints was immensely appreciated. Rival artists at once began to issue them. Yeishi produced his set of six whole-length figures of beauties, *Seirō Bijin Rokkasen*, which are among the finest of all his prints. Exquisitely printed, and with a great refinement of colour, these sheets have the aristocratic choiceness and elegance which distinguish Yeishi's style. Another beautiful set which followed this is the set of three, *Seirō San Shikibu*.

Chōki also designed some remarkable prints at this time on the yellow ground. One is reproduced in colour in the *Paris V.I. Catalogue*, Plate XXXIV. Shunyei and Toyokuni did not fail to adopt the fashion of the moment. There is a most effective print by Shunyei of a girl dancing with long ribbons swirling from two sticks held in her hands.

And Toyokuni rarely did anything finer, apart from the vigorous actor-prints which we shall record later on, than his set entitled *Fūryū-jin-gi-rei-chi-shin*, or " Popular Representation of the Five Virtues." One of this set, the " Wisdom " (*Chi*)—reproduced on Plate 37—representing a tall girl in a white dress with purple iris pattern on the skirt, looking back as she leaves a room, is a masterpiece. Of the same date is the set of four, *Fūryū Kin-ki-sho-gwa*, one of which is reproduced in colours by Succo (Toyokuni, Plate 34).

None of these masters approached Utamaro either in his peculiar intensity of conception or in his originality of design—the felicity with which his figures are related to the space they occupy, or to other figures, the variety of invention in their pose, gesture, and movement. But now in this wonderful year, 1794, Utamaro is challenged, and challenged with imperious power, by an apparition from the unknown. Sharaku bursts into the world of Ukiyo-ye.

Sharaku is something of a portent. With the other Ukiyoye masters we can trace a gradual development before their full force is matured, sometimes from what seem quite unpromising beginnings. But the genius of Sharaku starts full-blown, so far as Ukiyo-ye is concerned. What impelled this *Nō*-play dancer to design sets of prints of the actors in the popular theatres of Yedo, we do not know. Some Western writers have credited him with a savage scorn for the vulgar Yedo stage, as if his object had been to hold up these darlings of the mob to contempt by portraying them with no traditional idealization, but as they really were. The assumption seems perfectly gratuitous, like that which would impute Kiyonaga's retirement to a disdainful disgust with the degeneracy of the age. It is best to leave motives alone, since nothing can be proved, and in conjecturing what is in a Japanese mind from external evidence we are more likely to be wrong than right.

If conjectures must be hazarded, it might be as plausible to suppose that it was the new force, vitality and poignancy of Utamaro's latest work which provoked Sharaku to challenge him; as if he had said to himself: "What Utamaro is doing in the world of women, I will do in the world of the theatre." Or again, it might be conjectured that after the death of Shunshō, the great master of the actor-print, there was an opportunity to be seized of which Sharaku availed himself. What we know as actual fact is that his prints began to appear in the same month, the first of 1794, as the series *Yakusha Butai no Sugata-ye*, by Toyokuni. It would seem that there was a definite rivalry between the publishers, Tsutaya and Izumiya, if not between the artists, who portrayed the same actors in the same plays during two years. Toyokuni is here at his best, but pales before Sharaku.

It is usual to contrast Sharaku's "realism" with the "idealism" of his predecessors. Such terms as these mean different things in different contexts; it is therefore well to attempt a little greater precision.

If we turn back to the first actor-prints of Kiyonobu and Kiyomasu, we find that the faces of the actors, especially of those who played in the parts of women, are little individualized. The design is the main thing;

the actual hang and set of the dresses are subdued to the general flow of the sweeping outlines; no suggestion whatever of texture is given; and the faces also fall into the scheme, which aims at presenting a recognizable image rather portraying an individual person. When we come to Shunshō and his school, the prints approximate a stage nearer to actuality; hands and feet are more articulated, features are more expressive of character and personality, the individual is more differentiated. With Sharaku it is as if we were suddenly given a sharpness and intensity of vision quite beyond the faculty of everyday sight; the lineaments of his portraits leap into strange distinctness, as if we had looked through a lens. Design still controls the draughtsmanship, which still refrains from dwelling on accidents and inessentials; but in this heightened vision we observe how, for instance, the hair shows a little through the transparency of a comb, and the blue on a shaven crown or chin. Various writers have spoken of Sharaku's distortion and grotesqueness of feature, of the extravagant grimaces of his actors. But are not the same things to be found in the later prints of the Katsukawa artists? It is not these that differentiate Sharaku, but his searching vision, his penetrative insight into character and his power of expressing it. The more we contemplate his prints the more we feel in the grip of a powerful mind; for it is not a mere heightening of our senses that he gives us, he lends us his piercing imagination, which goes straight to the interior truth of what he contemplates. Sharaku was one of those rare artists who have a genius for veracity. Velazquez is another example. We do not impute to Velazquez a desire to expose the degradation of humanity in his paintings of the dwarfs and idiots who were pets in Philip's ceremonious court, because it is obvious that he enjoyed painting them; he saw them with a painter's eye and portrayed them without sentiment, without malice, and without extenuation. It is inconceivable that Sharaku did not enjoy drawing the Yedo actors. His was a mind, we feel, that was only happy in contact with reality. He could not have drawn them otherwise than he did.

Look at his portrait of Miya-uchi Dennai, director of the Miyako-za (first opened Dec. 3, 1793), announcing a new set of portraits of actors (reproduced by von Seidlitz, English edition, p. 146). And then turn to the old Tosa portrait of a priest in the Louvre, reproduced as frontispiece to the second volume of Fenollosa's *Epochs of Chinese and Japanese Art*, and compare it with the Sharaku. Given the difference in the type of person portrayed, how alike they are in their way of seeing and setting down the wrinkled old face! The manner of drawing the hands, one notes, is identical. The famous portrait of Shoichi Kokushi by Chō Densu is a similarly unflinching and veracious portrait of old age; and instances might be multiplied from the ancient art of Japan. There was nothing new to the traditions of Japanese portraiture in Sharaku's intense delineation. But, in this degree, it was new to Ukiyo-ye. And especially in the portrayal of women, or rather of actors in feminine parts. Before Sharaku came, these actors had been drawn in a more or less generalized manner, approximating to the female type in fashion among the artists of the day. With Sharaku it is definite portraiture.

It is difficult for us to realize the attitude of the Yedo public towards art, so utterly different was it from that of a Western public. What would our matter-of-fact public say to a representation of familiar handicrafts and industries in which women were substituted for men ? They would say it was absurd. Yet this is the constant custom of the Ukiyoye artists. The Yedo public were used to night-scenes in which everything was visible; they took it as a matter of course that artists should make their women all alike, and yet that in one year they should be exquisitely small and inconceivably fragile and in another massive and tall beyond the dreams of Japanese womanhood. Above all, they wanted something decorative. One sees in every detail of their household furniture how the sense of beauty sought and found satisfaction in form and pattern. The instinctive cry of delight which the average Western mind lets out before a favourite picture, " How like it is ! " finds little echo there. Sharaku's new vision of the theatre was not therefore one to find a natural response in minds prepared to move in that direction ; it gave a shock. It was not the squints and grimaces that offended; these they were used to on the stage, and in a few years they were delighted with these, even more emphasized, in prints by Toyokuni and his school. But searching, strongly characterized portraiture, this was a thing to which they were not used and for which they had no craving. Least of all in the actors of feminine parts, to whose features their eyes had always been willing to lend an appropriate charm.

The violent and sensational character of the Japanese popular drama partly accounts for the wrung features and desperate attitudes which we find in some of these prints—though not where it is not demanded for the character portrayed. But for Sharaku it was an opportunity of portraying the whole range of human emotions as written on face and form, and these he intensified to an extreme degree, without losing their essential truth. But we must not dwell on these prints exclusively as portraiture. We cannot sufficiently admire the unerring seizure of the one significant line that gives feature or expression (and note that, however extravagant the expression or posture, the delineation is reticent, the brush-line sober though intense) as if the whole force of the artist's mind were in the hand that traced it; just so Sharaku when he danced in the *Nō* plays would have concentrated the whole energy of his being in a gesture. But with this marvellous seizure of essentials which makes great portraiture is combined masterly design and magnificent colour. As an original colourist Sharaku is unsurpassed in Ukiyo-ye.

Since, so far as is known at present, no print of Sharaku's was published except in the two years 1794 and 1795, questions of date or development do not concern us. The prints are either in the form of *hoso-ye*, issued like Shunshō's in triptychs, or of upright *ōban*, whether whole-length figures or large heads, single or two together. The most famous series is that of the large heads on a ground made of powdered mica mixed with dull purple pigment; and it contains Sharaku's greatest works. But all his prints are on a wonderfully high level. It is true that a feeling of monotony and occasional repulsion is provoked by the subjects of his brush, and we cannot help regretting that Sharaku did not give us more portraits of men in ordinary life and not acting a part on the stage. The portrait of the theatre manager reading the advertisement, already mentioned, shows what masterpieces of the kind he might have multiplied for our delight.

The print reproduced on Plate 11 is, so far as is known, unique. It repeats on a larger scale and with different colouring the upper part of a whole-length portrait of the actor Yonesaburō as a tea-house servant (reproduced by Kurth, *Sharaku*, Plate 34). Perhaps it was made for a private patron; which would account for its extreme rarity.

It is significant that we now know that Sharaku, after ceasing to design prints, took up oil-painting. It betrays the Western affinities which were just what, in his prints, alienated the Yedo public. After two years of superb production he passes from our view for ever.

As we have seen, it was not Sharaku who invented or first produced the prints on mica ground, the *kirara-ye*. It is possible, however, that his famous set of large heads of actors was the first in which the dark mica ground was used.

Yeishi and his pupil Yeiri took up this new device, and some whole-length figures of Yoshiwara beauties standing against an opaque, reddish purple background are perhaps the most beautiful of all Yeishi's prints.

The print we reproduce in colours (Pl. 13) is sometimes found with this background, sometimes without, and variations in some of the blocks occur in different impressions.

Yeiri produced little, but his prints are very distinguished. His master-piece must have been a series of portraits of Yedo celebrities, *Yedo-no-hana*, two only of which are known. One is the portrait of a singer, repro-duced in the *Paris V.I. Catalogue*, Plate XIX. The other is the portrait of Kyōden, once famous in Ukiyo-ye as Kitao Masanobu, which is reproduced in the catalogue of the Haviland Collection (Deuxième Partie, 1923), No. 341. This last, though no doubt it owes much to Sharaku, is on a very high level indeed.

Yeishi, unlike Utamaro, was fortunate in his pupils. They were few, but they were well worthy of their master. Yeishō was as gifted as Yeiri, though of less fine fibre, and produced more than he.

Sharaku's influence was to be mainly on theatrical prints, but he came as a disturbing force to the whole of Ukiyo-ye. Chōki, holding his own as an independent master of real originality, seems to have been very im-pressionable. And while drawn to Utamaro, he was evidently overcome by Sharaku's fascination. Not that he was fortunate as a direct imitator in actor-portraiture, as in his Chūshingura series. The faces recall Sharaku, at a distance, but Chōki's gift did not lie in that direction. As a token of admiration he designed a pillar-print with a girl holding a fan on which is Sharaku's portrait of Matsumoto Kōshirō IV with a pipe in his hand and bandage round his head. Chōki at this time issued the finest of his designs, a group of prints of half-length figures with silvery mica ground, now among the collector's rarest prizes. One is the charming design of two girls sitting in the moonlight ; another is the famous night-piece the " Fire-Flies " ; a third is the " New Year Dawn," reproduced on Plate 12, in which the figure is beautifully related to the landscape, and which has an emotional quality rare in Ukiyo-ye. A later issue of this rare print, with alterations, is reproduced, *Paris V.I. Catalogue*, Plate XXXVIII. A noticeable mannerism of Chōki's is the placing of the upright line of a figure close to the margin and almost parallel to it.

About 1795, the year of Sharaku's disappearance from the scene, comes a sudden change over Ukiyo-ye. Times of stir and movement in Ukiyoye art had generally coincided with a change in fashion, expressed in a sudden preference for a certain type of figure, the proportions of which were heightened or reduced with a quite arbitrary choice. So it was now ; women's figures became once more immensely tall. Kiyonaga had set a similar fashion at the beginning of Temmei; but now the figures were not only tall but extravagantly slender.

Utamaro's set of the Twelve Hours of the Day, *Seirō Jūni toki tsuzuki*, illustrates the change. These prints are on a yellow ground, but this time dusted slightly with gold, a new refinement in single sheets.[1] On each is a bracket-clock, with a flower instead of dial, and below the clock the title of the series.

The daring attenuation of the girl-forms may disconcert those who love the normal. But which of the creative draughtsmen of Ukiyo-ye had ever treated the feminine form as mere matter for representation? Imagination had allowed itself full freedom to mould the type presented to the eyes into something adorable and strange. Harunobu had attenuated necks and wrists into an extravagant delicate slimness as of flower-stalks, and now Utamaro attenuated with a like extravagance the whole girlish form. Pontormo in Florence, El Greco in Spain, Blake in England, lengthened out their forms in similar fashion, obeying an impulse from within. The impossibility of such types in actual life is nothing against them in the world of creative art. Only if they have not a life of their own are we dissatisfied. In the best of these prints of the Twelve Hours Utamaro has created figures of enchanting *allure*. And the spacing, the colouring, the originality of the designs is of the finest order.

The same extreme slimness and tallness is in another set on yellow ground, called *Enchū Hassen*; a set of eight, in which beauties of the day are portrayed as *Sennin*, the "sages" of Chinese legend. Here the new types are less fortunately used, because the artist adopts something of the mannerism of the classic schools of brush-drawing, with its love for separate forcible strokes rather than continuous lines. One of the set, representing a girl as Sei-ō-bō the "fairy queen," is reproduced in colour by Fenollosa in his *Outline of Ukiyo-yé*; and Fenollosa uses it to point his moral that Utamaro was leading Ukiyo-ye into depths of degradation. He dares to portray a beauty of the Yoshiwara, a mere courtesan, as that supernatural creature, the theme of countless classic painters both in China and Japan. But what was there new in this? Was Sei-ō-bō as sacred a figure as Daruma, the great patriarch of the Buddhist sect of Zen? Yet Harunobu had made a print of a *geisha* masquerading as Daruma, crossing the sea from China to Japan on a reed—one of the classic subjects of the Sesshū and the Kanō schools. And Harunobu designed other prints in which he poked yet more irreverent fun at this

[1] It was used in the Shell and Bird books.

great and formidable saint. But besides Harunobu, which of the popular masters had not made travesties of the great figures of sacred legend? The Sennin were no more immune than the Seven Gods of Good Luck, who are universal themes of playful art. The feeling of the Japanese was much more like that of Christian medieval folk in this respect than that of our day. And, after all, Utamaro's "Fairy Queen" of the Green Houses is a sweet and serious girl, with no hint of burlesque intention on the surface. But Fenollosa was curiously unjust to Utamaro in his desire to exalt Kiyonaga, and reads in him all sorts of symptoms of "decadence" for which there is no justification. He most oddly accuses him of "naturalism" as opposed to Kiyonaga's "idealism." The terms, so applied, seem to have no meaning whatever.

Let us admit, however, that in this passing phase of extravagant elongation—for it was only a passing phase, and does not come towards the close of Utamaro's career as some writers have imagined, dating it after the beginning of the 19th century—let us admit that there was something perilous and extreme, which only a consummate genius could handle with felicity. The gulf between Utamaro and Yeishi can be measured in Yeishi's strained attempt to follow Utamaro's lead. At first he is fairly successful, imitating the swing of a figure across the design to foil the pose of another figure, in the way of Utamaro; but a looseness, a lack of organic structure in the drawing, is very perceptible. In the large print of unusual size, reproduced in the *V. and I. Paris Catalogue*, Plate VII, Utamaro's wonderful arrangements of figures, and mastery of a complex of lines diversely directed, are caricatured; the drawing, yet looser, communicating no sense of form. And in the series of Patterns of the Green Houses, *Seirō Moyō Awase*, easily recognizable by the red *sake* cup on which the title is written and the half-yellow, half-white background, the extreme proportion of the figures is allied not only to empty draughtsmanship, but to a peculiarly vacuous type of face. Utamaro was, indeed, far harder to follow than Kiyonaga. Yeishi was safe under Kiyonaga's stable influence, but as soon as that was gone he was never quite happy with his type of face, and it gradually tended to develop a rather silly smile. A well-known triptych of the Treasure-boat, seven girls masquerading as the Seven Gods of Fortune, in a rose-coloured barge with a peacock-prow, is Yeishi's most successful piece of this time.

His pupil Yeishō, who had been making some striking prints of large heads of girls with mica ground, produced one charming triptych in the

" tall " style of girls dancing under pink lanterns, one with a fan tied over her forehead. It is notable for its very pretty colour-scheme of rose and grey.

Chōki also published a triptych of girls surprised by a shower while stretching cloth in a garden ; a triptych happier in composition than most of this artist's, who sometimes became helpless and confused in grouping more than a couple of figures together.

Of Utamaro's triptychs in the tall, attenuated phase two are specially famous, the " Night Scene by the Sumida River," reproduced in the *Paris V.I. Catalogue*, Plate LVI—it is a challenge to Kiyonaga's early triptych of a similar subject—and " The Fireflies," reproduced on Plate LXXXI of the same catalogue. Fascinating compositions these are ; but they are not Utamaro at his greatest.

In his unique six-sheet composition of " The Bridge " the figures are tall and slender, but with no wasp-like contractions. There is only one other instance known of a six-sheet composition formed of two triptychs placed, not side by side, but one above the other, and that is a view of a theatre interior, and the audience, by Toyokuni.

In Utamaro's design we see groups of women and children standing on the bridge or leaning over the parapet ; below are groups in boats passing under it. In its complete state this composition is excessively rare. An example, very much faded, was shown at Yamanaka's Red Cross Exhibition in London during the war. But each triptych is a complete and delightful design in itself. Both are reproduced in colour in Vol. V of *Masterpieces of Ukiyo-ye*.

Another triptych of this time is one illustrating the " Three Lucky Things," Fuji, the hawk, and the egg-plant, remarkable for its colour-scheme of blue, purple, and green. Better known is the beautiful " Mosquito Net," a picture of ladies going to bed at an inn behind a great green net.

At the same time Utamaro was publishing great numbers of " Large Heads " of women, one of the most familiar sides of his work, but not really the finest. In these prints there was no scope for his marvellous composing gift ; yet what a splendid design is the head we reproduce (Pl. 36) !

Meanwhile, what was Toyokuni doing ? For in the eyes of the public he was the artist who stood out as Utamaro's closest rival. He had already won a great popularity. As we have seen, he had, like Yeishi and Chōki, competed with Utamaro for favour with some beautiful groups of **prints** on yellow ground. He had produced also some close imitations of Utamaro's half-length figures. But it was the theatre which more and more attracted him. We have seen how he designed a fine set of (whole-length) portraits of actors simultaneously with Sharaku. He pleased the public, and when Sharaku retired was undisputed master of the field, succeeding to Shunshō's place. But at the same time he did not cease his rivalry with Utamaro. Indeed, his fecundity of hand was amazing. During his career, from 1786 onwards, he was to illustrate three hundred and fifty volumes. This, one would have thought, was enough occupation. But apart from book-illustrations he published every year large numbers of nishiki-ye.

About 1795–97 Toyokuni produced some of his finest triptychs. Among them are two triptychs of girls imitating incidents in the life of the famous poet of the 9th century, Narihira; the passing by Fuji-san, and the crossing of the Tamagawa. These are schemed in a colour-design of purple, green, and yellow; pink and red are absent. The same colour-scheme is used in what is, apart from actor-prints, Toyokuni's master-piece, the "Wind among the Cherry Blossom." Girls are tying, according to custom, their little poems, written on tanzaku, to the blossoming boughs on a windy April day. One girl is lifted by a youth to reach the bough above her; another stands on a sake bucket and has to cling to the branch to steady herself in the gust; and the riotous wind blows through the design, tossing the girls' dresses into billowy curves and making a joyous rhythm flow through it all. Toyokuni is never exquisite: even here the line has nothing like the sensitiveness of Utamaro's: but in this composition the broad and simple rhythm is held and brought out with complete felicity. If it has no depths or subtleties, it has nothing of the cheapness which too facile production was soon to bring into Toyokuni's work; his powers were inspired to full fruition at a fortunate moment.

In another triptych of about the same time pinks are introduced with the purples. It is a party of holiday-makers on the seashore; an Awabi diver is seen swimming in the bay, and beyond the calm water are the clear outlines of the hills on the opposite coast. This, too, is a very attractive composition, though not so distinguished in colour, and lacking the inspiration in design which makes the Wind in the Cherry Blossom so completely charming. Of much the same date is the well-known "Bath" triptych in which cast shadows of the clothes hanging up on the wall are introduced.

Just a little later we may date the remarkable triptych of Blind Men Crossing a Wooden Bridge over a River, which, like some single prints of the same date, is a passing excursion into the style of Hanabusa Itchō (1652–1724).

Itchō was a Kanō painter who deserted the orthodox subject-matter of his classic school and delighted in spirited sketches of everyday life. He was a constant side-influence on Ukiyo-ye; Utamaro also occasionally adopted his manner. Toyokuni's " Blind Men," curiously parallel to the great Peter Brueghel's picture of the Blind Leading the Blind at Naples, is in Itchō's style of brush and humorous vein; the huddling crowd of sightless beggars crawl over the rough poles by which they make their precarious crossing, jostling and falling over each other. The beauty of a spring evening, with the young moon seen among the leafing willow-branches, adds by contrast a touch of pathos to those grotesquely groping figures who see nothing.

After all, however, it is not these triptychs that we think of as Toyokuni's most characteristic work; that is to be found rather in his actor-prints of the six years before the century closed. Few of these equal those in the series *Yakusha Butai no Sugata-ye*.

In this set, with grey or mica ground foiling already mentioned. Thirty-nine are known of the series, but most are rare. Admirably chosen colours in the dresses, there is dignity as well as force. We do not feel that Toyokuni is straining his powers, as we too often do in the large single heads of actors, or in the prints with two heads together, groups of which begin to appear almost at the same time. These heads are extremely striking at first glance, they are thrown on the page with great energy and boldness. It is only when we place them actually beside the Sharaku heads with which Toyokuni sought to compete that we realize their great inferiority. We are surprised too by the quietness of Sharaku's inevitable lines; Toyokuni's brush-strokes are violent and restless by comparison, they have no reserve of power behind them. It is the contained, interior force of Sharaku's conception, so unerringly and essentially expressed in every line, which impresses not the eye only, but the memory.

Meanwhile, another chapter was being added to the achievements of Kwansei period. This was the expansion of *surimono* designing, chiefly by Hokusai, though Shunman also had taken to designing in this form after about 1790. Exquisite are the small *surimono* signed " Sōri," then " Shinsai," then " Hokusai formerly Sōri," then simply " Hokusai," produced in the years from 1797 to 1800. Delicate colours are matched by delicate design. There is no sign of "decadence" here; rather of a new beginning. Scenes on the beach at low tide, with groups of figures among the weeds and shells and rusty anchors of the shore; or still life; or glimpses of distant Fuji; or doings of the New Year; walks in the snow; marketing at a fish stall; visions of cherry blossom from a verandah; all kinds of outdoor and indoor scenes become delightfully pictorial motives to Hokusai's all-observant eye and restless hand. Of the old "Shunrō" phase nothing is left; these are purely original. Sometimes, with his mania for changing his name, Hokusai signs "Kakō." Bearing this signature are one or two extremely rare full-size prints, in which the narrow type of face beginning to come into fashion is made interesting and individual. "Kakō" also signs a set of illustrations to the Chūshingura play (about 1798), which seem to be the earliest of several sets designed by Hokusai. These prints are on the uki-ye model, with red clouds, and with rather elaborate linear perspective very imperfectly grappled with. They seem curiously experimental for an artist now nearly forty, though there is great power in the night-scene of storm where Sadakurō kills Yoichibei; and some of the landscape backgrounds promise freshness and beauty of treatment.

To return to Utamaro, there is an interesting disclosure of his position and of his attitude at this period in the inscriptions on prints of an excessively rare series called "New Pattern of Brocade after Utamaro's style," Nishiki-ori Utamaro gata shin moyō. The prints are remarkable technically. Except for the face, arms, and hands, there are no outlines, and the face is outlined in red. They are on a yellow ground. Two of the set are reproduced in the Paris V.I. Catalogue, Plate XLIV, and one of them also in Kurth, Utamaro, Plate 31. This one has an inscription pouring contempt on the artists who try to make up for want of brush-power by dressing up their models in gorgeous costumes with painted faces; whereas a mere ink-sketch, if power be in the brush, will create living beauty. "My fee," says Utamaro, "is as high as my nose. Publishers who buy cheap must take the consequences; their proud noses will be crushed."

On the second print of this set there is a similarly scornful allusion to the bad artists "swarming like ants" who produce wretched prints and discredit the art of the nishiki-ye at home and abroad.

Only one other print of this series is known to us, and that in a single example, in the British Museum. It is the most beautiful of the three; a woman in a flowered dress of pale olive tint with black sash, holding a red and white fan. On it is an inscription which may be thus translated:

" There are only two ways of drawing beautiful women (*bijin*) : one is to delineate the features, the other to express the physiognomy. If, therefore, one draws a smiling face comprehensive of love, the person looking at the picture becomes excited ; and if to this is added a delicate and graceful form, he becomes infatuated. I want all ladies and gentlemen to offer their criticisms only after they have scrutinized my elegant style and compared it with the deformities of others."

These inscriptions remind us of what we are apt to forget, the masses of poor prints there must have been, now entirely perished out of memory and record, on the Yedo market.

We reproduce (Pl. 41) an interesting print by Shikō II of the year 1800. It is seal-dated Monkey Year, 1st month. It shows a group of three women sitting round the *hibachi* and examining their New Year purchases. One smells a packet of cosmetics, another opens a paper case of scent, while a third holds in her fingers a *bin-sashi*, the flexible little rod of metal, tortoise-shell or bamboo, which ever since early in Anyei had been used to keep the " wings " of the coiffure extended and in place. The seal-date is one of the earliest known, and the print is important on that account. It shows the type of face now in fashion among the print-designers, especially the followers of Utamaro, for Shikō was now more under the influence of Utamaro than of his master, Chōki. There is a decided change, in the direction of looser and less expressive drawing, from prints made by Shikō a few years earlier. Much the same types of face, whose thinness contrasts with the rounded cheeks of the beginning of Kwansei period, may be seen in Utamaro's five-sheet print, the *Susuhaki* or " House Cleaning " at the end of the year, an occasion for merriment and practical jokes, and in the twelve-sheet composition of " Silk-Worm Culture." Both of these date from about the end of the century, the former being a little earlier than the other ; and both, in the first edition, are designed in a colour-scheme of violet, blue, green, and yellow. Pink or red was introduced in later editions.

With the closing years of the century we find the themes of motherhood coming more frequently into Utamaro's work. Woman as existing for beauty and for passion he had portrayed in every phase and every intimacy ; but as if he felt that, to complete his portraiture of essential womanhood, the relation of mother to child must be pictured and explored, he goes on to design some of his most wonderful prints. There is the print of the mother at night holding in her arms the soft body of the baby, which rubs its sleepy eyes ; the print of the mother bending over with her child on her shoulder, her back towards us, to look at the image of the two faces close against each other reflected in the wooden cistern—one of those lovely, unexpected designs with which only Utamaro was inspired ; there is the print of the mother doing her hair in the mirror with a kind of fierce absorption, while the resenting child at her breast is being distracted by a toy held by a maid behind, who stoops her head down to smile at him ; and how many more, full of the tenderness of insight, designed by this " decadent " Utamaro !

And at the very end of the century, as if dissatisfied even with these intimate pages from daily life, as if seeking for some more essential and more primitive symbol of the maternal passion, Utamaro designs that strange group of prints, the Yama-uba series. He struck away from the world of Ukiyo-ye into the world of legend ; and he chose the story of the savage mountain-fairy who fostered and brought up in the wilds with a more than mother's devotion the " infant Hercules " of Japanese story, the Golden Boy, Kintoki.

Here was the maternal passion isolated and removed from all the dainty and delicate refinements of a city-life and home ; just the primitive, jealous, animal intensity of that love ; this alone could satisfy Utamaro's imagination. And marvellously is this passion expressed : the boy full of restless lusty life, the foster-mother with loose black hair giving him her breast as he turns his eyes, even in the act of suckling, with the curiosity and alertness of a wild creature, to something that calls his attention ; or they fiercely kiss ; or he climbs on her shoulder ; or they play together in their solitude. Besides the prints of ordinary size, of which there are many, there is the tall upright print in which the Yama-uba bends down and the boy reaches up to get the cluster of chestnuts which she holds in her hand ; a print often reproduced, and a magnificent design ; one of Utamaro's masterpieces.

In the same kind of vein, with a feeling of the elemental in its forms, is conceived the triptych which stands supreme among all the triptychs of Utamaro, the " Awabi Fishers," the central part of which is occupied by the half-naked fisherwoman suckling her child. Not so perfect perhaps as Kiyonaga's finest prints, this is something greater than Kiyonaga ever made ; for perfection implies a limitation. The group of nearly nude forms, with unbound hair, on the rocks, with infinite sea beyond them, yield a sense of latent and mysterious powers, as if they shared in the secrets of the deep waters which they are used to plunge in ; the human body appears strange and wonderful, a symbol more significant than ever it had been hitherto in the art of Ukiyo-ye. The theme is taken from daily life; there is a woman buying shellfish in the right-hand sheet, though she seems an insignificant intrusion from the superficial world; but the theme is indefinitely deepened and broadened into an imaginative " beyond," as, in the print, the sea-waves melt away into the unseen.

# CHAPTER VIII

# KYŌWA AND BUNKWA PERIODS

## FROM FEBRUARY 13TH, 1801, TO FEBRUARY 4TH, 1818

In the spring of Kwansei 13, which began on February 13th, 1801, Yeijudō Nishimuraya Yohachi published a volume entitled *Nishiki-zuri onna sanjū Rok'kasen*, the thirty-six famous poetesses, illustrated in colours by Hosoi Chōbunsai, with a frontispiece by Gwakyōjin Hokusai. In this book we see the last of Yeishi's work as a print-designer. During the remainder of his career, he devoted himself to painting. Two of his paintings have already been mentioned on pages 73 and 74. That in the British Museum of a corpulent man prematurely aged with flaccid cheeks, baggy eyes, bent back, and with a bloated and repellent aspect is inscribed: "Portrait of Utamaro painted by Chōbunsai Yeishi in the 60th year of his age" (Utamaro no zō Chōbunsai Yeishi gyōnen roku-jū sai fude).

At one time, before the date of this painting had been established as 1815, following upon the discovery of Yeishi's age at death and consequent birth, it was thought to be a portrait of Utamaro I; and this supposition was strengthened by the belief (now no longer held by the best native critics) that he had been turned out of home by his alleged father Sekiyen on account of his dissipated habits. It was looked upon as a true picture of the artist at the time of his death, after the term of confinement following a supposed dissipated life had enfeebled his constitution and brought him to a premature grave. Yeishi we assert doubtless intended this to be a portrait of Baigadō Utamaro II; for there exists another painting similarly signed, but without the age, which depicts a man of middle age, of serious demeanour, intelligent, and somewhat ascetic-looking, grasping in his left hand a rosary; undoubtedly a memorial portrait of the great master Utamaro I, painted just after his death on October 31st, 1806.

The fact that Utamaro's art shows an intimate acquaintance with the life of women, especially those of the pleasure quarters, has led some foreign writers to believe that he was addicted to sensuality. This, we repeat, is surely a mistaken opinion; for in those days it was the common practice not only for artists but also for writers to frequent these places, where they found material for their work unobtainable elsewhere. Jippensha Ikku (1765–1831), who came to Yedo in 1790, when he was lodged, fed, and clothed by Tsutaya Jūsaburō in return for his services as writer and artist (he designed some book-illustrations and a few prints, one of the latter representing Daidōzan Bungorō at the age of seven in 1794), tells us in his interesting introduction to the famous " Picture-book of the Green Houses and their ceremonial throughout the year " (*Seirō yehon nenjū gyōji*, two volumes, published in colours and in black and white in 1804, and illustrated by Utamaro, assisted by his pupils Kikumaro, Hidemaro, and Takemaro), that " This book is the outcome of what I have heard and seen these many years past," and he goes on to say, " I peeped through every hole I could find in the *shōji* so as to accurately spy out the rules and customs of each particular house." The same care to obtain first-hand knowledge was exercised by artists and writers on theatrical matters. Shikitei Samba, the author of two volumes entitled " Actors in the Third Story " (*Yakusha Sangai kyō*), illustrated by Toyokuni I and published by Nishimiya Shinroku in February, 1801, says in the epilogue, " From early morning, when the first strains of music are played by the orchestra, I sit close in front of the stage, regardless of being splashed by water and mud (from the stage), and content to bend my knees in a narrow seat and wash down a few bean-jam buns with tea sipped from a single cup. My friend, Mr. Toyokuni, is a man of the same kidney ; but he sits high up in the third story sketching actor's figures while I sit low down in the pit gazing at the actors and doing nothing. We are, nevertheless, of the same tastes ; he paints while I write." The fact that Utamaro designed a number of erotic pictures has no significance in relation to his morals, for every Ukiyoye artist from Moronobu onwards produced these, and some in far greater numbers than did Utamaro.

After Kwansei, we find no more prints from Yeishi's pupils nor from Rekisentei Yeiri, Tamagawa Shūchō, Yeishōsai Chōki, and some others ; but despite these losses, there remained sufficient talent during the first stage of the present period, i.e. up to 1806, as to render it interesting. Utamaro and Gwakyōjin Hokusai each produced some fine work at this time. Of special interest and artistic worth is a rare set of the Tōkaidō by the latter artist, consisting of fifty-one oblong prints on *surimono* paper, each $4\frac{3}{4} \times 6\frac{1}{2}$ in. ($5\frac{1}{4} \times 7\frac{1}{4}$ with margins), and eight of double this width, on which is inscribed in a yellow label the name of the post station, its distance in *ri* and *chō* from the next, and the signature generally " Gwakyōjin Hokusai gwa," or more rarely " Hokusai gwa," together with one or more poems chiefly referring to the products for which the particular place was noted. (For two of the set, see Plate 42.)

These delightful little prints are remarkable for delicate drawing and soft harmonious colouring, and were issued in February, 1804, by Gyoku-yōdō enclosed in a wrapper on which is the following inscription: " The fifty-three post-stations of the Tōkaidō with a record in *ri* of the distances en route, humorously drawn by Hokusai-ō." It is doubtful whether a complete set of this original issue with the envelope is now in existence. A later edition, with inscriptions removed but similarly signed, is more generally known; it is greatly inferior in every respect. *Nishiki-ye* in the true meaning of the word practically ceased after Utamaro's death, and it is rare indeed that we find a print worthy of the name after 1806. One of these rare examples is to be seen in Kunisada's " Girl trimming an *andon*," reproduced on Plate 43. Hurried work, coupled with the use of cheap pigments, resulted in an enormous output of crude and inartistic prints. Nor had the artists the ability to carry on the Utamaro tradition. Even the latter, after his release from confinement in the middle of 1805, dispirited and overwhelmed with commissions that he had neither the time nor energy to execute, was content to delegate the task in the main to his pupils who lacked the ability to carry out his instructions. Kiyonaga had retired; Shunyei did but little; Hokusai was chiefly employed in book-illustration and *surimono* designing; and the new artists were, generally speaking, wanting in talent and originality. The chief of these latter are enumerated below with such details as are available concerning their life-histories.

SHŌTEI HOKUJŪ, a pupil of Hokusai about 1800, at first designed *surimono*, one of which is dated the beginning of 1802. He worked till about 1834. Dates of birth and death unrecorded.

SEKIJŌ, SEKIHŌ, SEKIZAN, and SHINKŌ were pupils of Sekiyen as far back as the Temmei period; but the few prints from their hands date from the latter part of Kwansei to about 1807, and are not wanting in distinction.

HOTEI HOKUGA and AOIGAOKA HOKKEI were pupils of Hokusai about 1804. The latter was born in 1780 and died in 1850. He had as a pupil YASHIMA GAKUTEI, dates of birth and death not known, who used the *gō* of Harunobu, Sadaoka, and Gogaku. Each of these were chiefly book-illustrators, and specially noted as designers of *surimono*, which though of considerable merit have not the delicacy and refinement of the Sōri and Gwakyōjin type. Gakutei also took lessons from Hokusai.

YEIZAN, who became the leading designer of *bijin-ye* after Utamaro's death, was the son born in 1787 of Yeiji, a maker of artificial flowers, who had also studied the Kanō style of painting. He first received instruction from his father and later from Suzuki Nanrei; and finally established himself as an Ukiyoye artist under the name of Kikugawa Yeizan, and with the *gō* of Jūkyūsai, both of which names are found on his prints. These date from about 1804 till 1829, when he seems to have retired. He died on February 26th, 1867, aged eighty-one. He trained several pupils, amongst whom were Yeishō, Yeishin, Yeiri, and Yeichō, the Yei of whose names are written in the same manner as that of their master, and are to be thus distinguished from Yeishi's pupils.

TORII KIYOMINE was a pupil of Kiyonaga, after whose death (1815) he succeeded as the fifth of the Torii Line and took the name of Torii Kiyomitsu II. He was born in 1787, being the grandson of the first Kiyomitsu. Common name Shōnosuke; later Kameji. Died on January 3rd, 1869.

SHUNKYŌSAI RYUKOKU, BANKI II, and HYAKUSAI HISANOBU worked during Bunkwa. Dates of birth and death unknown.

HIDEMARO, SHIKIMARO, MINEMARO, and KANAMARO were pupils of Utamaro, and designed prints during Bunkwa. Dates of birth and death unknown.

BAIGADŌ UTAMARO, generally called Utamaro II, was first a pupil of Koikawa Harumachi, a noted book-illustrator and novelist who died in 1789, and from whom he received the name of Koikawa Yukimichi. His work, however, belongs to Bunkwa. On the death of Utamaro, whose pupil he may have been during Kwansei, he is said to have married his widow and assumed his name. Bakin, however, tells us that Utamaro had neither wife nor child. Dates of birth and death are unrecorded.

YOSHIMARU was first a pupil of Kitagawa Tsukimaro, when he was called Yoshimarō. In a book published in February, 1810, there is a note which says that " from this spring the artist Yoshimaru changed his *geisei* from Kitagawa to Ogawa." The book is signed " Ogawa Yoshimaru gwa at the age of eighteen," whence we learn that he was born in 1793. Later he changed his *geisei* to Utagawa, and later again to Kitao as a pupil of Masayoshi. After Shigemasa's death on March 8th, 1820, he assumed the name of Kitao Shigemasa II and the *gō* of Kwaransei, the first Shigemasa having been called Kwaran. Date of death is not known, but work extends from about 1807 till 1840.

SHUNSEN was first called Shūrin as a pupil of Tsutsumi Tōrin. Later he studied under Shunyei, from whom he received the brush-name of Katsukawa Shunsen (no connection with Shunsho's pupil Shunsen, the last character *sen* being written differently). He also used the *gō* of Kashōsai and Tōryūsai. After Shunkō's death on December 1st, 1812, he became Shunkō II. He worked during Bunkwa, and on retiring earned a living by porcelain decoration. Dates of birth and death unknown.

Of KATSU SHUNKYŌ nothing is known save that he designed very few prints during Bunkwa. He may be identical with Shunkyōsai Ryūkoku above.

Keisei Yeisen, whose real name was Isoda Yoshinobu, was born in 1790. As a youth he was a pupil of Kanō Hakkeisai, and later of Yeiji and his son Kikugawa Yeizan. He also studied the Tosa style and that of Hokusai; and then travelled in the country around Yedo in order to study Nature. About 1809 a publisher named Tomoyeya Nihei lodged him. Yeisen died in 1848, aged fifty-nine. His work extends from about 1810 till 1847.

UTAGAWA TOYOHISA, a pupil of Toyoharu, made a few actor-prints during Bunkwa.

KUNIMITSU, common name Kumazō, brush-name Ichiōsai, made a few prints during Kyōwa and Bunkwa.

KUNIHISA was an unrecorded female pupil of Toyokuni. Only two prints after her designs have so far been seen. These are signed " Toyokuni's pupil, Kunihisa gwa." They both represent actors in character, and may be dated August and September, 1804, and are of considerable merit. This artist is not to be confounded with another female artist of the same name who was later a pupil of Kōsotei Toyokuni (Toyoshige).

KUNISADA, whose real name was Sumida Shōzō, was born at Yedo in 1786. He left Toyokuni's studio about 1806, receiving as gō Ichiyūsai Kunisada. He illustrated a book in 1807. About 1813 he received from Shokusanjin the gō of Gototei, meaning the fifth ferry-house, in reference to his having inherited the licence of the fifth ferry (*Itsutsu-me*) at Honjō quarter, Yedo.

Before 1827 he was instructed by Ikkei in the style of Hanabusa Itchō, and changed his gō accordingly to Kōchōrō. On February 24th, 1844, he designed a triptych published by Yamamoto Heikichi and bearing the seal of the censor (*nanushi*) Fukatsu Ihei, on which he wrote an inscription stating that this being the anniversary day of his master's death (Toyokuni I died on February 24th, 1825), he, with the permission of Toyokuni's relatives, succeeded to the title. This interesting print is signed " Kunisada changed to (*aratame*) the second (*ni sei*) Ichiyōsai Toyokuni," and is sealed with the Toshi-dama red seal used by Toyokuni I, as his studio seal. It is related that one of Toyokuni's pupils, Daimyō Ishikawa Hyugano-kami, on one of his annual visits to Yedo, received news that it was a fruitful year for his rice crops at Kameyama, Ise province. This so delighted him that he styled his country *Toyo-toshi kuni* or " the country of a Fruitful Year " ; and turning to Toyokuni, he said : " I bestow upon you the word ' Toshi' as your seal " ; and forthwith drew a *Toshidama* (lit. year-jewel), which the artist adopted as his seal. Kunisada, who always refused to accept Toyoshige as the legitimate successor of his master, was, owing to the latter's adoption of the name of Toyokuni after the death of the first, in reality the third to bear the name. His death took place on January 12th, 1865.

KUNIYOSHI, whose real name was Igusa Magasaburō, was born at Yedo on January 1st, 1798, the son of a dealer in Kyotō-dyed goods, noted for their beautiful colouring, from which he is said to have acquired an early taste for painting. As a youth he eagerly examined the illustrations of Kitao Shigemasa, especially his warrior pictures, and the rapid brush sketches of Masayoshi ; and at the age of twelve he showed such promise in drawing and painting that Toyokuni took him into his studio, after having been shown a picture by the lad of the demon-queller Shōki. He remained with Toyokuni for many years, and finally about 1815 received his diploma and the name of Utagawa Kuniyoshi. His *gō* were Ichiyūsai and Chō-ō-rō. His earliest prints, about 1818, were two triptychs, one entitled " Taira no Tomomori no bōrei " (ghost), published by Kinshūdō (Azumaya Daisuke), and the other entitled " Sōshi Ōyama Ryōben "—depicting the celebrated waterfall, which was published by Kagaya Kichi-yemon, both of which were much admired. He died on April 14th, 1861.

KUNINAO, commonly called Utaizō and later Yoshikawa Shirobei, with the *gō* of Ichiyensai and Ichiyōsai, was a native of Shinano province and a fellow-student of Kuniyoshi in Toyokuni's studio. He was born in 1793. At one time he and Kuniyoshi lived together, the latter studying his style. He worked from about 1805 to 1840, and died on July 22nd, 1854.

KUNIYASU, personal name Yasugorō, brush-name Ippōsai, was born in 1794, and was a fellow-student of Kuniyoshi and Kuninao. He worked from about 1811, and for a short time called himself Nishikawa Yasunobu, soon resuming his former name. He died in 1834.

KUNIMARU, personal name Bunji, brush-name Ichiyensai, was a pupil of Toyokuni about the same time as the above. He worked from about 1809 till 1830, when he died well over thirty years of age.

KUNINAGA, brush-name Ichiunsai, and common name Hayanosuke, was born in Yedo. He was trained by Toyokuni during Kwansei. His work extends from 1801 till 1829, in which year he died when over forty years old.

UTAGAWA HIROSHIGE was born in 1797. He belonged to a family of fire brigade police, his real name being Andō Tokitarō. As he evinced an aptitude for drawing when a boy, his father sent him to be taught by his friend Okajima Rinsai of the Kanō school. At the age of fifteen he wished to place the boy under Toyokuni; but, as there was no vacancy, he entered the studio of Toyohiro, and at the age of sixteen obtained his diploma and the brush-name of Utagawa Hiroshige. This diploma still exists, and is dated April 20th, 1812. His earliest efforts were book-illustrations, and *bijin-ye*. Amongst these latter, which are signed " Hiroshige gwa," is a fine series of four prints entitled " Soto no uchi sugata hakkei," published by Azuma-ya Daisuke about 1815. One of these, generally called " The Girl awakening from Sleep," is described by Fenollosa in his *Masters of Ukiyoye*, as " startling in power, making us think in its intense feeling of Sir Joshua Reynolds' subject : ' Mrs. Siddons as the Tragic Muse.' " In this series there is an indoor and an outdoor (in a circular cartouche at top right-hand corner) view on each print with separate sub-titles, which, in the print referred to by Fenollosa, are Kinuginu no Banshō for the former, and Tampō no Rakugan for the latter; meaning, respectively, Parting of two lovers at dawn after mutually helping one another to dress, and Evening Bell, and Rice-fields and Homing Geese. The colouring of this series is very good. Hiroshige died of cholera on October 12th, 1858.

YANAGAWA SHIGENOBU, whose family name was Suzuki, was born at Yedo in 1784. He was a pupil of Hokusai about Kyōwa, and later became his son-in-law. He took the name of Yanagawa from the place in Yedo where he first resided. He worked chiefly at Yedo but for a time at Ōsaka, during Bunkwa and Bunsei, and died in 1832. He is said to have been a clever puppet maker.

UTAGAWA TOYOKIYO was son and pupil of Toyohiro, his common name being Kinzō. His work is confined to book-illustration and *surimono* during Kyōwa and early Bunkwa. He collaborated with his father and an artist named Bunyen in a long horizontal *surimono* invitation to a concert party about 1802, in which he displays considerable skill. He is said to have died at a comparatively early age, leaving behind a son, who later became Utagawa Toyokuma.

HARUKAWA GOSHICHI was a pupil of Harukawa Yeizan. He was first called Kamiya Hōshū, Kamiya being his real name, and worked at Yedo under this name and that of Harukawa Goshichi during Kyōwa and Bunkwa at designing *surimono* and actor-prints, one of the former, signed

Kamiya Hōshū, being dated 1802. During Bunsei he worked in Kyōtō. Dates of birth and death unrecorded. His *surimono* are of much merit.

After the production of the great " Awabi Fishers " triptych and the Yama-uba series, Utamaro's work no longer contains surprises, though before his imprisonment in 1805 he made many wonderful prints, and his extraordinary powers of inventive design never failed him. We are conscious, indeed, of a change in the type delineated ; it is becoming less attractive, less gracious ; but this change is not marked till the very end of Utamaro's career. It is much more noticeable in Toyokuni and in other designers of *bijin-ye*.

Utamaro and Toyokuni were now the supreme rivals in the public eye ; but though rivals they were on friendly terms. Utamaro had supplied two designs to Toyokuni's book of half-length portraits of actors, *Nigao haiyū*, in 1799 ; and a little later the publisher Iwatoya commissioned the two artists to contribute each a number of designs to a set of *hashira-ye* of special width.

Toyokuni, during the first three or four years of the 19th century, produced some fine triptychs, such as the " Picnic Party at Shichi-ri-ga-hama " with fishermen dragging great nets in the background, in which purple, green, and yellow predominate ; the " Actors of the Day sheltering from a Shower " under a great tree ; and the " Six Girls washing Clothes in the Tamagawa." Actor-prints he was also pouring out in great profusion ; and although these are often very effective in colour and design, an increasing haste or carelessness is perceptible ; what was a formidable intensity in Sharaku has become a rhetorical emphasis.

In essential qualities Toyokuni is, as ever, far behind Utamaro. In 1801 Utamaro published the book *Yehon shiki no hana*, which serves to give us the fashions of the day and contains charming designs. In the women's hair we note that the side-wings begin to have a slightly convex curve at their lower edges. By 1803 this curve is more pronounced, though the fashion is not universal.

Sets which contain beautiful prints are that entitled *Fujin sō gaku jittei*, " Ten Types of Feminine Physiognomy," and the well-known *Kyōkun oya no megane*, " Instruction through Parents' Spectacles," each print of which has the title inscribed within a pair of red-rimmed spectacles. Now, as ever, Utamaro is deeply interested in character as shown in the features ; and in the inscriptions on these two sets of prints he appears as something of a moralist, and deplores the degenerating manners of the day. One of the former set, a half-length figure of a woman, nearly nude, combing her hair, is of a grand simplicity.

Prints of mothers and children are plentiful in these years, and many of them are of great charm. We have less, however, of that elemental feeling of motherhood which the Yama-uba series expresses, and more of playful incident, as in that favourite print of the " darling child " who has upset the bowl of goldfish over the floor while his mother is asleep.

The triptychs of this period show no flagging of invention. One of these is the well-known " Night-scene on the Sumida," with a great fishing-net making the chief feature of the design. A fishing skiff has come alongside a large pleasure-boat, just as the fisherman hoists his net, slung on bamboo-poles, out of the water with one little fish in its meshes. Some confusion has arisen over a pair of triptychs representing the processes of the colour-print, since it is very rare to find either triptych complete, and separate sheets have been wrongly assigned. In one we see women, substituted for men, as so often in Ukiyo-ye, cutting blocks, sharpening knives, sizing the paper, and hanging it up to dry. One woman represents the artist sitting by a table, on which lie pressing commissions from publishers, and about to make his design. In the second triptych girls are taking impressions from the blocks, and others are selling prints to customers. A set of Utamaro's *Kintoki* prints is being shown. On the walls are prints in frames or mounted as *kakemono*. It is a scene to make water the mouths of collectors of to-day. Utamaros by the score, fresh from the block, in perfect condition, and how cheap !

To the year 1803 belongs a print by Utamaro which, though not in itself remarkable, claims our attention. Since the days of his youth Utamaro, like Harunobu, had disdained the stage. The print in question is a print of two actors in the parts of O Han and Chōyemon. Why did Utamaro, at the close of his career, break his rule and take a subject from the theatre ? The print is reproduced by Kurth, *Utamaro*, Plate 22, where it is assigned to " bald nach 1790," a patently impossible date. It was designed as a protest against the ugly realism that had become the fashion in actor-prints. One might at first blush have conjectured that it was directed against Sharaku. But one has only to look at the woodcut to see by the style and the types that it belongs to Utamaro's last years, nearly a decade after Sharaku's brief apparition on the scene. And, in fact, it celebrates a performance of the play entitled *Katsura-gawa imose no tsuki-mi*, produced at the Ichimura theatre from the 7th day of the 8th month of 1803. The actors were Ichikawa Yaozō the Third, who played Chōyemon, and Iwai

Kumesaburō, who played O Han. It was Yaozō's greatest success in his career.

On the print is an inscription which may be translated thus : " My picture of O Han and Chōyemon is not a mere unskilful imitation. The Chūsha (i.e. the Yaozō) belong to a family of handsome men, and Kumesaburō is a present actor of young women's parts. Both have an elegant stage appearance, and I sincerely desire by means of my insignificant brush to spread the beauty of our Yedo actors through all the coasts of our land."

What Utamaro thought of Sharaku we do not know. But we may conjecture that if, like Chōki, he could not help admiring that master's grand style and unmatched intensity of presentment, he regarded with disgust the now general fashion of theatrical prints designed by men who lacked Sharaku's style, but aped his realism and produced grimacing and squinting figures in increasing profusion.

Much has been made of Utamaro's evil influence during his leadership of Ukiyo-ye, and of his own decline of power in his latter years. Undeniably the general taste was changing for the worse ; but when we regard the actual prints, what do we find ? Utamaro alone stands out from the rest, composing with no loss of mastery to the end, even though as a draughtsman he was no longer what he was. The feminine types, with their narrow faces, have deteriorated from the sweet dignity of the Kiyonaga type ; but which of Kiyonaga's followers in the years about 1790, when so many charming prints were being published, was capable of so masterly and original a composition as the triptych of the " Persimmon Gatherers," which is one of Utamaro's latest productions, or the " Princess alighting from her carriage," or the many delightful compositions in the *Nenjū Gyōji* of 1804 ?

The famous Taikō triptych, hitherto assumed to be the cause of Utamaro's punishment, is of no great interest, except for historical reasons, but it betrays no enfeeblement ; nor do the offending prints reproduced here (Pls. 37, 38) for the first time. Only in the prints produced between the master's imprisonment in 1805 and death in 1806, of which the well-known triptych of " Girls on the Seashore at Ise " and the six-sheet print of " Marriage Ceremonies " may be taken as examples, do we find a real weakening ; and here it is not so much in the composition as in the detail of the drawing, which was entrusted to pupils.

Unfortunately for Utamaro's reputation, prints by the extremely feeble Utamaro II have been fathered on him ; his signature was forged in his lifetime by inferior artists ; and in his last years prints came from his workshop for which he had merely given the idea. Even Mr. Ficke in his book has given as one of his four illustrations of Utamaro's work a print (Pl. 41) which bears no trace of Utamaro's mastery, and is from the very end of his life and no doubt carried out by a pupil.

Alas for Ukiyo-ye ! In every period hitherto the triumphs of each group of masters were coincident with the rise of a fresh generation, equally gifted, and capable in time of taking their places and injecting new vigour into the traditions of the colour-print. But now the age was sterile. Utamaro's own pupils were singularly ill-fitted to succeed him. Nor, in the other groups, was there any fertile or distinguished talent. Kiyomine produced a few good and carefully-printed designs of *bijin ;* and the same may be said of Ryūkoku and the second Banki, but their production was very small, and Ryūkoku's prints, after Utamaro's death, are very bad. Yeizan, who succeeded Utamaro as the popular designer of *bijin-ye,* was an artist of no account.

Utamaro, of course, was a difficult master to follow. It was not a question of repeating in one group after another a felicitous type of womanhood, but of relating figures, lines, colours, empty spaces, and masses of black to each other with original invention ; and this was a thing not imitable. What the men of 1790, the followers of Kiyonaga, would have been able to achieve, had they chanced to arrive on the scene twelve or fifteen years later, we cannot tell ; their work would doubtless be far less attractive than it is ; but we cannot believe that they, or any former group of the minor masters, would have collapsed so completely as the men of 1806. For when Utamaro died it was a veritable collapse. Kikumaro's prints of 1808 are quite hideous, as well as deplorably feeble. Shuntei, who had been best known for legendary and heroic subjects, in the tradition of Shunshō and Shigemasa, published in 1807 a well-known triptych, the " Eel Restaurant," which has some merit and vigour ; but the general output takes on all at once an aspect of impotence and vulgarity combined which seems almost incredible by contrast with a few years before.

Seal-dates for these years of Bunkwa are found on many prints, and enable us to divide the prints preceding Utamaro's death from those which come after. The sudden change is astonishing.

Toyokuni surrendered with the rest. In fact, it would seem that he, more than any other, was responsible for the general depravation of taste. Even by 1800 his types of face, in *bijin-ye* and in idyllic scenes, were beginning to be little more than an insipid formula ; his actors were drawn with an increasing violence of emphasis which marked the lack of structure and significance. Contrast his work in the book called *Nigao haiyū* with the beautiful design by Utamaro which prefaced it. Even before Utamaro's death we find Toyokuni's faces tending toward that haggard, narrow, angular type with eyes exaggeratedly oblique and hard meaningless stare which after 1806 was to prevail throughout Ukiyoye design.

About 1810 Toyokuni published the well-known five-sheet composition "View of the Cherry Trees in the New Yoshiwara."

Fenollosa reproduced a sheet of this in his *Outline of Ukiyo-yé*, and very justly points out the tragic change that twenty years have brought. It seems scarcely credible that this is by the same artist as the five-sheet print of the same subject designed by Toyokuni towards 1790. But Fenollosa by making Utamaro, in defiance of the facts, live on to 1811, has involved him in a degradation in which he had no share.

From 1806 to 1825, when he died, Toyokuni's work is deplorable, whether in prints of actors or of women. It is callous and vapid, and has no real vigour even in its coarseness.

In the whole field of Ukiyo-ye there is only one sign of hope. That is Hokusai.

All through these early years of the new century Hokusai continued to produce *surimono*, side by side with books and paintings. There is a slight, gradual tendency to enlarge the scale of the figures, and *surimono* of long, oblong form became more common. But these prints still maintain something of the miniature in their design. Some of them are of "still-life" subjects, and the refinements of printing, the enhancements of silver and bronze dust, which were always a mark of these small prints, seem specially suited to such motives. The figure compositions rarely lack an outdoor setting, and the landscape element tends to become more important. The figures are sometimes not so much relieved against their surroundings as (so to speak) embedded in them. But in some of the most beautiful of the long *surimono* Hokusai places his figures prominently on a river-bank or cliff's edge, with a great depth of air behind them, through which the more distant scene appears, not in broad masses, but rather in delicately coloured hints and small, selected forms. None of these surpasses that one in which a little group of girls, with two servants, have come out on the cliffs to gaze at Fuji, white and far across the sea. The outline of the mountain and the wrinkled waves of the sea are indicated merely by blind-printed indentations of the paper; there is a faint flush of colour in the foreground with its blossom, but the bathing sense of atmosphere is what is mainly communicated.

The same kind of early spring colouring is in a set of *surimono* illustrating in analogues the Twenty-four Paragons of Filial Virtue. These are inimitable in their delicacy of design and tint. They are of about the same date as the small Tōkaidō set, of which we give two illustrations.

None of Hokusai's followers quite reached the quality of the master's *surimono* of this period, though Hokkei designed some very fine *surimono* indeed, and at his best did not fall far short of his exemplar. Hokkei's landscape *surimono*, designed in light, clear colours, show also a certain originality. Gakutei in this period designed some admirable *surimono*, especially of still-life. His best-known work of this kind is the print, rich in its fine detail, of the ill-fated Chinese emperor Ming Huang, seated by his adored mistress Yang Kuei-fei, and teaching her to play the flute.

But these artists and others of the same group tended to fall off sadly the more independent they became. With time their style coarsens. Hokusai's own style, too, becames more mannered, and the peculiar type of face which he affected becomes more pronounced. But his powers of design continue to expand. About 1815 he produced a wonderful series of *surimono* called *Genroku Kasen Kai awase*, " Choice Collection of Verse on Shells," for a poets' club. This set is easily recognized by the title, which is in red, with underneath it a little design of shells on a fan. It contains many delightful compositions, and the colour, less reserved than in the earlier *surimono*, is delicately harmonized.

Apart from *surimono* and books Hokusai produced few colour-prints during this period. One very rare diptych bears the seal-date for 1807. Its subject, taken from the legendary history of China, is " The Cruelties of T'a Chi, the Concubine." Here we find the curious types which Hokusai gives to the Chinese figures in the *Mangwa* and other books.

About 1810 he published a set of Six Poets, in which, after a fashion sometimes affected by Chinese and Japanese painters, the outlines of the figures are formed by the characters denoting the poet's names. Here Hokusai's mature style is seen for the first time in prints with large figures. This set is also rare. But before this he had published a set of prints which claim more detailed notice.

In 1806 the house of Tsuruya published a second Chūshingura set by Hokusai, which it is interesting to compare with the set, signed Kakō, of 1798. Hokusai's powers of design have greatly developed in the eight years' interval. The earlier set, as we have already noted (p. 131), is curiously tentative, considering that Hokusai was far from being a novice at the date of its production. When we turn to the present set we see at once that he is no longer distracted by problems of half-learnt perspective, and feels free to grapple with the core of his themes. There is a vivid sense of drama in all these scenes, and the persons " fill the stage " as they failed to do in the earlier prints. The colouring, too, is much more coherent. The best known of the set is the last scene of all, where the *rōnin* are scaling the snow-covered roofs of Moronawo's palace, and one of them heaves a huge mallet to break down the door. But others of the set are more interesting in respect of Hokusai's art and its development.

In the scene from Act I we see a terrace at Kamakura and look out over a wide prospect of sea and coast to Fuji in the far distance. In Act VIII Tonase and Konami are travelling the great Tōkaidō highway where it skirts the sea. The plan of this design is the same as that of the corresponding print in the earlier series, but what a difference in the carrying out ! In the finding of a convention to represent rock-masses and tree-shapes, in the relation of the human figures to the landscape, in the grasp of the scene as a whole, what an advance in confidence and mastery !

It needs but a slight alteration in the balance of interest to convert these prints from " figures in a landscape " to " landscapes with figures." Already we see the elements which, recomposed, will form the structure of the great designs of the " Thirty-six Views of Fuji."

This year, 1806, is, then, a date of great significance in the history of Ukiyo-ye. Utamaro dies, and with him dies that lovely world which we have seen in the mirror of so many an artist's mind ; the world of youth and charm, peopled by one generation after another of gracious forms in all the varied movements of life. For in the multitude of prints that are to follow there are but rare exceptions that can for a moment compare with what for so long had been a continuous stream of changing beauty. And in this same year we find, in this Chūshingura set of Hokusai's, the budding growth of that landscape art which was to be the glory of Ukiyo-ye in the 19th century.

# CHAPTER IX

# BUNSEI PERIOD

In the autumn of 1812 Hokusai, en route westwards, stopped at Nagoya, where he made the acquaintance of Gekkwōtei (also called Hokutei) Bokusen and Tōnansei Hoku-un of that city, both of whom became his pupils and forthwith assisted him in drawing the designs for the first volume of his masterpiece, the *Hokusai Mangwa*, which was published in the spring of 1814. This book, fifteen volumes in all, has justly earned a wide reputation both in his native land and abroad, and has been eulogized by several writers. Yet in no single case within the writer's knowledge has an entirely accurate account been given of the dates when the first editions of each volume were published, nor has any attempt been made to grapple with the question of the dates of subsequent editions. Even Katano Tōshirō of Nagoya, who inherited the copyright from his father Yeirakuya Tōshirō on January 10th, 1875, and who on September 26th, 1878, published the first edition of Volume 15, together with re-issues of Volumes 1 to 14, each with frontispieces setting forth the dates of the original editions of each volume, gives those of Volumes 8 and 9 as 1818 and 1819 respectively, whereas the correct date is 1817 for each. It is therefore desirable, in a work of this importance, that this matter should be adjusted; and with this object the following list has been prepared from first and other editions in the writer's collection. The dates of publication refer to the dates given at the end of each volume, where also appear the names of the artists and their pupils and of the publishers and booksellers. Dates of prefaces are apt to be misleading, as, for instance, Volume 1 has preface dated the 10th month of Bunkwa Mizunoe Saru, corresponding to November 4th to December 3rd, 1812, but close on fifteen months elapsed before the volume was published. Again, the preface of Volume 10 bears the date Bunsei 2, 10th month, i.e. November 18th to December 16th, 1819, but the volume was published in the spring of that year; the preface writer had made a mistake.

## LIST OF FIRST AND SUBSEQUENT EDITIONS OF VOLUMES ONE TO TEN

*Volume 1.* Bunkwa 11, which began on February 20th and terminated on May 19th, 1814. *Note.*—The only dated reissue of this volume was, as far as is known, made in the spring of Bunsei 11 (1828), and this is marked *sai-han*, which may mean either " second edition " or " republication."

*Volume* 2. Bunkwa 12 Kinoto I mō-shun, i.e. the first spring month of 1815, which began on February 9th.

*Volume* 3. Bunkwa 12 Kinoto I mō-ka, i.e. the first summer month of 1815, which began on May 9th. *Note.*—In the spring of Bunkwa 13, January 29th to April 26th, 1816, the second editions of Volumes 2 and 3 were published.

*Volumes 4 and* 5. Bunkwa 13 Ne natsu, i.e. the summer of the Rat year, 1816, April 27th to July 24th.

*Volumes 6, 7, 8, and* 9. Bunkwa 14 Ushi mō-shun, i.e. the first spring month of the Ox year, 1817, which began on February 16th. *Note A.*— In every record, both Japanese and Western, that has been examined, the date of Volume 9, one of the best of the series, has been given as 1819. This is the first record of the 1817 edition, and no other copy has been seen. *Note B.*—In the spring of Bunkwa 14, which began February 16th and terminated May 15th, 1817, the second edition of Volumes 4 and 5 and the third edition of Volumes 2 and 3 were published.

*Volume* 10. Bunsei 2 U haru, i.e. the spring of the Hare year, 1819 ; began January 26th and terminated April 23rd, 1819. *Note.*—On the same date were published the 4th edition of Volumes 2 and 3 ; the third editions of Volumes 4 and 5 ; and the second editions of Volumes 6, 7, 8, and 9.

*General Note.*—In Volume 1 the master had the co-operation of his Nagoya pupils Hokutei Bokusen and Tōnansei Hoku-un, and in Volumes 2 and 3 that of his Yedo pupils Uwo- (or Sakana-) ya Hokkei and Tōyenrō Hokusen in addition. Volumes 1, 2, and 3 in their first editions are signed " Katsushika Hokusai." The second and subsequent editions of Volumes 2 and 3 and all the editions of Volumes 4 to 10 inclusive are signed " Hokusai aratame (changed to) Katsushika Taitō," and are sealed with a seal usually described (perhaps from the difficulty in deciphering it) as a " square seal with reticules or interlaced lines." This seal reads " Fu-ji-ya-ma," written in a peculiar style of Hiragana, and is of interest as indicative of Hokusai admiration of the " Peerless Mountain." It is interesting, too, to note that in his second masterpiece, the " One Hundred Views of Fuji "—*Fugaku Hyak'kei*—he used a pictograph of Fuji as his seal, in which the white cone stands out in relief against a red ground.

After the publication of Volume 10, Sumi- (may be also read Kaku-) maruya Jinsuke ceded the blocks to Yeirakuya Tōshirō, who some years later republished the first ten volumes, but without date. On the last page of each volume of this new edition the artist's name is given as "Katsushika Hokusai," with the seal "Raishin." The master had taken the first of these names at the close of 1806 after bestowing his former name of Gwakyōjin upon a pupil, and that of Raishin, i.e. Thunder and Lightning, in commemoration of an escape from being struck by a great thunderbolt on his way to worship at the shrine of the god Myōken on Yanagishima in the Honjō quarter of Yedo.

Inasmuch as this Nagoya edition is scarcely inferior to the Yedo one, we may infer that it appeared within a year or two of 1819.

A considerable interval elapsed before Yeirakuya published the eleventh volume. This is undated, nor does Katano give any date. As, however, he assigns the spring of Tempō Kinoe Uma, i.e. February 9th to May 8th, 1834, as the date of Volume 12, it probably appeared some time previously. De Goncourt gives its date as 1834, but on what authority is not known. The twelfth volume is also undated; but the preface bears the date above assigned by Katano as the date of publication, which may therefore be taken as correct. When Siebold returned from Japan in 1830, neither of these two volumes had appeared. Volume 13 likewise is undated; but as the preface bears a date corresponding to a period from August 18th to November 14th, 1849, and as Katano assigns this as the published date, it is likely to be correct. There is no date of publication to Volume 14, nor is its preface dated; Katano also gives no date. De Goncourt mentions 1875, though as far as is known there is no authority for this date. It certainly appeared, however, before the fifteenth volume in the autumn of 1878. The *Mangwa* was issued in many other editions, most of them pirated; but these impressions are so bad as to demand no notice. Much may be gathered from the prefaces, written by contemporaries, regarding the master and his work, and the *raison d'être* of the book.

Hence a few brief extracts may be advisable embodying the salient features. "Everyone recognizes the rare genius of Hokusai-ō. During this autumn (1812), the master, so it happened, was on his way westwards and broke his journey at our prefecture (Nagoya) where he met Gekkwōtei Bokusen to their mutual joy. More than three hundred designs was the fruit of their conversations." "Nothing in Nature has been omitted. His brush has evoked the real spirit of all things—that truthful spirit which painters in recent years have been unable to grasp through an uncertain touch and a lack of ability to reproduce their ideas. . . . The volume is, indeed, a model for art students. The master himself chose the title of 'Mangwa.'" ... "What particularly strikes one is the excellence of the human figures of every station in life." ... "The master, Katsushika Hokusai, has reproduced with extraordinary deftness and fidelity all objects that his eyes have ever seen or his brain has ever conceived." ... "All know how devoted Katsushika Taitō is to his art. His works and prints published in Yedo are much prized and are in enormous demand; and his brush never lies idle." ... "From his boyhood, Taitō displayed a bent for drawing. He ate and drew, drew and ate, till finally he originated the Katsushika style and became famous." ... "Hokusai cared nought for *saké* and looked with contempt upon tea. Nor had pleasures and distractions any attraction for him—to art alone has he devoted fifty years." ... We are also informed that the *Mangwa* was the outcome of a demand by Hokusai's numerous pupils for drawings that might serve them as models and by studying which they might follow in his footsteps and perhaps eventually approach his skill; also that the Master's intention was to complete the work in twenty volumes.

Amongst the pupils of Toyokuni I who designed prints during Bunsei and Tempō were Toyoshige, Kunitsugu, and Kunitora.

TOYOSHIGE (personal name Genzō) was born in 1777. In addition to Toyoshige he used the *gō* of Ichiyeisai and Ichiryūsai, and as the adopted son of his teacher the signature "Toyokuni's humble son (*segare*) Toyoshige." On the death of Toyokuni he is said to have married his widow and to have received her permission to call himself the second Toyokuni, a title which the other pupils never recognized, deeming him to be an unworthy successor. He then signed his prints Kōsotei, Ichiyeisai, Ichiryūsai Toyokuni, or Toyokuni; but never, as far as is known, Toyokuni the Second; nor, it is believed, did he use his master's brush-name of Ichiyōsai, though some assert that he occasionally so signed. He died on December 20th, 1835.

Other pupils of Toyokuni who worked about the same time were KUNITORA, personal name Kumezō; and KUNITSUGU, personal name Kōzō, *gō* Ichiōsai, born 1800, died 1861.

KATSUSHIKA TAITŌ II, whose real name was Kameya Saburō, worked from about 1821 to 1853. He was a pupil of Hokusai and was first called Hokusen. In 1820 his teacher took the brush-name of I-itsu, at the same time bestowing upon his pupil his discarded name of Taitō. He owned one of the *hikite-jaya* or "guide tea-houses," so called from their being used by visitors for assignation purposes, in the New Yoshiwara. In the Kayei period he removed to Ōsaka where he designed some prints in imitation of his master's style which he signed with his name for which he had no authority. This earned for him the nickname of " Dog Hokusai." Opinions differ as to whether the well-known print " The Monkey Bridge," as it is usually called, is the work of Hokusai himself or of his pupil. There are two prints almost identical and each signed " Katsushika Taitō." In one the moon is small and the shadows of the boats are reflected in the water. This bears the *kiwame* seal and was published by Echigoya Chōhachi. The other was published by Izumiya Ichibei and has two censor seals. The superiority in drawing and colouring of the first points to its being the master's work about 1818. The second was probably not published till about 1842.

Bunsei is the period of Hokusai's splendour. During these years he produced the magnificent sets of colour-prints of landscape and of flowers on which his fame largely rests, as well as the *Mangwa.*

So far as the old tradition of *nishiki-ye* was concerned, production was as multitudinous as ever. But conception, design, and colour were equally debased.

Toyokuni lived on to 1825, but his work was virtually over before Bunsei began. Yeizan was the most popular designer of *bijin-ye* of the day ; but Kunisada was coming into prominence. Starting with theatrical prints, in which he followed Toyokuni very closely, Kunisada soon enlarged his range and produced many prints of beauties, mothers and children, etc., in the vein of Utamaro's last years. Occasionally one finds a print, or group of prints, in which Kunisada's gift is acceptable both as composition and as colour, especially those in which he has chosen small patterns for the dresses. Certainly Kunisada's earlier phases are quite superior to the last phase of Toyokuni. In 1825 he published a memorial portrait of Toyokuni, just after the master's death ; a whole-length portrait, standing, in Buddhist robes, with yellow ground. It is plain, unaffected portraiture, without being in any way masterly. Before this date Hokusai had begun to publish the first of his landscape prints.

In all the landscape sets of which we are now to speak there is a novelty which strikes the eye at once. This is the strong blue, " Prussian blue," imported from Europe apparently about this time. Hitherto only fugitive blues had been available, and none with any depth of tone. There is every reason to think that Hokusai was the first to employ this new colour. Before long it was to come into universal use in figure-designs, but we do not know of any figure-design in which it occurs of an earlier date than

1823, whereas prints of this kind which are known to be of later date are without it. In any case Hokusai was the master most fitted to use this new colour-resource.

Ukiyo-ye is the mirror of the transient world, the " glass of fashion," the art of the captured moment. What had it to do with the eternal hills ?

In Europe, in this same epoch, painters and poets were turning to the solitudes of sea and mountain as an escape from the world of mankind. But here was no Romantic Movement, no self-absorbed melancholy, no gesture of satiety and vague craving. It was, simply, the completion of Ukiyo-ye by the addition of the last province left to it. In Europe the passion for wild nature was new ; in Asia it was very old. And just as, at every stage, we have seen Ukiyo-ye challenge the classic schools in one field after another, so now it will rise to its last and greatest effort of self-vindication ; for in the Far East it is landscape which is held to be the supreme sphere of painting. As before, it will assert the Yamato genius ; it will be national. The Kanō academicians might go on for ever repeating their pictures of mist and peak and torrent from the China which they had never seen. The *Yamato yeshi*, the painter of Japan, would vindicate the beauty of his own land. It is no longer legendary sages and contemplative poets who haunt lake-shore or mountain-glen, but the ordinary traveller, bent on business or pleasure, who will be seen journeying the hilly roads, pilgrims resorting to shrines, *rōnin* with their curved flutes, coolies with packs upon their backs or straw-capes to protect them from the rain. It is Nature seen with the eyes of workaday Japan. It is Ukiyo-ye after all ; the pleasure of the people in their own doings and amusements completed by their pleasure in the world of nature about them.

For even in teeming Yedo, with its acres of streets and houses, there are glimpses to be had of Fuji-san, the peerless mountain, which for unnumbered generations has shone in its solitary altitude as a symbol of the soul of Japan, haunting the memory of her poets, and even for the humblest and poorest seeming a kind of heavenly possession of virgin beauty. And it was to the peak of Fuji-san that Hokusai turned when the impulse came to him to see what Ukiyo-ye could achieve in the art of landscape design. The famous Thirty-six Views of Fuji, supplemented by another ten views, were published during the years 1823–1829.

Hitherto the *uki-ye* had been the recognized type of landscape for the colour-print. We have noted specimens by various masters since the days of Okumura Masanobu in earlier chapters. Hokusai in the years when he was still Shunrō had designed them, and the Chūshingura set, signed

Kakō, belonged to this type, with its elaborate essays in perspective and bands of formal red cloud at the top of the design.

Now that Hokusai, with his powers fully matured, set out to design landscape in the medium of the colour-woodcut, what tradition did he build on? He retained when he chose the bands of cloud or mist, which had originally been a convention of the old Tosa school of painting, cutting into the design with clearly defined shapes, not melting and gradated as in the Chinese tradition. He made his masses broad and simple, with no small curves in their outlines; and with a few selected colours, boldly contrasted at will, built up a design not only admirably suited to the woodcut medium, but organically coherent. Accidents and " weather " he disregarded, pursuing rather characteristic structure and a sort of natural drama. The landscape art thus created was in the Japanese tradition, yet was like nothing that had been done before; it was in effect a new creation, a new synthesis of elements lying to hand in the art of the past. Just as Sōtatsu and Kōrin had fused Chinese breadth and unity of impression with Japanese motives and decoration for the special purposes of screen-painting, Hokusai combined these with hints from all the styles he had so eagerly studied to form a new and profoundly original manner of design for the special purposes of the colour-print.

As we look through the long series of the Views of Fuji, we see how with one part of his mind Hokusai is caught by motives that in other hands might have resulted only in something freakish, droll, or merely trivial. Travellers on a windy day, with their hats blown off into the sky and papers whirled up on the gust (a parallel motive had been turned by Masanobu and Harunobu to the prettiest account, with a girl for the wind's victim); a cooper caulking inside the huge round of a cask, through which distant Fuji appears; workmen repairing the roof of a building; sawyers at work on an enormous log tipped up on a huge trestle; a fisherman perched on a rock in the sea and pulling in his lines: the way in which the peerless cone would come into odd or fantastic relation with such sights of the everyday world entertained, one sees, the surface of the artist's mind; but no matter what the ingredients, there results, instinctively wrought out at a deeper level of his consciousness, magnificent design. This is Hokusai's extraordinary originality, his freedom from bias toward the accepted combinations of beauty. He takes the whole world of sight, decomposes it with a vigour like that of a potter kneading clay, and with a gust of creative energy composes it afresh, a thing of integral life. The presence of Fuji-san, now near, now remote, now dominating, now hardly seen on the horizon ; a blue silhouette on the evening sky beyond the long arch of the great bridge over the Sumida, watched by a crowd of holiday-makers in a ferry-boat ; a red, snow-streaked cone emerging from the plain ; a white apparition at the edge of a snow-covered world : the continued presence of this solitary form throughout the series gives to the whole array of prints a unity of theme, so that it seems irrelevant to complain of inequality in the series. Inequality there is, no doubt ; but it is the indispensable inequality of an epic poem, where we take for granted the lower levels, the tamer or more bustling scenes, because they fall into their place and do but enhance the strains of loftier feeling and sublimer rhythm. As if he could not help his deeper nature emerging to the surface, in spite of occasional proneness to be taken by whimsical juxtapositions or amusing incident, Hokusai again and again rises to the grandeur of simplicity, and in the culminating pages of this series answers the elemental in nature with an elemental power in himself. The Red Fuji in clear weather against a sky barred white and blue ; the Fuji above the Lightning ; and the deep-sea Wave toppling over the men rowing in their fragile boat ; these, by common consent, are the greatest prints of the forty-six, and are among the great landscape designs of the world. But even if these be abstracted, what a number of memorable designs remain !

The colouring of this set of prints varies much in different impressions, though a few are schemed in green and blue only, and therefore offer little scope for variety. The key-block is sometimes printed in black, sometimes in blue ; but neither of these must be taken as in themselves indications of early impression.

Before the publication of the Thirty-six Views was completed in 1829 Hokusai had published other landscape sets, the " Waterfalls " and the " Bridges," and apparently also the large " Flowers " and the small " Flowers and Birds."

The " Waterfalls " are even more original in design than the Fuji series ; some are even a little bizarre. They astonish by their force and boldness of conception. The spray, the sparkle, the drifting haze, the wetness of the falling water, are nothing to Hokusai ; what he sees, what he communicates, is its plunging mass, its weight, its energy. Tones of blue predominate in the colouring, relieved by green and pale buff. All is concentrated and intense. The " Fall of Yoro " is especially magnificent.

The " Bridges " are by comparison a tamer series, containing no great masterpiece, though never falling below a high level, for Hokusai's design is always interesting. The subjects perhaps tied him down too much, they did not supply the motives which inspired his supreme efforts.

The Large Flower set, published by Yeijudō about 1828, is, on the other hand, one of Hokusai's most satisfying works. There appear to have been earlier sets of flowers in Ukiyo-ye, by Shigemasa and by Shunshō, though they can only be traced in a few scattered specimens; and there is the incomparable Insect Book of Utamaro which contains exquisite flower-drawing. But nothing had yet been done of the grandeur and power of Hokusai's series. At this period he was saturated with the study of Chinese work; and it is probable that he now aimed at transcending the floral designs, familiar from such Chinese colour-printed books as the " Mustard Seed Garden." It is unfortunate that this series is extremely rare, for it shows the master at his most attractive, with very little of his peculiar mannerisms. De Goncourt says that it consists of ten sheets, and his statement has been generally accepted. These ten were perhaps the chief glory of the de Camondo collection, now in the Louvre; eight of them being reproduced in the *Paris V.I. Catalogue*. There are, however, at least eleven. Those in the Louvre are: Chrysanthemums and Butterfly; Irises; Lilies; Convolvulus and Tree-toad (reproduced in colours, Plate 15); Orange Orchid; Peonies; Narcissus; Sparrow and Fuyō (*Hibiscus mutabilis*); Poppies; Swallow and Hydrangea. The last three of these are in a rather different and more mannered style than the others. To these must be added the Kikyō and Dragon-Fly, an impression of which is in the British Museum. Some of the set are on a yellow, others on a blue ground. In the " Peonies " and in the " Chrysanthemums " a wind is blowing and makes the flowers on their pliant stems tremble and sway. Both of these are very nobly designed; but indeed the whole series is magnificent, both in design and colour. The " Lilies " especially have a simple grandeur, comparable to the vision of the red Fuji in the Thirty-six Views.

A set of very large prints, upright in shape, of birds and flowers and flowering trees, was published after Hokusai's death, but not designed for the woodcut. This set has sometimes been confused with the " Large Flowers "; and the same confusion has also arisen with regard to a set of oblong prints with a forged signature of Hokusai, made up from subjects in Taitō's *Kwachō Gwaden*, published at Ōsaka in 1848–1849.

About the same time Hokusai published, also with Yeijudō, another set of Flowers and Birds, generally known as the Small Flowers. These are also rare. Ten, probably the complete set, in brilliant impressions, are in the British Museum. These are fine in colour (varying in different impressions), but as design are not to be compared with the Large Flowers. They are charming rather than great. And in several cases the birds, though not the flowers, betray Hokusai's mannerisms. In drawing birds Hokusai exaggerates the eyes and gives a peculiar set to the head and neck, so that his birds seem to belong to a Hokusai world of their own.

The set of Eight Views in the Lu Chu Islands, the precise date of which is unknown, may be mentioned here. Presumably based on sketches or descriptions by another hand, they have not the interest of Hokusai's Japanese landscapes; but in their bright gay colouring of blue, white, and green, and their free and a little fantastic composition, they have a charm of their own, recalling Chinese landscapes.

Towards 1830 appeared the " Goblins," a set of which only five were issued. Perhaps, as de Goncourt surmises, these proved too terrifying to be popular. Yet, with all their power, one feels latent in them the sort of delight that children take in gruesomeness, rather than imaginative horror, though one must allow that the paper lantern decomposing into the features of the dead wife of the man who had offered it on her tomb is truly terrible.

And now we come to what is by many considered Hokusai's crowning achievement in the colour-print, the *Shika Shashinkio*, Living Images from the Poets of China and Japan. This set of ten *kakemono-ye* is indeed a magnificent array of most original and impressive designs, and taken as a whole is unsurpassed, though we may doubt if any single print among them quite vies with the " Wave " and the two red Fujis. The types, in the Chinese figures at any rate, are mannered and lack nobility. In the finest of the set, the " Toba," there is nobility and pathos in the principal figure, but then he sits on his horse averted from us, and we do not see his face. It is in the relation of the figures to the landscape that these prints are consummate. Neither element dominates the other; there is a sense of the power and vastness and mystery of nature—the moonlit sea melting into infinite distance, the waterfall plunging from huge heights, rivers flowing for ever, crags towering sheer from ocean into coils of mist—but there is also a sense of the strength and dignity of man, supported by his own spirit in exile and desolation, and though full of longings and experienced in grief still aware that " the world is all before him." In the " Tōru Daijin " and the " Tsuraki " there is a great calm and stillness, unusual with Hokusai. The " Shōnenkō," on the other hand, breathes of youth and movement. The " Toba " with its snow is a vision of one who has come to the end of things. The " Rihaku " contemplates eternity in the fall of the great stream.

One cannot help wondering what it was that inspired Hokusai to make this particular choice of subjects. Were these poets or poems—for in some cases it is a poet, in others a poem which gives the motive—already associated together in literary tradition ? If so, this has not yet been traced. In the case of more than one of these prints there has been misapprehension of the precise subject ; and it may be of interest to give here some notes on such of the prints as present a problem in this regard.

HAKU RAKUTEN. This is the Japanese name for the great Chinese poet, Po Chü-I. The print pictures the poet standing on a rock, while three attendants hold up a scroll inscribed with a poem. On a rock below sits a fisherman who points to the scroll. The explanation of this print, which has been incorrectly interpreted, is to be found in the *Nō* play, " Haku Rakuten," translated by Mr. Arthur Waley in his *Nō Plays of Japan*, p. 248, etc. Po Chü-I never visited Japan, but his poetry enjoyed immense fame there. " In the second half of the 9th century," says Mr. Waley, " the composition of Chinese verse became fashionable at the Chinese court, and native forms of poetry were for a time threatened with extinction." At the end of the 14th century, when Seami wrote this play, a similar danger threatened through the great wave of Chinese influence which swept over art and literature. In the play, Haku Rakuten is sent by the Chinese emperor to conquer Japan by his poetry. On the coast of Bizen he meets two fishermen, one of whom is really the god of Japanese poetry, whose home is the Sumiyoshi shrine, under this disguise. The fisherman salutes him by his name, to his great astonishment ; and when he displays a poem—that shown in Hokusai's print—about the moss that cloaks the shoulders of the rocks and the clouds that fold like a girdle round the crags, the fisherman reads it off at once as a Japanese *uta*. The poem, of course, is not a genuine poem of Po Chü-I's, but one ingeniously composed of such characters as might make verse in Japanese pronunciation. Haku is conquered by this proof of the vitality of the Japanese poetry. In Moronobu's book, *Onna Shōrei Shū*, the episode is given, with a different conclusion. The fisherman reveals his identity and entertains the Chinese poet at his shrine. There by a stratagem he causes the shellfish to start fighting ; whereon Haku exclaims, " What, can your very shellfish fight ? How much more your men ! " And he leaves for home forthwith.

Tōru no Daijin. Tōru no Daijin was son of the emperor Saga; he was born in 822 and died in 895. He amused his aristocratic leisure by building a palace at Rokujō, Kyōto, near the Kamo river, and laying out the grounds in imitation of Shio-gama Bay, famous for its salt-kilns. He filled a lake with sea-water brought from Ōsaka, and built kilns for manufacturing salt. Here he held revels and wrote poems with his friends by moonlight. In the *Hyakunin Isshū* he is represented by a poem in which he compares the confusion wrought in his thoughts by his love to the fern-patterns of Michinoku prints (Michinoku being the province in which is Shiogama Bay, and famous for cotton fabrics printed in intricate patterns by impression from actual ferns). But there is also a Chinese poem on the Moon by Tōru, a translation of which has been kindly supplied by Mr. Arthur Waley. It runs : " The fish that wander in the water suspect that it is a curving hook : The birds that fly in the clouds above in their panic mistake it for a bow." This poem is illustrated in Morikuni's book *Yoki-yoku-gwashi*. The crescent moon appears also in Hokusai's print, though otherwise there is no direct allusion either to the Chinese or Japanese poem. Both probably would be in the memory of those for whom the print was made.

Tokusa Kari. This seems to be an illustration of Jakuren's poem, which Mr. Waley thus translates for us : " Wetting the sleeve of the hemp garment of the man of Kiso when *tokusa* (rushes) are cut, the dew falls in pearls that need no polishing."

Ri Haku. This illustrates a poem by Li Po (600–760), the famous Chinese poet. The waterfall is the fall of Lo-Shan near the peak called Hsing-lu-feng in the Lu-Shan range, in the province of Kiang-Si. The poem is translated in *The Works of Li Po*, by Shigeyoshi Obata (New York, 1922), and contains the lines :

> As wind-driven snow speed the waters
> Like a white rain-bow spanning the dark.
> I wonder if Heaven's River[1] had fallen from above
> To course through the mid-sky of clouds.
> Long I lift my gaze. Oh, prodigious force !
> How majestic the creation of gods !

The last two lines seem specially to have been in Hokusai's mind.

Narihira. There seems to be no poem by Narihira which exactly fits the subject of this print. The building in the background has been recognized as Kinryūzan temple, on the Sumida River. If this actual

[1] The Milky Way.

locality be meant, the allusion should be to a passage in the *Ise Monogatari*, where Narihira tells how on reaching the Sumida at evening, in his long journey from Miyako, he felt homesick as he went down to the ferry. " My fellow-travellers and myself were calling to mind those we had left behind at Miyako, when we spied a flock of birds with red bills and legs which are not seen in Kyōto. So we asked the ferryman what birds they were, and he replied, ' Miyako-dori.' Hence I composed this verse : ' If indeed you be Miyako-dori, tell me, I pray you, if my beloved be alive or no.' " The only objection to this interpretation is that the birds on the shore are not *miyako-dori* (oyster-catchers), but wild geese. The flight of birds in the sky may be meant for *miyako-dori*, though one would expect them to be wild geese also. The women and boy beating cloth in the foreground give the sentiment of the scene ; the sound of the beating on an autumn evening being traditionally associated with moods of melancholy and longing. There are poems on this subject, but not by Narihira. The mood of longing for his absent love is expressed in a poem by him on the iris, where the word for iris is only introduced as a kind of acrostic, the separate syllables of the word forming the commencement of the several verses. It is unlikely, however, that this would not be illustrated by a picture of the poet contemplating the iris-beds. In any case there is no doubt about the mood intended to be conveyed.

TOBA. The print with the horseman in the big hat on a snowy hill-side has no sub-title. The poet is generally assumed to be Toba, i.e. the famous Chinese poet and caligraphist Su Tung-po.

Similar representations of Toba in exile are common in art. However, it is possible that it is not Toba who is here pictured, but that the print illustrates a poem by Tobo, i.e. the Chinese Tu Fu, another 8th-century poet who rivals Li Po in fame. A very similar design illustrating this poem is engraved in Hokusai's *Toshisen yehon-go-gon-ritsu*, Vol. III, published in 1833. The poem is supposed to be sent to an absent friend, lamenting that in time of war and disturbance he had left friends and kindred and had ridden out alone into a land of desolate winter, when the roads were hard to travel. The poem was sent to show what warm affection he had left behind.

SHŌNENKŌ. This is the Japanese name for a classic motive of Chinese poetry, " Youth setting out from home " ; there are about thirty versions of it by poets of the T'ang period, but it is not possible to say what particular poem, if any, Hokusai had in mind. The youth on his white horse has discarded his jewelled whip for a willow-branch. The print breathes the spirit of adventure, emphasized by the contrast of the youth setting forth into the world with the angler dozing over his rod.

The subjects of the other prints of this series present no difficulties. With this splendid set of designs, which have a completeness and solidity of effect, with their strong and sometimes strange colouring, hitherto unknown in Ukiyo-ye, Hokusai reaches the climax of his art, so far as the colour-print is concerned. He was still to produce a number of fine prints, but never again to touch quite so great a height.

# CHAPTER X

# TEMPŌ AND KŌKWA PERIODS

## JANUARY 25TH, 1830, TO FEBRUARY 4TH, 1848

The first Toyokuni was buried at Kōunzen-ji on Hijiri hill in Mita; and his pupils, consulting with his adopted son Toyokuni II, erected a stone monument to his memory in the grounds of Myōkendō, Yanagishima, Yedo, in mid-autumn of the 11th year of Bunsei (1828), beneath which were buried several hundred drawings left by their master. Engraved on the back of the monument are the names of booksellers, fan dealers, and pupils who subscribed, together with a notification stating that "names of other students not concerned in raising this monument are omitted." As this memorial affords a useful record of the artists upon whom devolved the duty of perpetuating the Toyokuni tradition during the periods under review, a complete list of their names are given below. The numerals in brackets do not appear on the stone, but are inserted to avoid confusion in the case of studio names used by two or more artists in after years.

*Students of Toyokuni I.*  Twenty-nine, including the second Toyokuni.

Kunimasa (I); Kuninaga; Kunimitsu (I); Kunisada (I); Kuniyasu (I); Kunimaru (I); Kunitsugu; Kuniteru (I); Kuninao (I); Kuninobu; Kuniyoshi; Kunitada; Kunitane; Kunikatsu; Kunitora; Kunikane; Kunitake; Kunimune; Kunihiko; Kunitoki; Kuniyuki; Kunitsuna; Miss Kunihana; Kunitame; Kunitaka; Kunihide; Kunikage; Kunichika (I).

*Students of Toyokuni II.*  Eleven in all.

Kunitomi; Kunitomo; Miss Kunihisa (II); Kuniharu; Kunihiro; Kunishige; Kunimori; Kunitsuru; Kunimichi; Kunikazu; Kunioki.

*Students of Kunisada.*  Eleven in all.

Sadatora; Sadafusa; Sadakage; Sadahide; Sadatsuna; Sadayuki; Sadataka; Miss Sadauta; Sadahisa; Sadanobu; Sadahiro of Ōsaka.

*Students of Kuniyasu.*  Six in all.

Yasunobu; Yasuhide; Yasuharu; Yasutsune; Yasukiyo; Yasumine.

*Students of Kunimaru.*  Three in all.

Shigemaru; Toshimaru; Teruhito.

*Students of Kuninao.* These are not named, but were probably Naomasa and Naofusa.

*Students of Kuninobu.* Five in all.

Nobukiyo ; Nobukazu ; Nobufusa ; Nobutoki ; Nobusada.

*Students of Kuniyoshi.* Eight in all.

Yoshiharu ; Yoshinobu ; Yoshifusa ; Yoshikiyo ; Yoshikage ; Yoshi-katsu ; Yoshimi ; Yoshitomi.

*Students of Kunitane.* Five in all.

Taneshige ; Tanemasa ; Tanekiyo ; Tanekage ; Tanenobu.

*Students of Kunikatsu.* Five in all.

Katsushige ; Katsunobu ; Katsuhide ; Katsuyoshi ; Katsumasa.

*Students of Kunitake.* Three in all.

Takeshige ; Takemitsu ; Taketora.

*Students of Kunimune.*
*Students of Kunitaka.* } Names are not recorded.

Several of these artists designed no prints. Others worked entirely at Ōsaka. Of those who worked at Yedo or at Yedo and Ōsaka the following alone are worthy of further notice.

*Pupils of the first Toyokuni.* Dates of birth and death in each case unknown.

KUNITERU, whose personal name was Jinyemon, is to be distinguished from a later artist of the same name, a pupil of Kunisada. He signed some of his prints Issai Kuniteru.

Kuninobu, real name Kaneko Sōjirō, at first used the *gō* of Ichiyōsai, and later that of Ichiyūsai.

KUNIKANE used the *gō* of Ippōsai. KUNIMUNE also studied under Kuni-naga. KUNIHIKO used the *gō* of Kokkisha ; KUNITOKI that of Ikkansai ; KUNITSUNA those of Ichiransai, Ichirantei, and Ichiyōsai ; KUNIHĪDE that of Ippitsusai ; and KUNIKAGE that of Isshōsai.

KUNICHIKA, who used the *gō* of Ichiyōsai, Ikkeisai, and Kaseisha, is to be distinguished from a later artist, pupil of Kunisada, the *-chika* of whose name is written differently.

KUNITAKA was an early pupil at the beginning of the 19th century. He is known only by an interesting *surimono* of the fifth Danjurō saluting his audience at the New Year of 1804. His age is given as fifty-four ; but as he was sixty-four in that year, either fifty-four is a mistake for sixty-four or the writer of the verse inscribed on the print has purposely substituted the earlier age in order to make it accord with the conceit of the poem, which reads thus : " A man from the East has come over the mountains and passed the fifty-three stations of the great highway."

*Pupils of the second Toyokuni*. Dates of birth and death in each case unknown.

KUNIMORI, who used the *gō* of Ippōsai and Kōchōrō, is identical with Hōrai Harumasu, who used the name of Kōchoyen about 1844, and who later studied under Toyokuni III (formerly Kunisada). He worked both at Yedo and Ōsaka.

KUNIHIRO, who usually signed " Toyokuni's pupil Kunihiro," also worked in both cities.

*Pupils of Kunisada*. Dates of birth and death in each case unknown.

SADAHIDE worked entirely at Yedo, using the *gō* of Gountei, Gokuransei, Gokurantei, Gokuran, and Gofūtei.

SADAKAGE (*gō* Gokotei) worked first at Yedo, but later and chiefly at Ōsaka.

Hasegawa SADANOBU worked mainly at Ōsaka.

*Pupil of Kuniyoshi*.

YOSHITOMI, who used the *gō* of Ichigeisai, worked at Yedo till about 1868. Dates of birth and death unknown.

The following additional print-designers appeared at Yedo during these periods.

Kwasentei TOMINOBU, whose biography is unknown, designed prints in a style between that of Yeisen and Kunisada.

Teisai SENCHŌ was a pupil of Yeisen. His prints of women follow closely his master's style.

Hokusanjin HOKU-I was a pupil of Hokusai, and worked from about 1830 to 1840.

Utagawa TOYOKUMA was the son of Toyokiyo and the grandson of Toyohiro. Upon his father's death, he was adopted by the first Hiroshige. He designed a few *surimono*, one of which is dated 1832 and another 1838.

Though Toyokuni was dead, and Yeizan retired, the Utagawa school was as active as ever, and the stream of prints of actors and *geisha* continued as before through Tempō. But for us the great event of this period is the rise to fame of Hiroshige, whose finest work was to be published during these years. This chapter will therefore be mainly concerned with Hiroshige's landscapes.

First, however, we must follow Hokusai's career. After 1830, when he was seventy-one years old, he produced comparatively few colour-prints ; but among them are some very remarkable designs.

First to be mentioned are a set of *kakemono-ye*, of which five are known, though all of the greatest rarity. These five are : A Falcon on a Perch under Cherry Blossom ; Tortoises under Water ; Carp and Waterfall ; Two Cranes ; and Horses. These are designed with superb bigness, boldness, and energy. They are all reproduced in the *Paris V. and I. Catalogue*.

Another set of five are fan-shaped designs. Two of these (also reproduced in the Paris Catalogue) are of cocks and hens, and are masterpieces of their kind. It is a pity that these prints also are rare in the extreme. So, too, is a set of small landscapes of fishing scenes, a little later in date, which are of great beauty. In one of them the downward rush of a long wave is given with tremendous force.

One of the prints of " Cocks and Hens " is dated " the year of the Sheep," i.e. 1835. To this year also is assigned, by de Goncourt, a *surimono* of an old fisherman smoking a pipe and looking up at the moon, which is supposed to be a portrait of the artist. During Bunsei Hokusai had turned again to *surimono* designing. These late *surimono* contrast with his earlier ones by their greater force of colour and by a certain angularity of manner derived from study of Chinese work.

But Hokusai's chief work during Tempō is the well-known series of prints entitled *Hyakunin Isshū Ubaga Yetoki*, " The Hundred Poems explained by the Nurse." Only twenty-seven of the series were published, though outline designs for others exist.

This series does not rank with Hokusai's greatest work, yet it contains many beautiful designs. Just as Harunobu and others of the older masters had invented analogues for classic themes in daily life, Hokusai translates the sentiment of the poems taken from the classic anthology of the " Hundred Poets " into homelier surroundings. And yet this is not quite a true description ; for though sometimes the original sentiment is frankly parodied, as in the " Yoshitake " (No. 50), where the blissful mood following a hot bath does duty for the first ecstasy of love, or as in the " Michinobu " (No. 52), where the lover's hatred of the dawn that ends the night is translated into the boredom of coolies and *kago*-bearers starting work at twilight—others of the series are quite seriously conceived, and some are direct illustrations of the poems, like the beautiful No. 5, where women listen to the cry of the stag on the hill on an autumn evening. Hokusai's way of treating his themes is exemplified at its happiest in such prints as the Toshiyuki (No. 18). The poet tells how shyly even his dreams steal to his Love, shy as the wave in the darkness steals to the shore of Suminoye Bay. The print shows a junk with full sail gliding past the coast, with a sunset flush in the sky. The Nakamaro (No. 7) directly illustrates the poem in which the exiled poet gazes at the moon and wonders that it can be the same moon that rises on the hills of home; a subject already treated in a grander design in the *Shika Shashinkio*. And others of the series illustrate the poems in a similar way. But Hokusai is generally more fortunate when he relies on a hint or allusion, or shifts the emphasis, so that another theme appears to replace the ostensible one.

Perhaps the finest of the series is the Takamura (No. 11), where women are diving for *awabi* from rocks, and boats rise and fall on the swell of the sea. This beautiful design is analysed by Sir Charles Holmes in the *Burlington Magazine* for April, 1907, where it is reproduced in colours. The poem, uttering the farewell of the poet to the fisher-folk, as he sails into exile, is here but hinted at. Again, the Girls gathering Lotuses in a Boat on a Pond (No. 37), a favourite print with collectors, alludes only indirectly to Asayasu's poem on the pearly dew.

There is a fascination of strange colour in some of these prints, with oppositions of dull orange or chocolate and pale blue-green, more subtle than in former sets.

Outline designs for other poems exist; some were formerly in Dr. Ernest Hart's Collection, and two are in the British Museum. Recently Mr. Shōtarō Satō has had four of these designs cut on wood, with the addition of colour-blocks. It may be of interest to record these prints, which are carefully and on the whole successfully executed. They are: Sosei Hōshi (No. 21), a guide with torches leading the poet to a shrine by moonlight; Atsutada (No. 43), a priestess hammering a nail into a great tree; Akazomeyemon (No. 59), a lady on a verandah by moonlight; and Masafusa (No. 73), cherry blossom on a hill-top, and holiday-makers.

The "Hundred Poems" virtually closes the chapter of Hokusai's colour-prints. It may have been observed that since the Views of Fuji, the Bridges and the Waterfalls, Hokusai has been drawing further away from Ukiyoye proper; invading more and more the classic themes of art, though always intensely original and entirely himself. He has his own peculiar convention, unlike anyone else's, for drawing everything in this Hokusai world—rocks and trees, men and birds and animals. But now we are to accompany the progress of an artist of very different temper, Hiroshige, who during these same years was maturing his mastery of landscape. And now we revert to a more truly popular art.

Hiroshige's original genius in landscape was first unmistakably announced in the set of *Tōtō Meishō*, Views of the Eastern Capital, published by Kawaguchiya Shōzō towards the end of Bunsei, probably about 1826. Before this he had made figure-designs of little distinction, remarkable mostly for the squat proportions of the figures and the unattractive types.

The *Tōtō Meishō* set heralds a kind of landscape which was new alike to Ukiyoye and to Japanese painting. In one print of the series, the "Sun-rise at Suzaki," one might trace a superficial influence from Hokusai, but the series as a whole reveals an essentially different mind and vision. Turner and Constable at the other end of the world were, during this same period, creating landscape masterpieces; and if Turner resembles Hokusai in unwearied fecundity, in passionate emulation of the masters of the past, and in creative reconstruction of what nature offered him (the differences might, of course, be equally emphasized), Hiroshige resembles Constable in freshness and integrity of eye, in his profound affection for the sight and scent and atmosphere of his native land.

When we look at one of Hokusai's landscapes, we are exhilarated by his creative energy, the novel and stimulating shapes, masses, and colours into which he has recast his world, and a sort of dramatic relation between the elements of his design. But Hiroshige's landscapes absorb us into a definite local atmosphere, into the mists, the sunshine, the windy clearness, the rain, the rice-fields, the indented coasts, the moonlight, the mountains, of Japan. With Hokusai the accidents of nature are an occasion for entertaining novelty of composition; to Hiroshige they are dear for their own sake. In this early *Tōtō Meishō* set there is a "Ryōgoku Bridge," in which the wooden piles are drawn with no schematic simplicity, as Hokusai would have drawn them, but with a dwelling on their knots and seams and stains of weather, not only on the lines of construction. Take, again, the "Full Moon at Takanawa," with the wild geese flying down into the foreground, and the wide curve of the bay beyond. The flight of the wild geese in the autumn moonlight is a motive repeated for centuries in Japanese painting; but how freshly Hiroshige uses it! There is nothing of the deftness of strokes learnt by heart, like a writing-lesson, that we find in countless pictures of the other schools; it is all felt and seen, the irregular hurrying motion of the birds following each other with necks outstretched. This rare set of prints is marked by red zigzag streaks of cloud in the skies, making a curious sort of pattern.

Some minor landscape sets, including two of Ōmi Hakkei, followed, before the artist changed the Ichiyūsai of his name to Ichiryūsai.

In the early years of Tempō, about 1832–1834, Hiroshige published a number of *Kwa-chō*, or Flower and Bird pieces, mostly in the shape of the narrow upright slips called *tanzaku*. Attractive and graceful as these are, they cannot compare for delicacy or firmness of design with Koryūsai's or Utamaro's handling of such subjects; they resemble the clever paintings of the Shijō school. On a larger scale is the celebrated " Bow Moon," an original and beautiful composition, and its companion-piece (no others of the series of " Twenty-eight Moonlight Views " are known), the moon seen through maple leaves drifting down across a waterfall.

But it is in pure landscape portraiture that Hiroshige's peculiar genius finds its true material.

In the early spring of 1834 there was published by Hōyeidō in two volumes the famous first Tōkaidō set, which immensely enhanced Hiroshige's fame. A copy in the possession of Mr. Hirose Kikuo is unique, so far as is known at present, in containing a preface written by Yomo no Takimizu in the 1st month (9th February to 9th March) of Tempō 5 (1834). The fifty-five prints had been issued as separate sheets before this, and their publication was probably spread over the year 1833. " Early in Tempō," we are told, the artist went to Kyōto by the great coast-road called the Tōkaidō. It was in some minor official capacity that he joined the retinue of a mission from the Shōgun escorting a horse which was being sent as a present to the Mikado. On this leisurely journey he made innumerable sketches; and after his return to Yedo he selected from these the series of designs engraved and printed to illustrate each of the fifty-three posting-stations along the route, with one for the starting-point at Nihonbashi and another for the terminus at Kyōto.

The enduring charm of this famous series lies, not in an array of masterpieces, but in the candour and freshness of vision by which they are inspired. There is an engaging sort of clumsiness about some of the compositions, and in all of them a complete absence of the callous cleverness into which the old traditions of Ukiyo-ye had sunk. Once again it seems as if Ukiyo-ye, in this new field of art, had renewed its youth. The Shōno (No. 46), with its rows of tall trees on a ridge tossing phantasmal in the rain, is admittedly the masterpiece of the series; but there is an even more intimate charm in some of those less striking scenes of lowland and prairie, or wide prospects at the fords of shallow rivers, breezy with wind or sunny with melting haze. And everywhere there is the sense of social life and intercourse on the great highroad, the true note of Ukiyo-ye. One marvels, too, at the delicacy of atmosphere, the sensitiveness to changing light and weather, which are communicated by such simple means. Truly Hiroshige owed much to his wood-cutters and still more to his printers, who, by grading the colours on the blocks, were able to achieve these hitherto unknown effects. But the point must be emphasized that the quality of these landscapes, just because of the subtleties of tone, can only be appreciated in fine early impressions, which, alas! are but seldom to be found.

Six or more of the blocks of the early part of the series seem to have been destroyed, perhaps by fire, and others were substituted, with in some cases considerable changes. The reasons for these variations are impossible to discover, as they are not improvements. And it is puzzling to find in the "Odawara" (No. 10), for instance, that the character of the distant hills is quite altered; instead of being sharp-edged and facetted, like bits of quartz, in a manner characteristic of Hiroshige's earlier mountain drawing, they are smooth and rounded.

The success of this series was so resounding that the artist was called on later to publish many more Tōkaidō sets, founded no doubt on the surplus of sketches made upon his journey; but none of the later sets approaches the first in closeness and intimacy of delineation.

Meanwhile other sets followed rapidly. First probably in date, perhaps in the course of 1834, comes the *Kyōto Meishō*. In this set is the well-known "Passenger-boat on the Yodo River," with a cuckoo flying across the moon. This is very typical of Hiroshige; the passengers, far from being sentimentalized, are shown busily eating and talking, while above them is the calm broad moon flooding the hazy water with its beauty. There is no note of irony; all is accepted; but the contrast enhances the enchantment of the summer night, and just the upturned head of the boatman poling on the prow, as he looks up at bird and moon, connects the silence of nature with the human creatures so absorbed in their own affairs.

The "Ōmi Hakkei," which may date from the following year, 1835, is in a different vein from any previous work. Here is an "ampler ether," a loftier sentiment, the appreciation of great solitudes and spaces.

Though individual prints from other sets surpass it, this set as a whole ranks, perhaps, above all others. The "Karasaki Pine Tree" in a vertical downpour of rain, all tones of blue and grey, is wonderfully conceived. The "Evening Snow on Mount Hira," all white, black, and grey with a lake of vivid blue, is unsurpassed among Hiroshige's mountain-scenes. There is a clear transparency, a breadth and sharpness of vision, a unity and completeness, in these prints which give them a place apart in the master's work.

The *Yedo Kinkō Hakkei*, Eight Views in the Environs of Yedo, is in Hiroshige's more personal and intimate style, and again is a set that ranks very high indeed. From Mr. Watanabe's catalogue of the Hiroshige Memorial Exhibition, held at Tōkyō in 1918, we learn that these prints were commissioned by a poet named Taihaidō, who with other poetizing friends chose the subjects and had their verses printed on the views. The set was afterwards reprinted with one verse only on each print. The lovely "Autumn Moon on the Tamagawa," with a solitary willow on the bank, is the crowning glory of this set. It is, indeed, exquisite in feeling, and of all Hiroshige's many moonlight scenes the most enchanting. It is one of the classic landscapes of Ukiyo-ye. Of extraordinary beauty, too, is the "Azuma no Mori," where, under the slanting rain, that drenches field and tree, travellers move along a raised causeway. It is a scene that in nature most of us would call dreary ; but Hiroshige seems to feel the rain as the trees feel it, drinking it into their fibres with a kind of patient ecstasy, though perhaps our chief satisfaction comes from the beauty and the unobtruded originality of the composition.

Of Views of Yedo, under various titles, *Tōto Meishō, Yedo Meishō, Kōto Meishō*, there is such a multitude of sets, dating from 1833 to 1843, that it is impossible to keep count of them. We can only mention as of special note such prints as the "Kameido Shrine in Snow," often reproduced, and the beautiful "White Rain on Nihonbashi," from a *Tōto Meishō* set published by Sanoki.

Of *Honchō Meishō*, Views of the Main Island, fifteen prints are known. Here are some prints with a new note of grandeur and solemnity, especially the impressive "Approach to Akiba Temple," where pilgrims go up the steep path between giant tree stems, and the tops of tall trees are seen rising from below against the mountain-side. This print is reproduced in colour in the *Paris V.I. Catalogue*, Plate LXX. It is interesting to find a sketch for this design in one of the five sketch-books by Hiroshige in the British Museum (formerly in the Arthur Morrison Collection), which contain many notes of landscape detail and a certain number of sketch-designs for complete compositions.

This sense of grandeur and solemnity is felt also in certain sheets of the Kiso Kaidō set, which was published somewhere about 1839, though the publication of the separate sheets was, as in the case of the Tōkaidō set, spread over a considerable time, probably three or four years. The Kiso Kaidō was the alternative route, by the mountains, between the two capitals; there were sixty-nine posting-stations, and the complete series of prints contains seventy sheets. Of these, twenty-three were designed by Yeisen, forty-seven by Hiroshige. Here again a number of changes were made in certain of the blocks. The first eleven numbers are all the work of Yeisen. There are many prints of little interest in this series, but a selection from it would contain some of Hiroshige's greatest works. Yeisen's work is competent and occasionally attractive; but most of his prints suffer from misplaced emphasis and lack of duly subordinated detail. This is just where Hiroshige's finest contributions to the series excel by contrast. We find a breadth and solidity of design, a reliance on planned masses, which we have seldom found before in his work; in the "Oi," for example—two travellers on horses in the snow between two great pines—which rivals Hokusai in largeness of conception; or in the white hill-masses of the "Wada." And in the huge pine avenue of the "Mochi-zuki," sombre in blue dusk with the moon rising beyond it, there is that sense of grandeur we have spoken of, allied to a sense of mystery. Again, we have designs in which a broad silhouette of shapes is the central feature; as in the rain-blotted "Suwara" with figures dark against wet mist, or the silhouette of trees in the misty moonlight of the "Miyano-koshi." More beautiful than these is the "Nagakubo," reproduced in colour on Plate 16 of this book. There is another state of the print in which there is a distant range of hills behind the figures on the bridge. This has been sometimes described as the first state. But if one compares the two states, one sees that in the one which we reproduce (without the range of hills) the further rail of the bridge is very subtly indicated, a delicate detail slurred and submerged in the other state, which is the state, moreover, in which the print is commonly found. Of misty moonlight scenes this is Hiroshige's masterpiece. Another exquisite moonlight scene, clear and windy, is the "Semba," approaching, but not quite rivalling, the "Autumn Moon on the Tamagawa" of the *Yedo Kinkō Hakkei* set. These prints, and one or two others, notably the "Shinmachi," with its dark trees on a river bank against a yellow twilight, make up an array of landscapes of peculiar impressiveness and charm.

Of about the same date is yet another set of Eight Views, the very rare and much-prized *Kanazawa Hakkei*, containing one of the most wonderful of Hiroshige's scenes of drenching rain, " Evening Rain at Koizumi."

Probably to the same time we may assign the two famous *kakemono-ye*, the " Kiso Gorge in Snow," and the " Monkey Bridge." Mr. Watanabe places the former of these much earlier, in the year 1832 ; but the signatures appear to be of the same time. The " Monkey Bridge " is especially admired ; and if the treatment of the chafing ruffled water is rather perfunctory, it is a fine composition.

About 1840, according to Mr. Watanabe, ten prints of Fishes were published, ten others having been issued earlier at the same time as the first Tōkaidō set.

In April of 1841 Hiroshige left Yedo for a tour in the province of Kai, returning in November of the same year. His journal of this tour is in a private collection in Tōkyō.

In 1842 was issued the sumptuary edict prohibiting the publication of prints of actors and courtesans, and limiting the number of blocks. The censors' seals now appear on the prints. An added stimulus was thus given to the designing of landscapes, also of heroic and legendary subjects.

As far as the production of actor-prints and *bijin-ye* is concerned, the prints of this period, down to 1842, are negligible. Yeizan had retired before the beginning of Tempō, and the field was left to Kunisada, Kōsotei Toyokuni, and other pupils of Toyokuni I, and Yeisen. But Yeisen's best work is not to be found in his figure-designs ; it is rather in prints of falcons, landscapes, and especially one or two *kakemono-ye*, of which the " Carp Leaping up a Waterfall " and the " Mountain Landscape " are celebrated.

Another fine *kakemono-ye* of a carp was made, perhaps in emulation, by Kuniyoshi. This artist had first become known through some triptychs issued about 1820. His early actor-prints were unsuccessful. In 1827 he produced some prints of " Heroes of the Suikoden," a Chinese romance popularized in Japan by the novelist Bakin. These made a hit, and Kuniyoshi was encouraged to publish a set of " One Hundred and Eight Heroes." These are melodramatic and sensational in conception, but tremendously vigorous both in line and colour. During Tempō he turned his attention more to the heroic episodes in Japanese history, and during the period of strict censorship, 1842–1853, became the pre-eminent master in this field.

A set of *Hyakunin Isshū*, the Hundred Poets, contains some fine designs, especially where the landscape element is strong, and the colouring is often original. Among single sheets may be mentioned the " Flight of Tokiwa " through the snow, from a series called *Kenjō Reppuden*, and " Kidomaru in Ambush," an oblong print. But perhaps the finest set by Kuniyoshi produced during this period is the Nichiren series, a set of ten scenes from the life of the famous Buddhist saint and reformer Nichiren. The last of these scenes, showing the exiled Nichiren toiling alone up a hill-side in the fast-falling snow, is justly famous and has been often reproduced. Few prints in all Ukiyo-ye have so much emotional and imaginative quality. There are two states of this print, one with a horizon-line to the sea, the other without. Whichever is the earlier, the state without this line, and with the sea melting into snow-filled sky, is certainly to be preferred. Here again the landscape element is the main part of the design ; and it is to be regretted that Kuniyoshi did not make more landscape prints. The few that he produced are so fine that they are comparable with Hiroshige's best. The " Anglers on the Rocks " and the " Shower on the Banks of the Sumida " are admirable prints ; but the most beautiful is the " Sea-weed Gatherers at Omori," which both in feeling and in composition is a masterpiece.

Even Kunisada, with whose figure-designs, for all his undeniable talent, one is so easily surfeited, could rise to greatness in landscape ; and we could wish that his beautiful and rare print of " Autumn Maples," so splendid in its colour, and the one or two other landscapes he produced, had more companions.

During this period Kuniyoshi began a great series of triptychs of heroic subjects, but as these were continued into the next period we will, for convenience' sake, speak of them in the following chapter.

# CHAPTER XI

# FROM KAYEI TO MEIJI 13

Upon the death of Hokusai in 1849, the fortunes of the Ukiyoye school rested almost entirely in the hands of the Utagawa artists, Toyokuni III, Kuniyoshi, and Hiroshige I, and in those of their pupils, some of whom have already been mentioned. As regards the remainder, the following are selected as the most noteworthy of those who practised in Yedo during the present periods.

*Pupils of the third Toyokuni (formerly Kunisada I).*

KUNIAKI I, family name Hirazawa, worked from about 1850 to 1860. His younger brother Onosaburō, who called himself Ippōsai or Hōsai Kuniaki II, was chiefly noted for prints of wrestlers.

KUNITERU II was born in 1830, his real name being Okada Tōjirō. His first brush-name was Sadashige. Died in 1874.

KUNISADA II was born in 1823, and at first signed his prints " Baidō Kunimasa III," or " Kunimasa, pupil of Kōchōrō." In 1852 he married his teacher's eldest daughter and received the name of Baichōrō Kunisada II. He died in 1880.

KUNIHISA, who used the *gō* of Ichiryūsai, Ippōsai, and Ichiunsai, married his teacher's third daughter. He was the first male artist of this name, and must not be confounded with the female pupils of the first and second Toyokuni.

KUNICHIKA was born in 1836 and lived well into the Meiji era. He used the *gō* of Ichiōsai, but not the school name of Utagawa. Before becoming a pupil of the third Toyokuni he had studied under Kano Chikanobu.

HARUMASA, though not listed as a pupil of Kunisada, appears from his prints to have come under his direct influence. He worked during 1840 to 1852 approximately, designing but few prints.

*Pupils of Kuniyoshi.*

YOSHIKAZU, who used the *gō* of Ichikawa and Ichijusai, was at work from about 1850 to 1870.

YOSHI-IKU worked at the same time, using the *gō* of Ikkeisai and Chōkarō, and later that of Keisai.

YOSHITORA, who used the *gō* of Ichimōsai and Kinchōrō, and after 1874 that of Mōsai, worked from about 1850 to 1880.

YOSHIFUJI, whose real name was Nichimura Fujitarō, used the *gō* of Ittōsai and Ippōsai, working about the same time as the above; as did also Yoshiharu, whose *gō* were Ichibaisai and Chōkarō.

YOSHITSUYA, whose real name was Kōko Mankichi, was born in 1822, and entered Kuniyoshi's studio at the age of fifteen, receiving his diploma when seventeen years old. He used the *gō* of Ichiyeisai. He died in 1866.

YOSHITSURU, whose personal name was Chōjirō, used the *gō* of Isseisai. He was a fellow-student with Yoshitsuya about 1834, and died at the early age of thirty-three. His work extends from about 1835 to 1855.

YOSHITOYO was born in 1830, his real name being Fukuyama Kanekichi. He first studied under the third Toyokuni, and then under Kuniyoshi; hence his brush-name of Yoshi and Toyo. He used the *gō* of Ichiryūsai. He died in 1866.

YOSHIMORI, whose real name was Miki Sakuzō, was born in 1831, and entered Kuniyoshi's studio at an early age. He died in 1885.

YOSHIHIRO, whose personal name was Jūbei, was born in 1838. As a child of six he used to amuse himself by drawing figures, birds, and flowers, and at the age of thirteen became Kuniyoshi's pupil, and was skilful when but fourteen years old, when he received his diploma. He used the *gō* of Itchōsai. He died in 1884.

YOSHINOBU, the last character being different from the former pupil of the same name already mentioned, was born in 1838, his personal name being Yasaburō. In his early years he studied under the first Hiroshige, and when eighteen entered the studio of Kuniyoshi. He used the *gō* of Ichiunsai. He died in 1890.

YOSHITOSHI was born in 1839, and was adopted when a child by the Tsukioka family and was called Tsukioka Yonejirō. He used several *gō*, chiefly Ikkwaisai, Kwaisai, and Taiso. He became Kuniyoshi's pupil in the autumn of 1850, but does not appear to have produced prints till some ten years later. He died in 1892.

*Pupils of Hiroshige I.*

HIROSHIGE II, whose dates of birth and death are unknown, was first called Shigenobu, and later Ichiyūsai Shigenobu. He was adopted by his teacher, after whose death he signed for a short period " the second Hiroshige," and more rarely " Ichiryūsai Hiroshige." In 1865 he retired to Yokohama, when he called himself Risshō and Hirochika II. He worked from about 1839 to 1864.

HIROSHIGE III, whose real name was Andō Tokubei, was an adopted son of his master, from whom he received the brush-name of Shigemasa. He was born in 1843, and died in 1894 at the age of fifty-two. Upon the retirement of the second Hiroshige to Yokohama he styled himself Hiroshige II, though in reality the third.

HIROKAGE, whose biography is unknown, worked from about 1851 to 1866.

Other print designers of this epoch were Sugakudō, Fusatane, Kyōsai, and Kiyochika.

SUGAKUDŌ is chiefly known by a set of Flower and Bird studies which are seal-dated 1859.

FUSATANE'S biography is unknown. He used the gō of Isshōsai and worked from about 1849 to 1859.

KYŌSAI, whose real name was Kawanabe Tō-iku, was born in 1831. While yet a child he entered Kuniyoshi's studio, where he remained but a short time. He received most of his training from Kano Tōhaku, and finally formed his own style. His early work is signed " Chikamaro," which name he used till the middle of 1863. He was addicted to drinking saké, and is said to have done his best work when under its influence. Many of his prints are signed " Shōjō (the drunkard) Kyōsai." He died in 1889.

KIYOCHIKA was born in 1847. He belonged to the military class, being the seventh son of a retainer of the Tokugawa family named Kobayashi Chōbei. As a boy he took a liking to Ukiyo-ye; and when as a young man he had to join the forces of the Shōgunate during the wars of 1867–1868, actually taking part in the engagements at Fushimi and Toba in the latter year, he would spend his spare moments in studying the various styles of the artists of that school. In 1869 he commenced his artistic career by illustrating the Iroha newspaper and continued in this occupation for some years. He began to design for prints about 1876, and continued to do so until his death at the close of 1915.

In 1852 Hiroshige again left Yedo, early in February, and made a tour in the provinces of Awa and Kazusa, returning in April. He made yet another tour—his last—in 1854 to inspect the rivers which cross the Tōkaidō ; and the journals of both these tours are in private collections in Tōkyō.

During Kōkwa (1844–1848) and the first four years of Kayei (1848–1854), he had been supplying various publishers in Yedo with an immense amount of prints, mostly Views of Yedo, Tōkaidō sets, or views in various provinces. Among them may be specially mentioned the fine Tōkaidō set published by Marusei. In some of these sets the figures are as important as the landscapes; for Hiroshige did not confine himself to landscape, and during Tempō had published a Chūshingura set in sixteen sheets and a set of ten scenes from the life of the great national hero, Yoshitsune. A very rare and remarkable set of six (or more) prints called *Waka Rōyei Shū*, contains the " Rocks in a Moonlit Lake," which we reproduce (Plate 44). It illustrates a couplet by the Chinese poet Liu Yü-hsi (772–842 A.D.), from a poem called " Afloat in Ships " :

> " *The mountain rises straight as a screen; the river is level as a mat.*
> *Plucking the strings, we come and go in the brightness of the moon's light.*"

(Translated by Mr. Arthur Waley.) The *Waka Rōyei Shū* was a compilation of Chinese verses and couplets, by Chinese and Japanese poets, set to music. It was made by Fujiwara no Kintō (966–1041 A.D.). Japanese *uta* were added to it later. Another of this set is a huge pine tree towering up into mist. These prints are full of poetry. They are notable also as being among the earliest of Hiroshige's upright compositions. Before this, all the great sets of landscape prints, apart from *kakemono-ye*, had been oblong designs. But from 1853 to his death in 1858 Hiroshige preferred the upright shape.

This change seems to coincide with a change of style, though really there is no sudden transition. The three great sets in the upright shape, produced in these last years, do, however, offer a marked difference from the first Tōkaidō and other famous early sets in the oblong shape. And this difference has led some critics to surmise that the Sixty Provinces, Hundred Views of Yedo, and Thirty-six Views of Fuji are not really by the master, but by the second Hiroshige. Mr. Strange took this view in his *Japanese Colour-Prints*, and in the *Paris V.I. Catalogue* M. Vignier has revived the theory, but in a more drastic form, for he would add not only these sets, but some earlier prints like those of the Kisō Kaidō to the work of a mysterious second Hiroshige, while the acknowledged Hiroshige II is degraded to Hiroshige III.

These reconstructions from the evidence of an artist's works, in disregard of other evidence, are always dangerous. We may recall from the history of Italian painting the case of Bonifazio. At first there was a single master; then two were invented : Bonifazio Veneziano and Bonifazio Veronese. Then Morelli, with his detective criticism, deduced from the actual paintings that there were not two but three Bonifazios. And finally an Austrian archivist showed from documents that there were neither two nor three, but one single painter after all. We have only to read the preface published with the contents of the Thirty-six Views of Fuji to be sure that Hiroshige claimed these as his own work. " One day," we read, " Hiroshige came to the publisher with Thirty-six Views of Fuji, which he said were his last work and asked him to engrave them. It was the beginning of last autumn, and at the close of the autumn he died, aged sixty-two."

It is, of course, true that this and the other two sets produced in Ansei period are inferior to the master's earlier work. They lack the sensitively scrupulous quality and regard for structure which we associate with the first Tōkaidō set and its companions, and replace it by a more fluent picturesqueness. But could we expect that an artist so exuberantly productive would not change, or not deteriorate in some respect? The facile and sometimes flimsy compositions of Corot's old age lack the austere delicacy and precision of his early work, but we have not yet learnt to invent a Corot the Second. Or take Toyokuni : what a contrast between his early and his late prints! M. Vignier relies on the change in the signature : Toyokuni's signature changes even more. No doubt Hiroshige was latterly helped by pupils ; also he made prints from other men's sketches to illustrate views in provinces where he had never been. But his own way of seeing and drawing and composing altered too ; and there is no question that none of the prints of the Ansei period can really compare with the great landscapes of his prime.

Nevertheless, there are many charming prints in the Sixty Provinces set, which Koshibei began to publish in 1853, and continued to publish after the artist's death, up to 1865. The Hundred Views of Yedo were published from 1856 to 1858. This set contains even finer things, such as the snowy coast-scene with the swooping eagle, the Shower on Ōhashi Bridge, the Fireworks at Ryōgoku Bridge (in its first state), and the Fire-breathing Foxes on a starry night, though a certain number of the prints are downright bad, with forced motives and unhappily capricious designs, and many are uninteresting—as, indeed, are many of the earlier oblong prints.

The " Thirty-six Views of Fuji," Hiroshige's last set, show a decided falling off in vigour and inspiration. From the preface, quoted above, we learn that the artist often talked of giving up painting rather than see his brush lose its power as age crept on him ; and this points to a secret consciousness of impaired vitality, though probably, like most artists, Hiroshige had a fondness for his latest offspring.

In 1857 Tsutaya Kichizō published the three famous triptychs, " Naruto Rapids," the " Moonlight on Kanazawa," and the " Mountains and Streams of the Kisoji." And though even these have not all the interior beauty of the earlier masterpieces, they are well worthy of Hiroshige's genius and rank high among his works.

The death of Hokusai in 1849 had left Hiroshige, with Kunisada and Kuniyoshi, paramount in Ukiyo-ye. Kunisada, during Ansei, produced a series of diptychs illustrating the Romance of Genji, which, coarse in type as they are compared with Yeishi's triptychs on the same theme, are original and sometimes distinguished in colouring, and are marvels of fine printing. Kunisada collaborated sometimes with Hiroshige. But in the domain of the figure-print it is the heroic scenes of Kuniyoshi which are the great achievement of this period. We have already mentioned Kuniyoshi's triptychs of these subjects produced during Kōkwa and Kayei, and now continued through Ansei period. All the chief episodes of Japanese history are illustrated in this long succession of prints ; and how rich in dramatic events and heroic characters that history is! The great struggle between the rival clans of Taira and Minamoto ; the battle of Ichi-no-tani, when, like the Persians at Thermopylæ, Yoshitsune and his followers found a mountain-path supposed impassable for men and fell on the Taira in the rear ; the single combat between the old warrior Kumagaya and the beautiful youth Atsumori in the shallow waves of the seashore ; the story of the Soga brothers' revenge ; the exploits of Yoshitsune, Japan's darling hero, and his giant follower Benkei ; and then, later, the struggle of the patriot heroes Kusonoki Masashige and Nitta Yoshisada against the intriguing Ashikaga Taka-uji, their tragic and devoted end ; these and many more historic and legendary scenes became vivid in Kuniyoshi's vigorous triptychs. Always with a bent towards the melodramatic, Kuniyoshi's conceptions seem to be somewhat coloured by stage representations. But, if occasionally violent to grotesqueness, Kuniyoshi is sincere. You feel that his sympathies go out strongly to his heroes, and most when they are in desperate situations, as in the print we reproduce, which is part of a triptych representing the last stand of the remnant of the Kusonoki against the Ashikaga power. And then, at his best, Kuniyoshi is a master of dramatic design. The fight between Yoshitsune and Benkei on Gojo Bridge ; the Ghosts of the Taira rising from the sea and defied by Yoshitsune in his ship ; the Fording of the

Uji River at twilight, with arrows hissing over the water out of the darkness ; the rescue of Tametomo by Tengu from a monstrous fish—these are splendid in their kind.

Ukiyo-ye had been the mirror of a people's daily life. Enlarging its range, it drew into its scope all the beauty of that people's native land, with Hiroshige's landscapes ; and finally it absorbed, with Kuniyoshi's triptychs, the consciousness of an heroic past.

Kuniyoshi survived Hiroshige but three years ; Kunisada, who had retired from active work, lived on another three years. But the achievements of Ukiyo-ye were complete. The successors of these three masters were powerless to give the exhausted tradition a new impetus or a new direction. Many symptoms betray the disturbing attractions and disintegrating influences of the Western world, of which Japan was beginning to be more and more keenly aware, and which herald the Restoration of 1868 and the opening of Japan to Europe and America.

Even so great a painter as Kyōsai, who was an enthusiastic collector of the older masters, could not revive their glory. He was trained in Ukiyoye style by Kuniyoshi, and for a short time designed prints signed Chikamaro ; but he soon abandoned the old traditions of the colour-print, and is better known by some later large light-coloured prints in the style of the older schools.

Probably, in any case, the Western contagion, bringing with it a sudden curiosity about such new wonders as steamships and daguerreotypes, would have ruined Ukiyo-ye. It was too powerful and disturbing. And we realize how fortunate for this art of the people had been the singular conditions under which it was produced ; the artificial isolation of the country, the absorption of the people in its own doings, the protection from distracting influences.

During the Meiji era there was a certain revival of the colour-print. The artists who designed these later woodcuts were men of graceful and facile talent. But there is no longer the old conception of design, in which the drawing was controlled by the fundamental idea of adaptability to the woodcut line. The contours are meagre and accidental, no longer firm and sweeping ; pigments are of a coarser and cheaper quality. The wood-cutters have become perhaps too accomplished ; they can reproduce any kind of painting ; and the designers, no longer needing to consider them, forget to think out their designs in terms of the woodcut. We reproduce, as a favourable specimen of the Meiji print, a charming night-scene with fire-flies, by Kiyochika (Pl. 46). This is of exceptional quality.

Looking back on the long and varied achievements of Ukiyo-ye in the realm of the colour-print, we are impelled to marvel more and more at the extraordinary amount of artistic genius devoted to this art. As pure design, this body of work is unrivalled in any other country, unless perhaps by the Greek vases. On the emotional, imaginative, " spiritual " side it is deficient, it is true ; perhaps the design is so consummate because it is little disturbed by other factors.

It is this devotion to design, this refusal to be seduced by the lures of picturesque naturalism, which give the colour-prints their unique distinction. In them, too, we can follow a special art from its very beginning to its extinction ; Ukiyo-ye has an unparalleled completeness.

But from another point of view, as the full, spontaneous, vivid expression of the moods of a people—or rather a certain section of a people—Ukiyo-ye has a singular interest. Regarded in this light we may well conceive of it as rising gradually to a culmination in Temmei period and declining gradually through the 19th century. But too great an insistence on the sociological aspect will deflect æsthetic judgment and give too little room to the significance of individual genius. In the limited number of Kiyonaga's central masterpieces we do, indeed, find a bloom as of perfect ripeness, which does not come again. Yet if we think of the chief masters of the colour-print in relation, not to the society which produced them and for which they worked, but to the art of the world, we are led to the conclusion that, in spite of the general decline of taste which began in Kwansei period, it is in Utamaro and in Hokusai that Ukiyo-ye finds its summits, the one supreme in figure-design, the other in landscape. And this not only because of their creative invention and a range far exceeding the other masters, but because in these two, even more than in Harunobu or Kiyonaga, there is a capacity to divine and to communicate the elemental powers in man and nature, and to rise at times into an imaginative world where life is more deeply felt and its mystery more deeply apprehended.

# THE KWAIGETSUDŌ PROBLEM

The biographical details concerning Kwaigetsudō given in native books are not only meagre, but, in respect to the period in which he flourished, contradictory. A careful comparison and sifting is therefore necessary in order to obtain a fairly trustworthy account, which is believed to be as follows.

Kwaigetsudō was an artist who lived in Suwō-chō, Asakusa, Yedo, during Hōyei and Shōtoku periods—1704 to 1716. His common name (*zoku-shō*) was Okazawa—some say Okazaki—Genshichi. He is said to have used the *gō* of Ankei or Anshi ; but the general consensus of modern opinion takes these to be meant for Ando, as this name is found on paintings, whereas the others are not. Some of his paintings are signed " Kwaigetsudō " only. There dwelt in the same street as himself a wealthy agent to several families, by name Heioku Zenroku, with whom he was on intimate terms of friendship. In the 4th year of Shōtoku—1714, he was in some way implicated in a Court scandal concerning the Lady Yeshima, who had allowed herself to be seduced by an actor named Ikushima Shingorō, both of whom were sentenced to exile. One account says that Kwaigetsudō received a like sentence and was banished to the island of Ōshima. Another account states that, owing to the favourable intervention of his friend Zenroku, he was afterwards lodged with a rice merchant. It is not clearly stated whether this means after sentence or after punishment, the phrase in the original being ambiguous. In any case, he appears to have continued soon after to exercise his profession.

All these biographies, however much they differ in detail, speak of one man only, namely Kwaigetsudō.

There are paintings signed Kwaigetsudō, Kwaigetsudo Ando, and Chōyōdō Anchi, prefaced by 'Nippon gi-gwa ; and paintings and prints which bear the names of Anchi, Dohan, Doshin, and Doshū, prefixed by the words " Nippon gi-gwa Kwaigetsu matsu-yō." This fact has led most writers to believe that these signatures belong to a group of different artists, who with Kwaigetsudō at their head formed a sub-school of the Ukiyoye school ; and that Anchi, Dohan, Doshin, and Doshū were Ando's pupils or descendants.

At the same time they agree as to the extraordinary similarity not only in the work of the alleged master and pupils, but also in the handwriting of their signatures.

One or two critics, on the other hand, deny the correctness of this view, contending that there was no sub-school at all and that these signatures are not those of pupils or descendants, but were special brush-names used occasionally by one artist only—Kwaigetsudō Ando.

The question is, which of these opinions is most likely to be correct? Let us first examine the school theory.

Dr. Julius Kurth, in his book *Der Japanische Holzschnitt*, 1910—new edition, 1922—emphatically asserts that "Kwaigetsudō is a school-name (*sippenname*), just as Hishikawa, Torii, or Okumura, but not an individual name (*einzelname*)." This argument, however, cannot be upheld; for there is no parallel between Kwaigetsudō and the names he quotes, inasmuch as the latter are family or surnames, whereas the former is what is known as a *dō-gō*, that is to say a pseudonym which it was the custom for scholars, artists, publishers, booksellers, and such-like to adopt. As examples, we have Okumura Masanobu, who as an artist used the *dōgō* of Hōgetsudō, and as a publisher that of Kwakujudō; Furuyama Moroshige's pupil Moromasa, who took Getsu-getsudō as his *dō-gō*; Tsutaya Jusaburō, that of Kōshōdō; Nishimura-ya Yohachi, that of Yeijudō—these two latter being famous publishers. Clearly Kwaigetsudō is the name of an artist, not the appellation of a school.

The next point for consideration is the true signification of the prefix "Kwaigetsu matsu-yō."

Kwaigetsu is, of course, an abbreviation of Kwaigetsudō, who is generally acknowledged to have been identical with the artist Ando. Matsu-yō means literally "last leaf" (as of a tree), and hence may be extended to mean "posterity" or "descendant," but hardly "pupil." It was the custom for an artist desirous of declaring in his signature that he was a pupil of a certain master to insert between his own and his master's name the words "*mon-jin*," literally "gate-man"—so-called because he had been allowed to enter the latter's "gate." For instance, we have such signatures as "Yeishi monjin Gokyō"; "Utamaro monjin Toyomaro; Toyokuni monjin Kunimitsu," and so on. Matabei (1572–1650), in his famous set of paintings of the Thirty-six Poets, executed in 1640, used the signature Ye-shi Tosa Mitsunobu (1434–1525) matsu-ryū Iwasa Matabei Shōi, meaning "Iwasa Matabei Shōi, a ' lower or inferior stream ' of the painter Tosa Mitsunobu." Of itself Matsu-ryū may also mean "posterity" or "descendant," but in that sense would have little, if any, significance here, seeing that Matabei was not born till forty-seven years after the death of Mitsunobu, and that the picture was not painted till one hundred and ten years after that event. Doubtless the artist used it in its literal sense and as a humilific. There is no record of any artist using this expression or that of " matsu-yō " to intimate that he was a descendant in the sense of " pupil."

The definition of *matsu-yō* by that eminent scholar Mr. Uyeda Bannen in his *Rōmaji Dictionary* (*Rōmaji-de-hiku kokugo jiten*), 1920 edition, is (1) last age or phase of life (*matsu no yo*); (2) posterity or descendant (*shison*, lit. children and grandchildren). There seems little doubt that this primary meaning is intended in the signatures Dohan, etc., and that their real interpretation is " Japanese amusement-picture (*nippon gi-gwa*); Kwaigetsu, in his last phase Dohan, etc., drew this (*kore wo zu-su*)."

As proof of this, one has but to examine certain paintings on which one or other of these signatures appear to discover that they are often followed by the seal " Ando," thus clearly indicating that he, otherwise Kwaigetsudō, was the painter.

Examples.—In Mr. Oscar Raphael's collection is a painting signed " Nippon gi-gwa Kwaigetsu matsu-yō Doshin kore wo zu-su," and sealed " Ando." In the illustrated catalogue of Japanese old fine arts displayed at the Japan-British Exhibition, London, 1910, is the signature on illustrated picture 118, " Nippon gi-gwa Kwaigetsu matsu-yō Doshū kore wo zu-su," and sealed " Ando." Illustrated picture 119 in the same catalogue bears the signature, " Nippon gi-gwa Kwaigetsu matsu-yō Dohan kore wo zu-su," and sealed " Ando."

It may be urged that Kwaigetsudō Ando permitted his so-called " pupils " to use his seal occasionally on their paintings; and, if we could be sure that these men were actually his pupils, there is precedent of this having been done in the classic schools. But the expression " descendant of Kwaigetsudō " connotes a considerable interval of time between master and descendant, whereas no such interval is here deducible.

In *Kwagai Manroku*, published in 1825, we are told that " Kwaigetsudō lived in Asakusa, Yedo, during the Genna period (1615–1624), and was the first artist of the Ukiyoye school in Yedo." If this statement is true and Dohan, Doshin, etc., were his descendants, then the expression Matsu-yō in this sense is quite proper, as they worked at the lowest computation eighty years later. Against this is the fact that no work of the Genna Kwaigetsudō is known to exist; and, though this is but negative evidence, still it cannot be ignored. If, again, we presume his reality, then the Hōyei-Shōtoku Kwaigetsudō Ando must have been the second and equally his descendant: yet he never subscribed himself as such. We are, therefore, forced to the conclusion that, as there was not sufficient interval of time between the work of Ando and that of Anchi, Dohan, Doshin, and Doshū to justify the use of Matsu-yō in the sense of " descendant," it should not be so interpreted : and that the correct interpretation is that Ando used it during the last years of his activity, being the equivalent, as Sui-insha shujin states in No. 55 of the magazine, *Ukiyo-ye*, published on 13th September, 1920, of *ban-nen* or " the latter part of his life."

In addition to the above considerations, we find these various signatures so exact a counterpart one of the other that only one thoroughly versed in the reading of Japanese handwriting can distinguish the names Anchi, Dohan, etc.; not only is the hand peculiar and sprawling, but it is precisely similar in each case. Enough has been said to prove that, from the point of view of signatures, the sub-school and master and pupils theory is untenable.

Let us now turn to the work in which these signatures are found. We notice that the female figures—and they are mostly such, either standing, stooping, or sitting—are all of the courtesan class ; are all clothed in heavy garments worn in the same way and manipulated in the same manner, and are all drawn in the broad style used in paintings known as " ema," done on *gaku* or tablets which were hung up in shrines as votive offerings. We notice, too, that the drawing of the face, hands, feet and poise of the head is identical.

Is it possible that five different men, no matter how skilful imitators they may have been, could have followed each other's mannerisms with such fidelity?

It may be asked, why did Kwaigetsudō change his signature so often? He, like Hokusai, doubtless had his reasons, at which we can only conjecture. It may be that after the Yeshima affair had blown over and he had resumed work, he thought it prudent to adopt these " gō " to hide his identity in view of his disgrace, still retaining that of Ando on occasions. It is noteworthy that the Ando seal is not found on prints, which fact may signify that these were a little later in date than those paintings upon which the names of Kwaigetsudō or Kwaigetsudō Ando only appear.

# THE SECOND KIYONOBU PROBLEM

A *hoso-urushi-ye* print that has come into the possession of Mr. Carl Schraubstadter, who has kindly furnished the writer with a photograph and has given permission to make such use of it as may be necessary for the present note, bears the signature " Ni-dai-me Torii Kiyonobu fude," that is " drawn by the second generation Torii Kiyonobu." The value of this print in regard to the problem under review depends upon the genuineness of this signature.

In the opinion of the owner and of the writer there is no doubt about this ; but Mr. F. W. Gookin, to whom the latter is indebted for many valuable suggestions in regard to the problem, writes as follows in this connection. " When I had an opportunity to examine the Ni-dai-me Torii Kiyonobu print in a strong light, I found that the ' Ni-dai-me ' is not printed but written with a brush. Although I more than half suspected this from the photograph that was sent me, I had to see the print to make sure. The inscription does not appear to be modern, but the question ' When was it done ? ' is rather a vital one, is it not ? It involves the further question as to whether the one who wrote it was correctly informed. I very much fear that we cannot safely draw the conclusions from the written statement that we could from a printed one, and especially so if you are right in your contention that the print depicts Masugorō in the Kaomise play for 1727." Another impression of the print was seen by the writer in a private collection and bore the same signature, though unfortunately no opportunity was afforded of placing the two impressions side by side in order to see whether there was any variation in the same, which would have probably been apparent had the " Ni-dai-me " been written with a brush.

The print represents Ichikawa Masugorō, the son of Ichikawa Danjūrō II, in the rôle of Kusunoki Masatsura, and Hayakawa Denshirō as his opponent in a *shibaraku* act. Inscribed on the print is a declamatory speech (*serifu*), which transliterated reads as follows :

## TRANSLITERATION

Tō karan mono wa Tenjiku Ryōjūsen no suteppen daishō seson Shaka-muni-nyorai no nattō-beya te yotte kike. Chikakuba yotte Sakai-chō Saruwaka Kanza ga kidō-guchi wo oppiraite yoku miro. Katajikenaku mo Bidatsu-Tennō byo-ei Ide-no-Sadaijin Tachibana no Moroe-kō no koin Kawachi no kuni no jū-nin Kusunoki Tamon byo-ei Masashige ga

chakushi dōmyō Tatewaki Masatsura to iu shin aragoto hyaku rai san-dai-
me no Danjūrō to ho-ho uyamatte mosu. " Nanda ore wo koshō tsubo ʔ
Sonnara unura udon da na dori de, hana ga shita ga nobi ta wa yo ! Yai ! !
Hari wa chisakitte mo nomarenu ! Sanshō wa kotsubu demo waruku
yotte ka ! Kujira ni shachiburo to dotepara ni ana ga aku bei ! Kusunoki
Tatewaki Masatsura ni mukatte ichi-ban kyōtte mibei to wa oyakata ā
tsugu mo nai ! "

### TRANSLATION

You who are distant ! listen well at the steamed-bean chamber of the
great Sage Shakamuni-nyorai on the summit of Ryōjū mountain in Hindu-
stan. You who are near ! push aside the theatre door of Sakai-chō Saruwaka Kanza and have a good look in. The third Danjūrō that is to be
(ha ! ha !) as Kusunoki Tatewaki Masatsura, heir of Kusunoki Tamon
Masashige a dweller in the province of Kawachi and remote descendant of
Ide-no-Sadaijin Prince Tachibana-no-Moroe descendant of the awe-
inspiring Bidatsu-Tennō is respectfully declaiming in a new style of *aragoto*
like a hundred thunders thus : " What ! am I a pepper-pot ʔ If so, you
fellows are nothing but vermicelli—fools that you are ! Out upon you ! !
A needle small though it is cannot be swallowed ! A pepper-corn (here
a pun on his *haimyō* of Sanshō) may be small, but it is mighty pungent !
A grampus can bore a hole in the belly of a whale ! You will be a great fool,
you big fellow, if you would oppose Tatewaki Masatsura."

This last exclamation and probably the whole of the *aragoto* declamation
is addressed to his opponent Denshirō, who in the print is depicted being
trampled upon by Masugorō in the rôle of Masatsura.

Now Masugorō played the rôle of Masatsura upon the occasion of his
first appearance on the stage at the age of seven in the Kaomise performance
of " Yatsumune Taiheiki," produced at the Nakamura theatre in Kyōhō
12, i.e. December, 1827 ; when, as recorded in *Kabuki nendaiki*, vol. 2,
page 5, the audience were amazed at his " *aragoto* (violent) *no serifu* "—
doubtless that referred to above.

The toy windmill (*kaza-guruma*) and tambour (*denden-taiko*), shown on
the print at Masugorō's feet, clearly hint at his extreme youth.

Mr. Gookin suggests that the *serifu* was probably written by his father,
who, by his reference therein to the third Danjūrō, intended to hint that
Masugorō was to be his successor, which he in fact became in the 4th
month of Kyōhō 20 (1735). We entirely agree with this suggestion, the

more so as his father did the same thing later on. The only other occasion upon which Masugorō played the part of Masatsura was in the Kaomise play " Shihon Taiheiki " in Kyōhō 18 (December, 1733) ; but this was produced at the Ichimura theatre, whereas the words " push open the stage door of Sakai-chō Saruwaka Kanza " evidently indicate that the scene depicted was from a play produced at the Nakamura theatre, formerly called the Saruwaka theatre, under the proprietorship of Nakamura Kanzaburō.

We know that the first Kiyonobu died on August 11th, 1729 ; and, as this print was according to custom designed soon after the scene it depicts, its date may be safely fixed as either the close of 1727 or the beginning of 1728. If then the signature is, as we believe, genuine, apart from the question as to the Ni-dai-me having been printed or written with a brush, the inference is that Kiyonobu I had retired as an *inkyo* (one who has renounced his right as head of the family) during 1727, and that the artist whoever he may have been succeeded to the title with his approval. Now Kiyomasu was the eldest son and natural heir to the title, and history records that he was his father's successor. Mr. Gookin makes the follow-ing interesting suggestion.

" If it be true that, having become an *inkyo* in 1727, Torii Shōbei (i.e. the first Kiyonobu) gave the Kiyonobu *gō* to his son, theretofore known as Kiyomasu, then it must be that there was a *nidaime* Kiyomasu as well as Kiyonobu. That the two *gō*, Kiyonobu and Kiyomasu, could have been used off and on, alternately, by the same person I do not believe. But it may be that after Kiyomasu I was made Kiyonobu II, one of the other pupils of Kiyonobu I—perhaps Kiyotada—was made Kiyomasu II. Japanese usage permitted much liberty in the assumption of names, but there were some conventions that it was not possible to violate, and that any Torii artist should have had two Kiyo *gō* in use at the same time is incredible." The above has reference to a theory put forward by the writer that it was Kiyomasu who designed the print in question and signed " Ni-dai-me Torii Kiyonobu," to indicate his succession to the title. It seems inconceivable that during his father's lifetime he would have been passed over in favour of a pupil, especially as he had proved himself to be a capable artist and hence was a worthy successor. There exist at least two prints which are signed " Torii Kiyonobu," but sealed " Kiyomasu." Moreover, from about 1727–1728 there is a continuous and characteristic parallel in style between prints bearing either of these two signatures. The alternate use by one artist of two Kiyo *gō* is difficult to understand—and resolves itself into the possibility of such a phenomenon having actually occurred. In considering whether it was on a pupil other than Kiyomasu that the right to use the brush-name of the second Kiyonobu was conferred, it would have to be proved that the pupil had abandoned his former *gō* before using the latter ; otherwise the difficulty of the alternate use of two *gō* would again arise. In the case of Kiyotada, for instance, his activity is given in the Chronicle of Ukiyoye artists that forms an appendix to No. 55 of the *Ukiyo-ye Magazine* published in September, 1920, as extending from 1716 to 1745, which, if correct, and we assume that he was made Kiyomasu II, presents a parallel difficulty as regards alternation of signatures.

Though it may be premature to conclude that the identity of the second Kiyonobu with Kiyomasu is established by this print without other independent corroborative evidence as, for example, a print signed " Kiyomasu aratame (changed to) Ni-dai-me Kiyonobu," yet it is thought that the evidence of the print, providing always that the signature is genuine, makes this highly probable. In any case its importance in the solution of the problem cannot be overlooked.

An important contribution to the problem under discussion appeared in Vol. 2, Nos. 3 and 4 of the Ukiyoye Society of Japan's quarterly journal, *Ukiyoye no Kenkyū*, published at Tōkyō in July, 1923, from the pen of Mr. K. Inouye, under the title of " Torii Kiyonobu and Torii Kiyomasu," supplemented by " Generations of the Torii line."

Unfortunately a copy of the journal did not reach the present writer till the middle of August, by which time the manuscript for this book had already passed into the publisher's hands, thus precluding anything more than a brief summary of the salient points, and excluding any sifting of the evidence produced by the author in support of his opinions.

The subject is treated under six headings. (1) The father of Kiyonobu I. (2) Kiyonobu I. (3) The elder brother of Kiyonobu II. (4) Kiyonobu II. (5) Kiyomasu I. (6) Kiyomasu II. Certain biographical and other details are given under these headings as follows. The words in brackets are comments by the present writer.

(1) The opinion that Kiyomoto, the father of Kiyonobu I, died on May 24th, 1702, at the age of 58, receiving the posthumous name of Gen-tetsu, and that his wife died in 1721, aged 65, receiving Myō-ō as her posthumous name, is to be discredited for the following reason. (On the front face of one of the two tombstones of the Torii family, now in the Somei cemetery on the outskirts of Tōkyō, these names

appear below the posthumous names of Kiyonobu I and his wife respectively.) Supposing for the moment that these dates and ages are correct, Kiyomoto must have been born in 1645 and his wife in 1657. According to the Torii records they were married in 1661, and their son Kiyonobu I was born in 1664, at which date his father would have been 20 and his mother but 8—an obvious absurdity.

Kiyomoto's common name was Shōshichi. Date of his death and his posthumous name are matters for investigation.

(2) Kiyonobu I was a son, perhaps the second, of Kiyomoto. He was born in 1664. Common name, Shōbei. Married in 1693. Wife, born in 1675, died on 28th day of 5th (not 1st) month of Shōtoku 6 (July 7th, 1716), aged 42; her posthumous name was Yō-kō-in Myō-gi Nit-ten. She bore him either 3 sons and 1 daughter or 4 sons and 2 daughters. (Perhaps Gentetsu and Myō-ō referred to in No. 1 were the posthumous names of his eldest son and second daughter.) Kiyonobu I died on 28th day of 7th month of Kyōhō 14 (August 11th, 1729), aged 66, and received the posthumous name of Jō-gen-in Sei-shin Nichiryū.

(3) Kiyomasu I was eldest or second son of Kiyonobu I. Common name, Shōjirō. Born about 1696; died on 25th day of 5th month of Shōtoku 6 (July 3rd, 1716), aged about 21. Posthumous name: Is-san Dō-mu (on left side of the first Torii tombstone).

(4) The elder brother of Kiyonobu II (the designation adopted by Inouye) was the 2nd or 3rd son of Kiyonobu I. Common name, not clear. Born c. 1699; died c. 1724, aged c. 26. Post. name: Taitoku.

(5) Kiyonobu II was the third or fourth son of Kiyonobu I. Common name, Teishirō; afterwards Shōbei. Born about 1702; died on 1st day of 6th month of Hōreki 2 (June 30th, 1752), aged about 51. Posthumous name: Chi-ryō-in Hō-gen (on right side of first Torii tombstone).

(6) Kiyomasu II was born in 1706. Common name, Hansaburō. The "Torii gwa-kei-fu" states, without discriminating between a first and a second Kiyomasu, that he was adopted as *muko* (son-in-law marrying into his wife's family) by Kiyonobu I upon marrying his eldest daughter; that his wife was born in 1707, bore him 4 sons and 6 daughters, and died on 14th day of 8th month of Hōreki 11 (September 12th, 1761); and that late in life he removed from Naniwa-chō (where Kiyonobu I had resided) to Sumiyoshi-chō. He

died on 2nd day of the 11th (not 12th) month of Hōreki 13 (December 6th, 1763), aged 58. Posthumous name : Sei-gon-in Sō-rin Nichi-jō (on front face of the second tombstone).

Whether Mr. Inouye's opinions will bear the test of future criticism or not, he has certainly presented the problem surrounding the names of Kiyonobu and Kiyomasu in a new light ; and, though Kiyomasu is spoken of as but one artist throughout the body of the present work, the possibility of there having been two should not be overlooked. We would remark, however, on (5) that prints signed Kiyonobu were published at least as late as the spring of 1757 ; e.g. a print. in the Ritchie collection, sold at Christie's in 1910, of Onoye Kikugorō in a part played by him only in the first month of Hōreki 7, or February–March, 1757. There are also three little picture-books of plays in the British Museum, dated in MS. 1755, 1757 and 1758. If, therefore, Kiyonobu II died in 1752, we have to presume a Kiyonobu III. But who can this artist have been? Was he Kiyomasu after all? Or, if Kiyonobu II lived on after 1752, who was the Chi-ryō-in Hō-gen of the tomb-stone?

# NOTE C
# THE SHIKŌ-CHŌKI PROBLEM

In a paper read before the Japan Society of London on April 21st, 1922, the present writer expressed the opinion that there were two artists who used the name of Shikō; the first a pupil of Toriyama Sekiyen, and who some time between 1784 and 1789 had assumed the name of Chōki; the other a pupil of his to whom he had given his discarded name.

The following arguments were advanced in support of this opinion:

1. That the writer Shikitei Samba (1775–1822) had declared that Chōki's first name was Shikō.

2. That Shikō is recorded in books from 1772–1784, illustrated by Sekiyen, as having assisted in the designs as the latter's pupil.

3. That in a book, *Tenka ichimen kagami umebachi*, three vols., 1789, Chōki appears as the illustrator—the first known use of this name.

4. That prints signed Chōki are clearly earlier than those signed Shikō, and follow the manner of Kiyonaga and Yeishi, whilst the latter are more like those of Utamaro in the latter half of the Kwansei period (1795 to 1800).

5. That a book, *Ikebana tebiki-gusa*, five vols., 1800, is illustrated by Momokawa Shikō, and that there is a Shikō-signed *surimono* dated 1798, i.e. twelve and ten years respectively after Sekiyen's pupil had taken the name of Chōki.

6. That there is a print signed " Shikō " and dated Monkey 1, which from its style can only be referred to the Monkey year of 1800.

7. That at least two prints exist signed respectively Yeishōsai Chōki and Yeishōsai Shiko, the latter at least ten years later in date.

8. That in a book, *Shibai kummō zui*, compiled by Samba between 1803 and 1805, Yeishōsai Chōki appears as the *hissha* or *copyist*, having apparently given up print-designing for this metier.

9. That the frontispiece to a novelette, *Futari Kamuro*, 1802, is signed " Shikō gwa," followed by a seal Shi (the same ideograph as that of the Shi in Shi-kō), Mon, and Shi (Jap. *uji*, meaning family name or Mr.); the reading being " Family name Shimon or Mr. Shimon." But, it was argued, as there is no such family name (the Editor here remarked it would be safer to say—as the existence of such as a surname is highly improbable), it was interpreted to mean that the artist

here acknowledged that he was the *mon* (-jin) or pupil of Mr. Shi (-kō), who could be none other than Chōki, formerly Shikō, the pupil of Sekiyen.

Taking these points into consideration, the writer felt that the pupil theory was far more likely to be correct than to assume that for some unknown reason Shikō had, after changing to Chōki prior to 1789, reverted to Shikō about 1795—for which there was no precedent. The recent discovery, however, of the above-mentioned print signed Ni-dai-me Torii Kiyonobu reopens the question. For if it be true that Kiyomasu and Kiyonobu II are identical and that he continued to use both signatures after his father's retirement, then may not Shikō have acted somewhat similarly and reverted to this name after having discarded it? It is true that the two cases are not exactly parallel, since in Kiyomasu's case it is a question of an arbitrary alternate use of the two signatures, whereas in Chōki's case there is no such systematic alternation, but rather reverting to a discarded name with pronounced interval between the discard and the reversion. Still, the two questions are sufficiently allied to demand further investigation into the latter before the pupil theory can be accepted. It may here be remarked that nearly all the problems that confront the student of Ukiyo-ye are bound up with the apparently (from our want of knowledge of customs) arbitrary and capricious manner in which artists adopted, dropped, and reassumed their *gō*. As several such cases will be noticed during the perusal of this volume, one example in explanation will suffice. A calendar *surimono* of 1765, referred to in the body of the work, is signed on the right " Ishikawa Toyonobu," seal Ishikawa, and on the left " Kyosen renjū, Rinkō " (latter in seal).

Another calendar for the same year is signed Gihō, and sealed Rinkō, thereby indicating one individual, which it would have been impossible to have known if, as is often the case, the seal Rinkō had been omitted.

# THE REAL CAUSE OF UTAMARO'S IMPRISONMENT

The late Mr. Sekine Shisei (died 1893) records in his work *Meijin ki shin roku* that Nishikiye of the Taikō and his five wives after designs by Utamaro were put on sale on June 23rd, 1804, and that the artist was censured and sentenced to three days' imprisonment and confinement to his house under handcuffs, which latter expired on August 12th—that is, for a period of fifty days. The writer, doubtless, refers to the well-known but little-understood triptych entitled *Taikō go sai Rakutō yūkwan no zu*, i.e. " A picture of the Taikō (Toyotomi Hideyoshi) and his five wives pleasure-viewing at Rakutō," in which the artist depicts an incident that actually occurred on April 10th, 1598, when Hideyoshi, accompanied by his legitimate wife, and four concubines—in their order of rank, Kita-no-mando-koro, Matsu-no-maru, Sanjō-dono, Yodo-dono, and Kaga-no-tsubone (called Kana-dono in the triptych)—sought a few hours' relaxation from the cares of State in the peaceful temple grounds of Sambō-in at Rakutō Daigo, east of the Kamo River, Kyōto, where a banquet was served in a screened-off enclosure beneath the flowering cherry trees. Some writers have thought that this picture in some subtle way was regarded by the Government as a reflection upon the dissolute life of the reigning Shōgun Iyenari, and that in consequence of this Utamaro was punished. The picture, however, is perfectly straightforward and cannot possibly be interpreted in this way.

The real reason why the authorities suppressed it was that it transgressed the law and had not received the censor's approval.

As far back as the Tenshō period (1573–1591) an edict had been issued forbidding the names and *mon* of high personages, warriors, and others who had rendered conspicuous service to the country to appear on prints or in books ; and, as these were shown on this triptych, it was suppressed and the artist and publisher (Kinshodō, whose trade-mark Yama-jin is stamped thereon) were arraigned and punished. In proof of this, the censors were notified at the same time as the triptych appeared that " since Tenshō the disclosure on *ichimai-ye* and in illustrated books (*yezōshi*) of the names and *mon* of warriors, etc., has been strictly forbidden " ; and they were enjoined to exercise the utmost vigilance to put a stop to such a practice.

From whatever source Mr. Sekine obtained information that Utamaro was imprisoned and confined under manacles for designing this triptych, his account certainly differs entirely from those recorded in *Honchō Ukiyo gwajinden* (pub. 1899), *Hōsei ron san*, and *Ukiyo-ye bikō* (1898), in each of which the following details are given of two single-sheet prints, but no mention is made of the triptych.

Firstly, a picture of the Taikō taking by the wrist Ishida Mitsunari, whose hair is dressed after the manner of a page (this is not so in the triptych) and whom he has received in audience ; and a female attendant (*jijo*) who holds a long-handled *saké*-pourer, and who hides her face with her sleeve (i.e. to conceal her amusement).

Secondly, a picture of Katō Kiyomasa in armour seated at a feast ; and a Korean harlot playing the *samisen*. The two first books further state that for these *nishiki-ye* Utamaro was summoned, tried, and sent to jail (the *Hōsei ron san* says for three days) ; and that on being released from prison was confined to his house in handcuffs, while the *nishiki-ye* were ordered to be seized, and the publisher was fined 15 *kwammon*. The *Bikō* states that Utamaro was immediately censured on the appearance of these two prints which were directed to be confiscated ; and that he was afterwards, for designing other prints, sent to jail, from which he was soon released and sent back to his house. It is to be noted that the *Ukiyo-ye ruikō* also speaks of two separate offences for which he was censured by the authorities, but does not enter into details either as to the prints or as to the punishment. Bakin (1767–1848), a contemporary of Utamaro, tells us in his *Iwademo no ki*, published in 1820, that " Utamaro was tried for some *nishiki-ye* that appeared in the spring of 1805, and sentenced to imprisonment ; and that these *nishiki-ye* represented personages taken from the *Yehon Taikō ki*" (" a picture-book of the history of the Taikō "). Shokusanjin (1748–1823), a still earlier contemporary, makes no mention of imprisonment, merely stating that Utamaro was confined to his house in handcuffs. Taking this evidence as a whole, meagre and conflicting though it is, it would appear that Utamaro was censured for the triptych published in June, 1804, and imprisoned for three days and handcuffed in his house for fifty days for the single-sheet prints, which are probably those referred to by Bakin as having appeared in the spring of 1805. However this may be, there exists a series of three very rare single-sheet prints published by Moriya Jihei, whose trade-mark appears thereon, two of which are most certainly those described above. Two of the series are here reproduced for the first time (Pls. 37 and 38). The one, inscribed Mashiba Hisayoshi—an intentional transposition for Hashiba Hideyoshi, the name by which he was known when serving under Nobunaga—agrees exactly as regards the Taikō and Ishida Mitsunari, whose *mon* is visible on his sleeve with the first of those recorded in the above-mentioned three books. The female attendant, however, though she wears a long-sleeved dress and displays a slight smile, is not shown as trying to conceal the same with her sleeve, nor does she grasp a long-handled *saké*-pourer. There is, moreover, a retainer of whom no mention is made in these books.

Possibly the original writer, whom the others followed, had not himself seen the print, but had heard of it and was describing it from hearsay ; or, if he had seen it, he had not it before him at the time of writing, but described it from memory. What lends colour to this suggestion, apart from the partial correctness of detail, is that the second print, which has been seen but is not available for reproduction, tallies almost exactly with the description given in these books. It represents Katō Kiyomasa in armour seated fan in hand with a retainer kneeling beside him, and two Korean harlots, one of whom, kneeling, is playing the *samisen*, while the other standing holds a transparent fan.

The inscriptions on the second of the two prints here reproduced read Shibata Shuri-no-shin (his title) Katsuiye and Otani-no-kata. Katsuiye was Nobunaga's most famous captain, who after his lord's assassination in 1582 found service under Hideyoshi whom he hated too irksome and rebelled ; but, being beaten and beleaguered in his castle at Kitanoshō, Echízen, decided to kill himself by committing *seppuku*, and to set fire to the buildings so that his corpse might not fall into the hands of his foe.

Otani-no-kata was the sister of Nobunaga, and had first been the wife of Asai Nagamasa, to whom she had borne three daughters. After Asai's death she was married to Katsuiye and was at this time along with her three daughters in Kitanoshō. Her husband endeavoured to induce her to escape with her children ; but, while permitting the girls to go, she herself determined to die with her lord. The courageous couple feasted and drank wine during the night, together with some trusted retainers ; and in the morning, after Katsuiye had directed the firing of the castle, they committed suicide with the same dirk. In the picture the devoted wife is shown presenting a long battle-sword to her husband, thinking that he intended to sally out to battle ; but the latter is shown holding his short sword reserved for the *seppuku*. If we compare these prints with the triptych, we can readily understand the authorities taking a more serious view of the former, more especially as they apparently constituted a second offence. Still, as in the case of the triptych, its gravity lay in the displaying of names and *mon*. In proof of this and incidentally as affording an interesting sidelight on the methods of censorship, we may mention that the single-sheet prints of the Taikō and Kiyomasa (and probably, too, that of Katsuiye, though such has not yet come under observation) were reissued by the same publisher some years later, when the inscriptions were removed and the prints were stamped with the censor's *kiwame* seal of approval. The sticking out of the tongue on the part of the retainers is a mark of good-humoured derision, intended in the one case to ridicule the notoriously immoral relations that existed between the Taikō and his favourite, and in the other the fidelity of husband and wife, so rare in those days of loose conjugal ties. These pieces of satire doubtless weighed with the judge in delivering sentence.

# A LIST OF CHOICE COLOUR-PRINTED BOOKS AND ALBUMS

## ARRANGED IN CHRONOLOGICAL ORDER WITH BRIEF DESCRIPTIVE DETAILS OF THE ORIGINAL ISSUES AND THE COLOURS EMPLOYED

### MEASUREMENTS ARE GIVEN IN INCHES
### VERTICAL MEASUREMENT FIRST

1. YEHON BUTAI ŌGI, " Picture Book of Stage Fans " ; 3 vols., 10½ × 7. Two prefaces each of three pages, the last dated Tiger first month, i.e. January 27th to February 25th, 1770. Five preliminary illustrations in colours, the first signed Katsukawa Shunshō, and the fifth sealed Mori (family name of Ippitsusai Bunchō). One hundred and six fan-shaped prints each occupying one page and sealed either Mori or with the jar-shaped Hayashi seal used by Shunshō. Finally, one page of an actor standing with an open fan in his right hand ; this picture is signed " Bunchō gwa " and sealed " Ippitsusai." Two pages of postscript followed by 7 pages of *haikai* (17-syllable) poems, amongst which is one by Shunshō and one by Bunchō. On the last page is inscribed : " Meiwa 7 Tiger year, beginning of Spring," i.e. January 27th, 1770. Engraver : Yendō Matsugorō of Kanda ; Yedo bookseller Kariganeya Ihei of Koishi-kawa Denzuin-mae." Colours : yellow, green, beni, black, grey, purple, pink, chestnut-brown, and Indian red. Mica is applied as a ground to the fans of the actor's portraits, and their names are inscribed in white.

*Note.*—A supplement in 2 vols. was published at Kyōto by Kikuya Yasubei in 1778.

2. YEHON SEIRŌ BIJIN AWASE, " Picture Book comparing Beauties of the Green-houses " ; 5 vols., 10¾ × 7⅓, in dark blue covers. Each volume has a frontispiece with a *haikai* in white on a light blue ground, composed by Saren. The book is divided into the four seasons as follows : Vol. 1, Sakura (Cherry) for Spring ; Vol. 2, Hototogisu (Cuckoo) for Summer ; Vol. 3, Tsuki (Moon) ; and Vol. 4, Kōyō (Reddening of Leaves), both for Autumn ; Vol. 5, Yuki (Snow) for Winter. Following the frontispieces are portraits of the courtezans, each inscribed with a *haikai* by Saren. The pictures are distributed thus : Vol. 1 with 39 figures, 2 of which are standing and 37 sitting ; Vol. 2 with 37 figures, 10 standing and 27 sitting ; Vol. 3 with 14 sitting figures ; Vol. 4 with 14 standing and 9 sitting figures, 23 in all ; Vol. 5 with 49 sitting figures. Number of coloured illustrations, 167. The first volume is prefixed by a 2-page preface undated and un-

signed, in which Harunobu is given as the artist. The last page of Vol. 5 contains the following : " Engraver, Yendō Matsugorō ; (Date) Meiwa shichi kanoe tora nen roku-getsu kichi-nichi, i.e. a lucky day in 6th month of the Tiger year Meiwa 7, which began on June 23rd, 1770. Sold by the Yedo booksellers Maruya Jimpachi of Tōri abura Street and Koizumi Chūgorg of Yoshiwara book-store, and by the publisher Funaki Kasuke of Suruga Street." Colours : *beni*, green, blue, pink, yellow, light brown, dark brown, orange, black, purple, slate-blue, and greyish blue. *Gauffrage* is applied to the white portions of the dress in two cases only—one on page $\frac{13}{2}$ of Vol. 1, and the other on page 77 of Vol. 5.

*Note.*—Harunobu died on July 7th, 1770. Kasaya Saren was a famous *Haikai* composer and an intimate friend of both Harunobu and Kyosen, with the latter of whom he collaborated in the *Haikai* poems of the 3-vol. book entitled *Segen Jūi*, published in 1758. Apart from its artistic excellence this book affords an important insight into Harunobu's drawing and colouring. Volumes 3 and 4 representing Autumn are sometimes bound in one volume.

3. SAIGWA SHOKUNIN BURUI, " Various Classes of Artizans in Coloured Pictures " ; 2 vols., $11\frac{1}{10} \times 7\frac{1}{2}$, in light blue covers ornamented with dark blue geometrical designs at top and bottom. Two prefaces, both dated December, 1770, the latter by Minkō himself. Each volume has a page of contents, followed by double-page colour plates, 15 in Vol. 1 and 13 in Vol. 2, of artizans engaged in their respective trades with inscriptions setting forth their origin and development. On some of the plates women and children are interested spectators or the actual workers. The last page, which is preceded by a postscript dated the 12th month of Meiwa 7 (began January 16th, 1771), eulogizing the work, reads as follows : " Artist : Gyokujuken Tachibana Minkō, (sealed) Tachibana Masakatsu (his real name) ; Engraver : Okamoto Shōgyo, (sealed) Kai-in ; (Date) Meiwa shichi kanoe tora nen rōgetsu, i.e. Meiwa 7 year of the Tiger 12th month, which corresponds to January-February, 1771. Yedo booksellers Uyemura Tōsaburō and Sawa Isuke. The plates are printed from stencils in the following colours : red, green, light blue, pink, grey, black, orange, light brown, dark brown, pale green, pale yellow, and a tint approximating to peach or pale salmon.

*Note.*—A second edition, quite unworthy of comparison, was issued by Uyemura Tōsaburō in 1784, with a preface by Shokusanjin who relates that the first edition was almost entirely destroyed in a conflagration at Yedo in 1772. This book and a calendar print for 1765 are all that remain of Minkō's signed work ; and as the print is not characteristic of his style, being one of a set of six illustrating " The Fox's Wedding," the book is of considerable importance and utility in detecting the hand of the artist from among the number of *nishiki-ye* which appeared unsigned at this period.

4. SEKIYEN GWAFU, "Sekiyen's Picture Book"; 2 vols., $12\frac{1}{2} \times 8\frac{1}{2}$. Three prefaces; the first dated the first day of the last winter month of Mizunoe Tatsu, i.e. December 24th, 1772; the second dated the beginning of Spring of Mizunoto Mi, i.e. January 23rd, 1773; and the third, which is written by Toriyama Sekiyen, is dated the 1st month of the Snake year of Anyei, i.e. January–February, 1773. One page of contents of Vol. 1 and 2. Vol. 1 contains 12 double-page pictures of human beings, monkeys, birds, and landscapes in the *fuki-bokashi* style of gradation printing, said to have been the invention of the artist. Some of these are in monochrome, others in colours. Vol. 2 contains 13 pictures in the same technique, of which 12 are double-pages and one a triple-page in colours of Peafowl and Peonies. Then follow 2 pages of postscript; and on the last page is inscribed: "Toriyama Sekiyen Toyofusa," with the seals "Toriyama shi" and "Toyofusa," "assisted by his pupils Shikō, Sekichō, and Gessha. Engraver: Ryok'kōdō Tōyei; (Date) Anyei san kinoe uma no toshi (i.e. the year of the horse Anyei 3 = 1774). Owner of the blocks, Yūriyen Toshū." Colours: *beni*, green, yellow, grey, brown, orange, and black.

*Note.*—The pupil Shikō changed his name to Chōki some time between 1784 and 1789. There are, however, several prints from about 1795 to 1802 which are signed "Shikō," which raises a problem that has been discussed in Note C.

5. NISHIKI HYAKUNIN ISSHŪ AZUMA-ORI, "Brocades of one hundred Poets' stanzas woven at Azuma, i.e. at Yedo"; 1 vol., $11\frac{1}{4} \times 7\frac{3}{4}$, in light blue covers. A 2-page preface written by "Katsukawa Shunshō Ririn under the cold lamp light in the waiting-for-spring month of the 2nd year of Yasuku nagaki," i.e. the last month of Anyei 2, which began on January 12th, 1774. This preface is sealed "Ririn Shunshō." Then follow 6 coloured illustrations with the poems of the Rok'kasen or Six Great Poets, and 100 portraits of poets or poetesses each inscribed with a stanza of their own composition. The last page reads: "Artist: Ririn Katsukawa Yūsuke Tō Shunshō of Buyō (i.e. of Yedo); Engraver: Inouye Shinshi-chirō of the same city; (Date) Anyei shi kinoto hitsuji mō-kon, i.e. the beginning of darkness in the Goat year Anyei 4, corresponding to October–November, 1775; Bookshop Kariganeya Gisuke of Yedo, Koishikawa Denzuin-mae." There is a note stating that the book is ready in two kinds, viz. in colours and in black and white. Colours are red, yellow, grey, mauve, black, light brown, green, orange, and blue.

*Note.*—Of this original issue only one copy has so far come under observation. The poems as well as the prefaces are in the handwriting of the artist. Later editions—and they were several—all bear the date of the original. They have, in addition, an introduction written by " Watanabe Hiroshi, a pupil of Sayama," which is dated the beginning of spring (i.e. February 11th, 1774) in Anyei 3. The poems in these editions are in the handwriting of Hiroshi's teacher Sayama Chikayuki, the second son of Sayama Ryuchi, a famous calligraphist in the Ōhashi style of writing invented by Ōhashi Shigemasa. The colour-scheme is practically identical with the original.

6. SEIRŌ BIJIN AWASE SUGATA KAGAMI, " A Mirror reflecting the forms of Fair Women of the Green-Houses "; 3 vols., $11 \times 7\frac{2}{5}$, in pale blue covers splashed with gold and ornamented with a touch of shrubbery. Vol. 1. A 3-page preface by Kōshōdō dated Anyei 5, 1st month which began on February 19th, 1776. One page of Spring Flowers and 10 double pages of women in Spring costumes ; one double page of Summer Flowers and 8 double pages of women in Summer dress. Vol. 2. One page of Autumnal Flowers and 12 double pages of women in Autumn garments ; one double page of Winter Flowers and 10 double pages of women in Winter garb. Vol. 3. One page of the Shin Yoshiwara Ō-mon-guchi or Great Entrance Gate of the New Yoshiwara, and 3 double pages of women clad in Winter dress ; followed by $26\frac{1}{4}$ pages of poems recited by the women at the four seasons. Last page reads : " Ukiyoye Masters Kitao Kwaran Shigemasa (and) Katsukawa Yūji Shunshō, (sealed respectively) Kitao Shigemasa (and) Katsukawa Shunshō ; Engraver : Inouye Shinshichi ; (Date) published in the first month of Spring in the Monkey year Anyei 5 (began February 19th, 1776) ; Yedo Booksellers Yamazaki Kimbei of Honseki Street (and) Tsuta-ya Jūsaburō of Ō-mon-guchi Shin Yoshiwara—joint publishers." Colours : *beni*, blue, pink, yellow, light brown, green, black, grey, stone, mauve, dark brown, and a touch of tan on flowers in last plate of Vol. 1. *Gauffrage* is used on some white fans in the Summer section, and mica is applied to some icicles and a block of ice in the winter section.

Note that in the preface and at the end of the book Shigemasa's name precedes that of Shunshō. The former designed the pictures for Spring and Autumn, the latter those for Summer and Winter.

7. YOSHIWARA KEISEI SHIN BIJIN AWASE JIHITSU KAGAMI, " A Mirror comparing the handwriting of new and beautiful courtezans of the Yoshi-wara "; an album, $15 \times 10$, in dark blue covers with a suggestion of gold cloud effects and a yellow label on which is inscribed the title, followed by the words " First Series complete." Two pages of preface by Yomo sanjin (i.e. Shokusanjin) dated the commencement of spring in the Dragon year Temmei 4, i.e. January 22nd to February 20th, 1784. Seven plates, $15 \times 20$ each, each with 2 celebrated courtezans, their Shinzō and Kamuro

of seven famous houses of the Yoshiwara. On last page a postface by Shurak'kwan shujin (the Master), and the names of the artist " Kitao Rissai Masanobu," sealed " So-seki," and of the publisher " Kōshōdō Tsutaya Jūsaburō," with his new address of the south side of Tōri-abura Street, whither he had removed from the Shin Yoshiwara Ōmonguchi in September, 1783. The colours, of extraordinary richness and purity, embrace the following : Light and dark blue, orange, pink, olive, bluish grey, purple, dark green, black, *beni*, crimson-red, yellow, brown and light red. *Gauffrage* is applied to the white portion of some of the robes, and the writing-table at which one of the courtezans is seated has its mosaic pattern sprinkled with mica.

*Note.*—There is no date of publication, but it was certainly issued in the spring of 1784. On the last plate is an inscription on a pillar corresponding to March, 1783, and on two others is the publisher's trade-mark with Ōmonguchi inscribed above—thus proving that the blocks were engraved before his removal to Tōri abura-chō in September, 1783. These 2 plates alone bear the artist's signature " Kitao Rissai Masanobu gwa " and his seal " Soseki," and have, moreover, a title reading Seirō Meikun jihitsu shū, i.e. " A collection of the autographs of famous fair ones of the Green-Houses." No second series has so far come to light, though apparently one was contemplated, judging from the words on the title-label above quoted. A 2nd edition in wholly inferior colours, with the title " Seirō Meikun jihitsu shū," appeared some years later, in which the words " Ōmonguchi " over the publisher's trade-mark are significantly omitted, and in which the beautiful orange is replaced by a disagreeable yellow and the blue by a crude green ; the black, too, lacks depth.

8. GENJI HYAKUNIN ISSHŪ NISHIKI-ORI, " Genji and 100 Poets' stanzas woven in brocade " ; 1 vol, 10¾ × 7⅖, in dark blue covers. A double page with portraits of the 3 gods of Poetry, viz. Sumiyoshi, Tamatsushima, and Kakinomoto, in a circle on a white ground surrounded by a mosaic pattern of dragons, etc. A double-page frontispiece of Waka-no-ura. Four single-page illustrations of court ladies with each a poem composed by herself and topped by explanatory text occupying half of each sheet. These poems are for the 4 seasons. One page of text concerning the 100 Poem Anthology and its compiler, the Deputy Chunagon Fujiwara no Sadaiye, commonly known as Teika. On the lower half of each page of the remainder of the book are portraits of the 100 Poets, each inscribed with his poem. The upper halves contain portraits of the Sanjū-rok'kasen ; the Onna Sanjū-rok'kasen ; the 54 episodes of the Genji Monogatari ; illustrated poems of the 12 months ; illustrated poems on the 10 Buddhist regions or states of existence (Jikkai) ; an illustrated poem for each of the 4 seasons ; together with several illustrated instructions for the upbringing

of girls and their duties as wives, their accomplishments, and so on. On the upper portion of the last page are the portraits and poems of the Rok'kasen, and on the lower portion the name of the artist, Kitao Kōsuisai Shigemasa Tairei Kitabatake of Yedo ; the engraver Inouye Shinshichirō ; the date, a lucky dragon day in the 1st month of the Snake year Temmei 5 (began on February 9th, 1785) ; and the booksellers Okumura Kihei and Mayegawa Rokuzayemon with their addresses at Yedo. Colours : blue, *beni*, yellow, purple, light red, black, olive, light brown, and green.

9. TEMMEI SHINKEI GOJŪNIN ISSHŪ ; AZUMA-BURI KYŌKA BUNKŌ, " A new series of 50 poets' stanzas of the Temmei period ; a bookcase of humorous poems in the Azuma (i.e. Yedo) style " ; 1 vol., 10¾ × 7, in salmon-pink covers. One page repeating the title thus : Azuma-buri kyōka gojūnin isshū. Two pages of preface by Yadoya Meshimori. Fifty pages each with a portrait in colours of the poets with their pseudonyms and one of their poems. One page inscribed as follows : " A second series of Kyōka gojūnin isshū will shortly be published in colours. Artist : Kitao Denzō Masanobu (sealed) Santō Masanobu no in. Engraver : Seki Jiyemon. (Date) The first spring month of *hinoe uma* (Horse) year Temmei 6 (i.e. January 30th, 1786). Published by Kōshōdō Tsutaya Jūsaburō of the south side of Tōri-abura Street, Yedo. Colours : *beni*, dark green, sepia, blue, yellow, grey, light green, chocolate, purple, black, light blue, and Indian red.

*Note.*—The second series advertised is not now extant, if indeed it was ever published.

10. KAIKO YASHINAI GUSA, " The Cultivation of Silkworms," 1 vol., 11 × 8, in dark blue covers. Two pages of preface dated Temmei hinoe uma haru, i.e. the spring of the Horse year in Temmei, which began January 30th, 1786. Twelve pictures in colours, 6 signed " Katsukawa Shunshō " and 6 signed " Kitao Shigemasa." On last page is inscribed ; " A lucky day in the first month of the Horse year of Temmei 6," i.e. January-February, 1786. " Published by Mayegawa Rokuzayemon, 3rd street section to south of Nippon Bridge, Yedo." Colours : purple, *beni*, yellow, green, and brown.

*Note.*—These colour-prints were issued separately, two on a sheet, to be divided if required, some 14 years previously. An alternative title is Sanyō zu-ye gwa-hō nō-ru, under which a previous edition in book form (1 vol.) was, according to Friedrich Succo (*vide* p. 77 of his book, *Katsukawa Shunshō*, 1922), issued in 1776 ; but this edition has not, so far, come under observation. Still another alternative title to the 1786 edition is Takara no itoguchi.

11. HYAKUNIN ISSHŪ ; KOKON KYŌKA-BUKURO, " One poem by 100 poets ; a sack of ancient and modern humorous poems " ; 1 vol., 10¼ × 7, in

light blue covers, on the front one of which is the above title, together with the name of the compiler, Yadoya Meshimori, and a table of 27 books which served in the compilation. A double-page preface enclosed within plum and cherry blossoms in colours is signed by Yomo sanjin, i.e. Shokusanjin. Five preliminary pages as frontispieces with pictures of festivals in which women and children are shown interchanging New Year visits, going to gather shells at ebb-tide at Shinagawa, boy's festival, the *tanabata* festival, and the chrysanthemum festival—each with descriptive text and poems above the pictures. Then follow the portraits of the 100 poets, each with his pseudonym and one of his stanzas inscribed above. One and a half pages of postscript, and the names of the compiler, Yadoya Meshimori, and of the artist, Kitao Denzō Masanobu. One page with the name of the publisher, Tsutaya Jūsaburō, of Tōri-abura Street, 8th section of the north side of the Main Street, Yedo; and a list of 10 of his publications for sale. Colours: light blue, *beni*, olive, black, grey, Indian red, sepia, yellow, purple, light brown, green, stone, peach, and chocolate. Mica and *gauffrage* are sparingly used.

*Note.*—Though this book is not dated, its date can be fixed as the spring of 1787; for, in the postscript, mention is made of No. 9 above as having appeared last year, i.e. 1786, and that this year (i.e. 1787) the compiler has collected a further lot of 100 comic poems which here appear.

12. SAISHIKI MITSU NO ASA, " The Three Mornings, in colours "; 1 vol. in album form, 10 × 7¾, with a preface (*sui-jo*, literally an intoxicated preface) by Tsuru-tayū, and 7 prints representing scenes enacted on the 1st, 7th, and 15th mornings of the New Year fêtes—in this case of the year Temmei 7 which began on February 18th, 1787. Each plate, 10 × 15¼, is unsigned except the last representing the shop of the publisher Yeijudō Nishimuraya, which bears the title and the signature " Torii Kiyonaga gwa." The scenes represented comprise : (1) First writing in the New Year. (2) Yoshiwara women paying and receiving New Year visits. (3) First archery practice of the year. (4) First opening in the New Year of a merchant's shop. This shows a ledger marked with the E-to of Temmei 7. (5) First horseback exercise in the New Year. (6) Ladies' first bath and toilet in the New Year. (7) As above noted. On the last page the signature " Torii Kiyonaga " and the seal " Kiyonaga "; the date, " spring of the Goat year," i.e. 1787; and the name of the publisher, " Yeijudō of Yedo." Colours : red, pink, green, black, *beni*, light blue, yellow, orange, and grey.

*Note.*—This series was also issued in single sheets enclosed in a wrapper.

13. YEHON MUSHI ERABI, "A Picture Book of Selected Insects," 2 vols., $10\frac{1}{2} \times 7\frac{1}{2}$. Preface by Yadoya Meshimori, and 15 double-page illustrations as follows : Vol. 1 : (1) Three wasps, *hachi ;* and a hairy caterpillar, *Kemushi*. (2) A grasshopper, *Umaoi-mushi ;* and a centipede, *Mukade*. (3) A mole-cricket, *Kera ;* and an earwig, *Hasami-mushi*. (4) A dragon-fly, *Tombo ;* and 2 white butterflies, *Chō*—the wings of both species glisten with mica. (5) A white caterpillar, *Imo-mushi ;* and a horse-fly, *Abu*. (6) A cricket, *Matsu-mushi ;* and 2 fireflies, *Hotaru*. (7) A mantis, *Tōrō ;* and a small grasshopper, *Batta*. (8) A cicada, *Higurashi ;* and a spider, *Kumo*. Vol. 2 : (9) A red dragon-fly, *Aka-tombo ;* and a rice locust, *Inago*. (10) A snake, *Hebi ;* and a lizard, *Tokage*—their bodies glisten with mica. (11) A basket-worm, *Mino-mushi ;* and a helmet beetle, *Kabuto-mushi*. (12) A noisy cricket, *Kutsuwa-mushi ;* and a snail, *Katatsumuri*. (13) A singing cricket, *Kirigirisu ;* and a cicada, *Semi*. (14) A black cricket, *Kōrogi ;* and an earth-worm, *Mimizu*. (15) Two frogs, *Kairu ;* and a golden insect beetle, *Koganei-mushi*. Postscript by Toriyama Sekiyen. Last page : Artist, Kitagawa Utamaro ; Date, the 1st month of the year tsuchi-no-e Saru, Temmei, which began on February 7th, 1788. Compiler (and selector of the poems which accompany each picture) : Yadoya Meshimori. Publisher : Tsutaya Jūsaburō Kōshōdō of Tōri-abura Street. Sekiyen's postscript, which is sealed (after his signature) Toriyama Toyofusa, and is dated the winter of the Goat year of Temmei 7 (began November 10th, 1787), significantly alludes to the artist as " my pupil Utamaro." On the inside of the back cover is an advertisement of a list of books already published by Kōshōdō, among which are Nos. 9 and 11 above. Colours : yellow, brown, greyish purple, pink, green, red, blue, pale yellow, lilac, and black. *Gauffrage* and mica are used here and there with telling effect. Besides the insects, each plate contains some variety of edible fruit or flowering plant, as well as a humorous poem concerning each insect.

14. YEHON WAKA YEBISU, "Picture Book of Poems of the Common People " ; 1 vol. in album form, $9\frac{9}{10} \times 7\frac{1}{2}$, containing a double-page preface and the following 5 plates : (1) A nobleman riding towards a mansion where are seated some court ladies and nobles and some visitors. (2) People looking on at some men performing the Lion dance outside the house. (3) Manzai dancers visiting a household on New Year's Day. (4) A snow scene : Man, carrying a girl pick-a-back, about to cross a plank bridge ; 2 other men and 2 dogs outside a house, from the corner verandah of which a woman is watching. (5) A monkey trainer putting

his animal through his tricks before a party of ladies. A postscript by Yadoya Meshimori; 5 pages of humorous poems; and the names of the artist, Kitagawa Utamaro sealed Bokuyen, and of the publisher, Tsutaya Jūsaburō, of Tōri-abura Street. Colours: pale blue, green, brown, yellow, dark blue, red, light green, pink, brown, purple, and black.

*Note.*—Though 1786 is given in the Hayashi catalogue and elsewhere as the date of publication, the book has no date either at the beginning or at the end. Perhaps the introduction of the Monkey in the last plate may signify that the volume was for the spring of the Monkey year of Temmei 8, which began on February 7th, 1788. This date accords with the style of the pictures.

15. YEHON KWACHŌ KAGAMI, "A Picture Book Mirroring Flowers and Birds"; 1 vol. in album form, $9\frac{7}{8} \times 7\frac{3}{8}$, with 12 plates as follows: (1) Two Chinamen on the seashore, one leading a goat by a rope and the other carrying a basket containing dead fowls still in plumage. (2) Three Chinese by the seashore, one standing and two seated on a tree-trunk, and in front a caged bird. Inscribed on the top in Dutch are the words "Chinese immigrants from Nankin." (3) Jutai-chō (a sort of Magpie) on a pine tree. (4) Gwabi-chō (a species of Bunting) and Cherry. (5) Kwa-uri (a species of Bush Warbler) and Peonies. (6) Sekirei (Wagtail), Iris and Lotus. (7) Two Silver Pheasants. (8) Chikukei (Quail) and Convolvuli. (9) Hakutō-ō (an unidentified bird) and Loquat berries. (10) Jūshimai (a species of Finch—Fringilla sp.) and Maple. (11) Yōkin (Falcon) and Camellia. (12) Two partridges (Shako) beside a cascade. Each plate is unsigned; later editions are signed "Keisai utsushi." At the end the following details. These were originally drawn from life by Kiyō Ishōsai Shūsen; collected by Seki Yeibun, and copied a second time by Keisai Kitao Masayoshi; after which they were engraved by Shumpūdō Ryūko and published by Gungyokudō Matsumoto Zembei in the 2nd month of tsuchinoto Tori (Cock year) Kwansei 1 (which began on February 25th, 1789). There is also an advertisement of a second and a third supplement, which, however, were never issued. These supplements are entitled in the advertisement "Raihin zue," which is the title given to the album when it was republished in 1793 with an additional volume of text only and explanations. For particulars of the 2nd edition see Sotheby's catalogues of the Happer and Kington-Baker Collections sold in London in April, 1909, and March, 1916, under Lots 398 and 191 respectively. Colours: red, green, yellow, pink, brown, blue, and peach, with fine *gauffrage* and heavy embossing here and there.

16. SANJU ROK'KASEN, "The Thirty-six Poets"; 1 vol., $11\frac{3}{4} \times 8\frac{1}{4}$, in pale blue silk covers. Seven pages of preface by Sayama Chikayuki (*vide* note to No. 5 above), who also was the calligraphist of the poems. A frontispiece portrait of the compiler of this anthology Dainagon Kintō, followed by a single-page introduction by Katsu Shunshō. Then follow the 36 portraits of the poets, each on a page, with one of their poems on the reverse page. On last page is inscribed: "Yedo Jōgwasei Kyokurōsei Katsu Yūji Shunshō; engraver, Shumpūdō Ryūko; (date) Temmei 9 year tsuchinoto tori (Cock year) early spring (began on February 25th, 1789). Published by Yamazaki Kimbei of Yedo, and also sold by Katsunuura Jiyemon of Kyōto and Ōgawa Yōzayemon of Ōsaka. Colours: black, yellow, *beni*, grey, peach, green, blue, purple, stone, olive, and persimmon (*kaki*).

17. YEHON KYŌGETSUBŌ, "Picture Book of the Mad Full Moon"; 1 vol. in album form, $9\frac{9}{10} \times 7\frac{1}{2}$, containing 2 pages of preface by Kino Sadamaru, 5 double-page illustrations, and 72 humorous poems on the moon. The plates are as follows: (1) The chūnagon Yukihira on Suma beach gazing at the moon and men attending to the salt-pans. (2) A party viewing the moon from the balcony of a Yoshiwara house. (3) A faggot gatherer crossing over a bridge spanning a waterfall, his form silhouetted against the full moon. (4) A mother holding up her baby boy who is pointing to the full moon and another boy gambolling beside her, whilst her "man" washes vegetables in a stream in which the image of the moon is reflected. Hills in the distance on the left, and their hut close by on the right. (5) The Emperor Genso, accompanied by a Taoist magician, crossing the aerial bridge towards the Palace in the Moon (Gekkūden). Signed on last page "Kitagawa Utamaro" and sealed "Toyoaki" and "Utamaro." Dated the 8th month in autumn of the Cock year tsuchinoto-tori of Kwansei, which began on September 19th, 1789. Published by the Yedo bookseller Kōshōdō. Colours: pale blue, green, yellow, brown, dark blue, red, black, pink, light green, purple, and grey, enhanced here and there by *gauffrage* and metallic printing.

18. YEHON GIN-SEKAI, "A Picture Book of the Silvery World"; 1 vol. in album form, $9\frac{9}{10} \times 7\frac{1}{2}$, containing 5 plates, with a preface by Yadoya Meshimori, dated 1st month of the Dog year, which began on February 14th, 1790; and 8 pages of humorous poems at the end. On last page the names of the artist and publisher as for No. 16 above. The pictures are: (1) A court lady rolling up the reed blind for the Emperor to view the garden under snow. (2) Two men towing a boat upstream (in graded black and

grey). (3) Shadows of people on the *shōji* of a tea-house, and a *geisha* peeping out to watch the falling snow. (4) People promenading on the bank of a river on which is a boat. (5) Children making a snow dog, rolling a ball, and fighting. Colours are similar to No. 16 above, and the pictures are enhanced with embossing and metal printing.

19. FUGEN-ZŌ, " The Image of Fugen " ; 1 vol. in album form, $9 \times 7\frac{1}{10}$, containing preface by Tsuburi no Hikaru, dated 3rd month of the Dog year, which began on April 14th, 1790, with 5 plates and 10 pages of humorous poems at the end. Plates as follows : (1) A procession of courtezans down the centre street of the Yoshiwara, and women looking down from a balcony on the tops of the umbrellas which conceal the procession. The cherry trees in full bloom. (2) A picnic party of men watching an approach of women and girls. (3) Returning from the picnic, one woman overcome with *saké* being helped along by two others, and men in rear. (4) Two women viewing the cherry blossoms and men in rear with picnic materials. (5) Cherry blossoms at Goten-yama. Signed : Kitagawa Utamaro ; published by Kōshōdō. Colours similar to No. 16, with gold-sprinkled clouds.

*Note.*—Though the preface is dated as noted, the book itself bears no date of publication.

20. MOMO CHIDORI KYŌKA AWASE, " Birds compared in Humorous Songs " ; 2 vols. in album form, each $10 \times 7\frac{1}{2}$. Vol. 1—first series—contains a double-page preface by Akamatsu no Kinkei and the following 8 plates, each with a humorous ditty supposed to be sung by the birds themselves. (1) A couple of Quail (*Uzura*) and grasses on right and a Skylark (*Hibari*) amid grasses on left. (2) Japan Tit (*Yamagara*) on a bough on right and Japan Bush-warbler (*Uguisu*) on a branch on left. (3) Japan Hawfinch (*Mamemawashi*) on a pine tree on right and a Woodpecker (*Kitsutsuki*) on trunk of same tree on left. (4) On right a Cormorant (*U*) diving after a shoal of fish ; on left 2 Snowy Herons (*Sagi*) in a pool. (5) Japan Wren (*Misosazai*) on a bough on right and a couple of Snipe (*Shigi*) in a marsh on left. (6) A pair of Eastern Chimney Swallows (*Tsubame*) in flight on right and a Green Pheasant (*Kiji*) amid grasses on left. (7) Jay (*Kashi-dori*) on a branch on right, and Owl (*Fukuro*) on another branch of same tree on left. (8) A domestic Cock and Hen (*Niwatori*) on ground to right and Japan Bunting (*Hōjiro*) on a bamboo on left. Last page has an advertisement of this book, and 3 others of which one is No. 18 described above, and an announcement inviting customers to inspect several other choice picture books recently published. Then follow the

names of artist, Kitagawa Utamaro, sealed Utamaro, and of publisher,
Tsutaya Jūsaburō, with address as already noted. Vol. 2—second series—
contains a double-page preface by same writer as the first, and the following
7 plates : (1) Falcon (*Taka*) on right and Bull-headed Shrike (*Mozu*) on
left, both perched on a plum tree. (2) Manchurian Great Tit (*Shijūkara*)
hanging head downwards from the stem of a white chrysanthemum on the
right and Japan Robin (*Komadori*) on a bamboo on left. (3) Two Copper
Pheasants (*Yamadori*) on a rock on right and a Wagtail (*Sekirei*) below
rock on left. (4) An Owl (*Mimizuku*) on a tree trunk on right and 2 Eastern
Bullfinches (*Uso*) on a bough on left. (5) Three pigeons (*Hato*). (6) Japan
Long-tailed Tit (*Enaga*) on bamboo on right, and three Japan White Eye
(*Mejiro*) on twig on left. (7) Couple of Wild Duck (*Kamo*) on bank of
stream on right and an Eastern Common Kingfisher (*Kawasemi*) on stalk
of a plant overlooking water on left. Last double-page identical with that
of the first series described above. Colours : Cinder-grey, pale yellow,
black, bright yellow, sandy-brown, grey, red, olive-green, dark brown,
slate-black, soft green, light brown, ruddy gold, indigo blue, greenish
black, pale orange, pink, and a greenish lilac, besides other reflecting tints
baffling description.

*Note.*—This book bears no date, but probably appeared in spring of 1791, as the third
book advertised at end of each series, viz. *Yehon Fukujusō*, 1 vol., in colours by Kitao
Shigemasa, was published in early spring of that year. A later edition in 2 vols., with a
preface by Hajintei (the *nom de plume* of Kishi Bunshō, a *kyōka* pupil of Ippitsusai Bunchō),
who also signed Tsumuri no Hikaru, is dated 1st month of Kwansei 8 (1796). There was,
it is thought, an intermediate edition without date, but about 1793.

21. SHIOHI NO TSUTO, " Presents of the Ebb-tide " ; 1 vol. in album
form, 10¼ × 7½, with a double-page preface by Akera Kankō, and 8 plates
as follows : (1) People gathering shells at Shinagawa bay at ebb-tide.
2 to 7 consist of a variety of shells, seaweeds, etc., lying on the sea-bed
with a wavy convention at the top to represent the surface of the water.
(8) A party of ladies engaged in playing the shell game (*Kai Awase*) or in
conversation, and on the left 2 female attendants, one carrying a pet dog
on her shoulders. Last double page contains a postscript by Chiyeda at
the request of the circle of poets called the Yaegaki-ren, whose poems are
inscribed on each plate ; and the names of the artist Kitagawa Utamaro,
sealed Jisei Ikke (Self-made House, meaning that he had founded a school
of his own), and of the publisher Kōshōdō Tsutaya Jūsaburō of the same
address already noted. Colours : purple, red, pink, black, orange, blue,
brown, green, black, pearl-grey, grey, and several indescribable tints.

*Gauffrage* and gold dust applied here and there, together with silver and mica.

*Note.*—Later editions omit the conventional wave lines. The work bears no date, but probably appeared in the spring of 1790, the Dog year of Kwansei 2, the dog introduced in the last plate possibly signifying this year (*vide* note to No. 14 above).

22. OTOKO TŌKA, " Name of a dance performed by men on the 15th day of the 1st month " ; 1 vol. in album form, 10 × 7⅖, in dark blue covers with a suggestion in gold of shrubs and clouds. A double-page preface dated the 1st month of Kwansei 10, which began on February 16th, 1798. Six plates, interspersed with poems, as follows : (1) A court lady admiring a blossoming plum tree from the verandah of a house ; signed " Hakuhō son Yekiga." (2) Leading the sacred white horse of a Shintō shrine ; signed " Kitao Kōsuisai (i.e. Shigemasa)." (3) A courtezan in an interior with her Shinzō and Kamuro ; signed " Chōbunsai Yeishi." (4) A lady holding up a caged bird for another to see, a girl with a bag of food, and a female servant holding a pestle (an object ever provocative of ribald laughter amongst low-class women) in her right hand for another kneeling in the doorway to see, both women concealing their mirth behind their sleeved left hands held before their mouths ; signed " Utamaro." (5) A thatched hut beside a winding rivulet spanned by a bridge, under which a man is washing a basket, and upon which are standing 2 men and a woman. In the foreground a picnic party of women and children ; signed " Hokusai Sōri." (6) A rain scene. Two men playing *go* and a boy being dressed by his mother on the verandah of a house, and a female servant waiting outside in the rain with an open umbrella ready to take the boy out ; signed " Tōrin." At the end of the volume is the date : " A day in spring of Kwansei tsuchi-no-e uma, which began on February 16th, 1798. Published by Tsutaya Jūsaburō." Colours : purple, *beni*, yellow, light green, red, blue, brown, black, dark green, and cream.

23. NISHIKI-ZURI ONNA SANJŪ ROK'KASEN, " Brocade Prints of the 36 Poetesses " ; 1 vol., in album form, 9½ × 7¹⁄₁₀. Three pages of preface. A double-page illustration of 7 retainers of a *daimyō* crossing a plank bridge spanning a stream, one carrying a boy on his back ; on the further bank 3 boys pointing and poking fun at them ; signed " Gwakyōjin Hokusai." Thirty-six double pages, each with a portrait of a poetess on one page and her poem on the other. Two postscripts, the last dated the mid-winter of the Snake year, hinoto mi, Kwansei 9, which began on December 18th, 1797. Then follow the undermentioned particulars :

" The foregoing poems are in the calligraphy of 36 young girls (not over 15 years of age), pupils of the Yedo ode composer Hanagata Shodō, and were examined by the master Hanagata Giyū. The illustrations are by Hosoi Chōbunsai of Yedo (i.e. Yeishi), and the book engraved by Yamaguchi Matsugorō and Yamaguchi Seizō." (Advertisement 1.) " Brocade-printed portraits of the 36 poetesses to be shortly published complete in one volume." (This is the present work.) (Advertisement 2.) " The poems of the 36 poets in the calligraphy of the master Sayama and with illustrations by Katsukawa Shunshō has been previously published complete in one volume." (This refers to No. 16 in this list.) (Date) " This work was begun in the Horse year, tsuchinoe uma, Kwansei 10 (1798), and published in the spring of the Cock year, kanoto tori, Kwansei 13 (which began on February 13th, 1801)." " Published by Yeijudō Nishimura Yohachi, wholesale bookseller of Bakuro Street, 2nd section, Yedo ; the firm was founded by Nishimuraya Dembei." Colours : Practically identical with No. 21, but red predominating. *Gauffrage* used in the first plate.

## A BRIEF ACCOUNT OF OTHER COLOUR-PRINTED BOOKS DEEMED WORTHY OF ATTENTION

1. YEHON SAKAE-GUSA, 2 vols. ; 15 ills. by Katsukawa Shunchō ; pub. by Izumiya Ichibei, 1790. (See Duret, No. 134.)

2. YEHON FUKUJUSŌ, 1 vol. ; 7 double-page ills. by Kitao Kōsuisai Shigemasa ; pub. by Tsutaya Jūsaburō, 1791.

*Note.*—2nd edition entitled " Yehon Takara no nanagusa," was published in 1804.

3. YEHON MATSU NO SHIRABE, 2 vols. ; 24 single-page illustrations by a " certain person " as related in the preface by Musashi no Shōfu, dated 1st month of the Hare, Kwansei (began February 19th, 1795). Musashi no Shōfu was one of Shigemasa's *gō*, and probably he humbly describes himself as a " certain artist." Other attributions are Utamaro (very unlikely), Masayoshi, and in Hayashi Cat., lot No. 1590, Shikō. These pictures were also issued as separate prints, when they are sometimes signed with the forged signature of Shunshō, who died in beginning of 1793. A later and much inferior edition with the same preface, but signed by Rokujuyen, is dated 1802.

4. YOMO NO HARU, 1 vol., with 7 plates by several artists, pub. in 1795 by Kōshōdō. (See Hayashi, No. 1751.)

5. YEHON SHIKI NO HANA, 2 vols.; 4 single (of flowers) and 7 double-page ills. by Kitagawa Utamaro; pub. by Izumiya Ichibei in 1801.

6. HAIYŪ SANGAI KYŌ, 2 vols.; 2 single and 20 double-page ills. by Utagawa Ichiyōsai Toyokuni; pub. by Nishimiya Shinroku in 1801.

7. YEHON IMAYO SUGATA, 2 vols.; 2 single and 24 double-page ills. by Utagawa Ichiyōsai Toyokuni; pub. by Izumiya Ichibei in 1802.

8. TATSU-NO-MIYA TSU-KO, " Servitors of the dragon palace," really fishes; 1 vol. with 30 double-page ills. by Keisai, sealed Soshin (i.e. Masayoshi); pub. by Suwaraya Ichibei in 1802.

*Note.*—Care must be taken to distinguish between this rare original issue, with preface by Ichiyōsei Sōgwai and with poems on the plates, and later editions with same date, but without the preface and poems and with such titles as Gyokai-fu, Gyokai ryaku gwashiki, etc., all of which are much inferior. These are not rapid brush sketches (*ryaku gwashiki*); for, as the preface says, " the rapid sketches (*ryaku gwa*) of the master Kuwagata Keisai are well known to the public. These only showed the meaning, but not the reality of form; whereas here we find all copied to the life with each scale accurately and faultlessly drawn. . . . Keisai has with remarkable spirit depicted the finny tribe leaping between the shores as poems floating on the waves. Hence have we called the book *Servitors of the Dragon Palace.*

9. SEIRŌ YEHON NENJŪ GYŌJI, 2 vols.; 19 double-page illustrations by Kitagawa-sha Murasaki Utamaro with the assistance of his pupils Kikumaro, Hidemaro, and Ṭakemaro; pub. by Kazusaya Chūsuke in 1804.

*Note.*—Was also published at the same time in black and white.

10. YEHON KYŌKA YAMA MATA YAMA, 3 vols.; 28 double and 4 single-page ills. by Hokusai; pub. by Kōshōdō Tsutaya Jūsaburō (II) in 1804.

11. ŌSON GWAFU, 1 vol.; with 25 double-page ills. by Hōitsu (Ōson being another name); pub. at Nagoya and Yedo without date by Yeirakuya Tōshirō.

*Note.*—This original edition is very rare; that generally seen was published at Yedo by Izumiya Shōjirō in 1817. The pictures are in the beautiful Kōrin style.

# INDEX AND GLOSSARY

# INDEX AND GLOSSARY

# INDEX AND GLOSSARY

# INDEX AND GLOSSARY

# INDEX AND GLOSSARY

# INDEX AND GLOSSARY

# INDEX AND GLOSSARY